THE
MORE
PERFECT
UNION

By R. M. MacIver

Towards an Abiding Peace

The Web of Government

The More Perfect Union

R. M. MacIver

Robert Morrison (handwritten)

THE
MORE
PERFECT
UNION

*A Program for the Control of Inter-group
Discrimination in the United States*

THE MACMILLAN COMPANY
New York · 1948

Contents

204696

Acknowledgments

THE OPPORTUNITY to undertake the work here presented
and the research assistance needed to carry it through I owe
to the Rockefeller Foundation, and I am particularly grate-
ful for the sympathetic cooperation of Dr. Joseph Willits.
The initial impulse was greatly strengthened by the support
of my friends of the Institute for Religious and Social Studies,
especially Louis Finkelstein and Lyman Bryson. I am much
indebted to Professor Gardner Murphy, who not only gave
me his advice throughout but also enabled me to enlist the
services of a team of psychologists. These were Dr. L. Joseph
Stone of Vassar College and Drs. Eugene Hartley and Bohdan
Zawadski of City College. The reports prepared for me by
these scholars were most helpful, and no less was the critical
examination they gave my own work. Two of the appendices
are contributions by collaborating scholars, one by Dr.
Robert Bierstedt of the University of Illinois and one by
Dr. Stone.

While I have made much use of the aid and counsel thus
generously provided the sole responsibility for the statements
and findings of the text rests with the author.

R. M. MacIver

Chapter One

The Challenge

MANY HISTORICAL FORCES combine to make the relation of group to group the central issue of modern society. This issue takes different forms in different lands, but it besets them all. And in a special way it challenges the United States of America. Our people are mostly unaware of the nature of the challenge. They are mostly unaware of the threat to the integrity of this nation that lies in the existing relations of its groups. They do not perceive that its unity, its well-being, its creed, and its historical tradition are together menaced.

Mankind has made great advances toward the solution of many of its ancient problems. But *this* problem is not only unsolved, it has become greatly aggravated. The aggravation has come in the train of technological and social change. The different groups—ethnic groups and culture groups and interest groups—becoming more mobile, coming more into contact with one another and at more points, find far more occasion for clashes than in the simpler, more insulated, and more communized life of earlier days.

In our time groups and interests are more together and yet more apart. More together because the world has narrowed while interests have expanded, because every considerable community is now composite, multigroup; more apart because every interest and every group become more concentrated, more compartmentalized, more organized. Take the modern city; with every calling and every mode of life stratified: physicians congregate mainly with physicians, teachers with teachers, labor leaders with labor leaders, brokers with brokers, businessmen with businessmen, garment workers with garment workers, amusement caterers with amusement caterers—and not even in their common capacity as providing the same service for the community, but mostly in the several subdivisions into which their occupations fall. Or take the nonoccupational categories, which again are crisscrossed by divisions so that we find, say, an Italian-American Democratic Club or a Greek Fur Workers Union Local, and so forth. We are not for a moment suggesting that such modes of organization are undesirable. What we are pointing to is the danger inherent in the multiplicity of compartmented groups unless some way is found of evoking the primary sense of unity that far transcends them.

For these conditions strengthen the natural tendency to group-bound thinking, the gravest peril in the social orientation of modern man. We tend to view the members of other groups as—members of other groups, rather than as persons. They are workers or they are employers; they are miners or teamsters or elevator operators, not individuals; they are manufacturers or bankers or civil servants, not fellow men. We see them in the light of the alleged attributes of their group, with all the distortions fostered by difference of interest or of station. The tendency itself is as old as human nature. It is as old as the first Cain who was a tiller of the ground and looked askance on the first Abel who was a keeper of sheep. But modern organization has enormously extended its range and intensified its expression. It is the business of every organization to assert its own interests over against the interests of other organizations—this principle has just as much sway whether we live in a socio-capitalist or in a socialist economy. The executive of every organization is an agency trained and specialized for this process of assertion. Practically every organization labors to promote in its membership the sense of the paramountcy of the group interest. Thus there are many forces assiduously at work to propagate group consciousness and indirectly to minimize and to weaken the integrity of the greater community.

It is a simple corollary that group differences are magnified out of all proportion to their significance, with the consequent development of inter-group tensions and antagonisms. Every group has its antithetical group and similar processes are at work on both sides of every group demarcation. On this point we quote from a letter to the author from Professor Gardner Murphy:

"It seems to me that whenever people are handled and reacted to as groups . . . the emphasis is bound to be on differentiating factors. Consequently, if my group is good, the other group, which does differently, is bad. The result is to set up a countermovement. Actually both groups are doing the same thing at the same time; no one begins it. But the majority group—or, if in possession of power and prestige, the ruling minority—may be more active in the process. It succeeds in due time in inducing resentment, compensatory behavior, and other traits characteristic of the sense of injury or injustice. These traits react back and increase the sharpness of differentiation. It is a good deal like Newton's Third Law. Most people forget that the gun kicks when fired, and that the minority group plays its large and psychologically inevitable role in the creation of group tensions."

In the face of all this concentration and compartmentalization of group interests the common interest suffers and the community is in danger of being torn apart. It is easy to see the danger in the economic area, where the consequences of the exclusive organization of group interests strike home to everyone, where a dispute affecting the trucking industry or the coal mines or the shipping industry or the operation of elevators can paralyze the whole economy. But we do not so readily perceive the more insidious danger presented by the clashes and tensions of ethnic groups, racial groups, culture groups, even though it was revealed in the red glow of the greatest of world wars. Most of the countries of the world are confronted with this problem of inter-group solidarity, with the cracking of their internal nationalisms while they are making excessive nationalistic claims in their external relations—the latter phenomenon being itself in part a reflection of the former.

The issue exists on a world scale. It is recognized as such by the United Nations, though how far it can be dealt with through international machinery remains problematical. One of the early actions of the General Assembly was the unanimous adoption of a resolution (November 19, 1946) declaring that "it is in the higher interests of humanity to put an immediate end to religious and so-called racial persecutions and discriminations" and calling on all governments "to take the most prompt and energetic steps to that end." The Social, Humanitarian and Cultural Committee of the U.N. is designed to deal with cases of discrimination. Both in the Security Council and in the Assembly considerable attention has already been given to the subject. It was involved in the controversy over Iran. It was directly presented in the charge brought against South Africa in the Assembly concerning the treatment of Hindus. It lies in the background of some of the most serious questions of international relations, and there are indeed few countries that can, or at least should, feel at ease when the issue appears on the agenda.

Whatever may be achieved on an international scale, clearly the main advance or retreat will depend on the domestic attitudes and policies of the various countries, and particularly on those of the greater powers. In this work we are concerned solely with the United States of America. The United States is the supreme example of a multigroup social order. Other countries, such as Russia, are composed of many ethnic groups, but in most of them these groups are relatively localized, territorially compact, each maintaining in a particular area the long-established tradition of its own culture. In the United States the peoples are brought together, mingled everywhere in the local communities. Thus has America grown, thus has it developed its tradition, on this basis has it set up its Constitution. But the United States is facing anew, in a new age, a challenge it met with considerable success in the last century. This time the challenge is greater. There are more groups, and more cleavages.

The cleavages we shall here be occupied with are not economic as such—they are not the divisions between employers and employees. Nor are they the divisions between social classes, of the kind that has played so large a role in the history of many other countries. They are the cleavages that exist between groups because they have different derivations. At one time the peoples these groups represent lived in different parts of the earth and learned different ways and different modes of speech. Now the descendants of these peoples have come together, learning the same modes of speech and many of the same ways, but the prejudice of origin keeps them apart, fostering tensions and antagonisms, grievances and frustrations.

In the next chapter we review the simple facts of the situation. No one can look honestly on these facts and not realize that they constitute a momentous danger to everything for which the United States stands before its own citizens and in the eyes of the world.

Before its own citizens. Let us cite only two cases, for many will appear in the body of this work. The capital city of the nation cherishes its many memorials to liberty, to heroic struggles for the rights of man. The city of Washing-

ton has one legitimate theater. No Negro can enter it as a
member of the audience. That is one of the prerogatives of
the White, and in Washington the Federation of Citizens
Associations is at the time of writing engaged in a campaign
to prevent the doors from being opened to Negroes. The
city of the Lincoln Memorial carries segregation to a point
where it defies the most elementary considerations of humanity—and of religion—as the following incident reveals:

On a wintry morning of 1945, a colored woman in labor,
unable to find a cab, set out in the company of her sister for the
maternity ward of the Gallinger General Hospital. Reaching the
vicinity of a church-supported hospital, the women discovered
that the birth was so imminent that the expectant mother could
not reach Gallinger in time. The sister rushed up the steps of the
denominational hospital and sought admission for the suffering
woman as an emergency patient. This was curtly refused and
the baby was delivered on the sidewalk in front of the hospital.
Its staff supplied a sheet to cover the mother and child until the
municipal ambulance arrived to take them to Gallinger.[1]

In these days the rest of the world watches with new eyes
the discrimination we practise at home. The United States
has become, by destiny and not by design, a world power. It
has corresponding responsibilities. It is so deeply impli-
cated in world affairs that its good relations with other
peoples have assumed the greatest significance. But it carries
a heavy handicap that not all its good services or its fair professions can overcome. The countries of the Orient, which
contain the major populations of the world and which have
become increasingly important in world affairs, discount our
friendliness and distrust our words. For in this country they
are treated as no American is treated in theirs, treated in a
way that would arouse in us, were we in their place, the
liveliest resentment—treated in effect as pariahs. Again, we

[1] Reported by Joseph D. Lohman and Edwin R. Embree in the *Survey
Graphic*, January, 1947.

have, with a generous initiative most rare in the historical record, renounced our dominion over the Philippines, have in turn liberated them from Japanese dominion and rendered many other services. But what does it avail if we bar the Filipinos among us from the elementary courtesies of social relationship? The peoples of Latin America share the feelings of the peoples of the Orient. We proclaim toward them the "good neighbor" policy, but the one thing beyond all others that stalls our endeavors on behalf of this policy—though this thing does not figure prominently in diplomatic exchanges—is the simple fact that the members of these Latin American countries, when they are admitted as immigrants, are assigned to a lower caste and, so far from being regarded as "good neighbors," are not thought worthy of eating in the same restaurants or residing in the same hotels that serve the White people of the United States. What leadership, what influence, can we then expect to have in the American hemisphere? And how can we stand for democracy or for human liberty before Latin America when we contradict our principles as soon as the citizens of these states cross our borders?

If we could add to these international impairments the incalculable losses that inter-group discrimination and prejudice inflict within the American community—not only economic losses but the wastage and attrition and frustration of personality, as these human costs cumulate within the social order—we would have an irresistible case for the enlistment of every open-minded citizen in the battle against our ethnic and racial cleavages.

There are already important forces on this side. There are also considerable inertia and evasion and there is much simple unawareness of the magnitude of the issue. It is the hypothesis of this work that if the potential resources available for combating discrimination could be evoked and effectively organized they would put to rout the enemy forces.

Only by doing so can the United States maintain and advance
its health and strength at home and its leadership abroad.
This country has the opportunity and the supreme need to
rediscover its unity by removing the barriers of discrimination that separate its many groups. By doing so it would give
the world guidance toward the solution of a problem that
afflicts, though in different ways, many other countries as
well.

The claim is made in some quarters that Soviet Russia has
solved the problem and that by following this example we
can solve it too. The claim is valid only in a sense that makes
the example of the Soviet Union of little or no value to the
rest of the world. It is true that ethnic differences are mini-
mized and ethnic prejudices are thoroughly discouraged and
kept entirely in the background. So far this is a gain, and it
can properly be counted as a distinction of the Soviet Union.
The dominance of any nationality group within it is, as such,
rejected. But the condition is the acceptance by all groups
of the same overriding ideology and of the same Party dominance. All ethnic groups have in principle equal rights and
the principle is vigorously applied, since ethnic differences
have no dynamic for the ends of the Soviet state. But all
ethnic groups must be equally submissive to the cultural as
well as the economic dictates of the Party. The ethnic groups
retain no effective cultural spontaneity. "The interests of
socialism," said Lenin, "are indeed superior to the right of
self-determination." Where it suits these interests the cultural
values of the group are exalted. When it does not they are
abased. Stalin has driven the lesson home. Thus the boun-
daries of the constituent states are changed without respect
to ethnic considerations. As Stalin has explained in *Marxism
and the National and Colonial Question,* the region, not the
group, is the basis of what passes for autonomy. "The obliga-
tions of Social-Democrats, who defend the interests of the

proletariat, and the rights of a nation, which consists of various classes, are two different things."

So the gain is that an individual is not subject to open disprivilege or disparagement because he is a Ukrainian or a White Russian or a Georgian or a Jew (though there may be occasional violations of the principle here) or because he is a Tartar or a Turcoman or a Pole or belongs to any other of a hundred ethnic groups. And this is indeed a signal advance over anything that has been achieved in a country like ours. But there is a serious offset to the gain. The members of all groups have equal rights and substantially equal opportunities. But the rights of individuals and of groups are minimal. The ethnic group can enjoy its own language and its own customs—provided they became the media for the expression of the doctrines and policies of the Party. It can choose its own leaders—provided they are subservient to the leadership of the Kremlin. The demands of a rigid orthodoxy make no distinction between group and group. But it is only in the realm of cultural liberty that the fundamental problem of a multigroup society can be solved.

When we speak of the cultural liberties of the group are we then envisaging a society that is a patchwork of many cultures? Is the multigroup society a system of "cultural pluralism"? Or how shall we render to the group the things that belong to the group and to the community the things that belong to the community? Participation is the primary thing, and participation flourishes on the acceptation of difference. The goal is not conformism, not assimilation in the sense of reducing differences into the undifferentiated common, certainly not "coordination" as proclaimed by the Nazis and as, except in the external matters of language and local coloration, practised by the Communists. Neither is the goal a cultural pluralism, in which each group cultivates its particularism in a kind of federated community. The objection to both these alternatives is that they alike, though in different degrees, reject the spontaneous processes that from the beginning have built up community life. Only when differences are free to stay apart or to merge or to breed new variations of the community theme can human personality have fulfilment and creative power, drawing its sustenance where it finds its proper nourishment, neither clinging to likeness nor worshipping difference. In this whole matter we are still socially uneducated. We are the victims of the primitive necessities of socialization, where we learn, children and adults alike, to love what is ours by repudiating what is theirs. In the multigroup society we have to learn that the primitive necessity no longer holds, in this any more than in other relations. Men must somehow be taught that difference is not separateness and that community is not identity. They must learn to make these distinctions just as they learn to distinguish the clutch pedal from the gas pedal. Most men have to learn this simple mechanical distinction because they live in a mechanized society. And most men are under no less necessity to learn—because they live in a multigroup society—that their attachment to the group is a different thing from their attachment to the community and that the former must be duly adjusted to the latter if they wish to enjoy the benefits and the liberties of the civilization they have inherited.

Chapter Two

The Inquiry

1. THE THEME

THE MAJOR theme to which our inquiry is addressed is the relation of group to group in the United States. More particularly, we are concerned with the tensions, rifts, and cleavages between groups of different origin, stemming from different peoples or races. We are not concerned with the rivalry and strife of parties nor with the conflict of creeds or schools nor with the various forms of economic or "class" struggle, except in so far as these are accentuated and made more divisive by differences between groups that rest on conceptions of them *as different kinds of human beings,* on conceptions of them as races, peoples, or ethnic groups. Other forms of conflict, bitter as they often are and serious as some of their consequences may be, do not in our judgment present the same threat to the democratic faith, the historical process, the integrity, and the very being of the American people. The discrimination we shall be concerned with is based not on *intrinsic* differences between groups nor primarily on differences of policy or of interest or of faith. The divisions we have in view become in effect caste divisions. The Negro-White relationship in the United States has predominantly a caste character, and there is a quality of caste in claims of dominance or superiority made on ethnic grounds. In this way caste, mitigated or unmitigated, plays a larger role than class as such in the social cleavages of America.

It will be observed that we have not included religion along with race and ethnic origin as one of the major bases of inter-group discrimination in the United States. We do not dispute that difference of religion is sometimes a determinant of the type of discrimination we have in view. A Protestant employer, for example, may reject the most qualified applicant for a position solely because he is a Roman Catholic, and the Roman Catholic employer may similarly turn down the Protestant. But we do not find sufficient reason to regard religion *by itself* as of crucial importance in provoking the tensions and cleavages manifested in the everyday relationships of American society. It is natural enough for people to give general preference to those of their own kind, whether the congeniality be that of religion or political affiliation or anything else. These universal tendencies are taken for granted unless they become sharpened into the concerted and manifest discrimination of group against group. In particular areas of the United States religious discrimination may reach this level, but not, in our judgment, in the country as a whole. There is, moreover, a special reason for not regarding difference of religion, at least in North America, as coordinate with difference of ethnic origin or of presumptive race. The reason is that if we give prominence to the category of religious discrimination we are likely to include under it many cases that more properly belong elsewhere. We notice, for example, that in the statistical reports of the New York State Commission Against Discrimination, where the categories employed are creed, color, and national origin, the vast majority of cases under the first head are listed as Jewish. It would be entirely erroneous to conclude that with respect to these cases the basis of discrimination is religion. No doubt it is not strictly correct to

speak of the Jewish people as a "national origin" group.[1]
And again the term "race" is likely to carry false implications.
But discrimination and the prejudice back of it do not rest
on the distinctions drawn by anthropologists or political
scientists. They spring from the consciousness of difference,
not from the scientific fact. The anti-Semite regards the Jew
as a different type of human being, not as a fellow man who
professes another religion. It is therefore much more appropriate to classify the Jewish cases under some inclusive category such as "ethnic origin." Some cases of discrimination
listed as directed against Roman Catholics are likely to belong
under the same category, say where the individuals affected
are Italian or Polish or possibly—in some areas—Irish. In
short, the coordinate use of the category of creed, alongside
ethnic origin and race, leads to confusion and misinterpre-
tation.

Group conflict has many manifestations and we shall focus
our inquiry on one alone of these, the aspect of discrimination. Our problem is the social control of discrimination and
the attitudes and interests that lie back of it concern us only
as conditions of that problem. We take the fact of discrimination as evidenced by much testimony and by numerous investigations. We shall not add to that evidence—it is more
than sufficient for our purpose. Nor shall we be directly
dealing with the control of the prejudicial sentiments that
are the psychological background of discrimination. Our
focus is on the social act rather than on the psychological
attitude. It is obvious that we cannot affect the one without
affecting the other. They are interactive as well as interdependent. Discrimination breeds prejudice just as prejudice
breeds discrimination. In seeking for means of reducing
discrimination we shall be planning also for a flank attack
on prejudice.

We select the aspect of discrimination because it is more

[1] See Appendix 1, Race and Ethnic Group.

overt, more public, and particularly because it has such
effects on those exposed to it that it plays a major role in the
development of the cleavages of American society. Inter-group
prejudice may exist without specific discrimination, whether
because the prejudice is less extreme or because, for one reason or another, it is not permitted to express itself in that
way. Furthermore, discrimination can be made, within limits,
subject to controls even while the prejudice that promoted
it still endures. Discrimination is the concerted behavior of
a group, guarded by social sanctions and sometimes by legal
enactments. Prejudice is a way of feeling, a bias of disposition, with many variations from individual to individual,
even though they may all be susceptible to group indoctrination. Discrimination, in its more public forms, can be the
object of legal and other institutional restraints. Prejudice
is not controllable in that sense; it has numerous modes of
expression; it exists wherever groups exist, wherever families
exist. It has relatively innocent expressions and also highly
detrimental ones. Anyone who knows the jealous prejudice
of family toward family where three or four of them constitute a little settlement or who has watched the ways of boys
at school cannot but acknowledge that prejudice springs up
everywhere when groups of any size or kind come into close
contact. Every group has its own sense of superiority, and
it sustains that sense by invocation of prejudice. But prejudice, unless sustained by social usages and sanctions, is fluid
as well as variable, and it is transferable from one direction to
another. Under certain conditions it is strongly canalized as
ethnic or racial prejudice, under others it does not take that
route. In France or in England, for example, there is not
the same caste attitude toward the colored man that prevails
in the United States. In the early days there was not in California the widespread antipathy to the Japanese that appeared later. But when ethnic or racial prejudice arises it

entrenches itself in customs and institutions in accordance with its larger scale, and thus becomes more enduring than other types. The main feature of this entrenchment is a system of discrimination, in the extreme case going as far as segregation. This system is highly developed in the United States.

When therefore we select the aspect of discrimination we are dealing with a problem that concerns the whole structure of a community. In the United States it is a *national* problem. It is from this viewpoint we approach it, not as affecting particular groups, whether they are discriminators or the victims of discrimination. Our problem is that of the unity of the American people, the unity that entitles them to be called one people, the unity that is rendered ineffective in action and weak in spirit by all divisions that deny to any groups the freedom of opportunity in the service of the whole.

We are not disputing the value of investigations directed to the lot of particular groups suffering from discrimination. But the overriding issue is one that cannot be broken up into the question of the Jews *and* of the Negroes *and* of the Mexicans, the Italians, the Orientals, and so forth. We suggest that the frustrations and hardships to which these groups respectively are submitted are more likely to be overcome if attention is turned from the particular to the universal damage resulting therefrom, if in other words the rest of the people could be brought to realize the hurt it does to them as members of the greater community. The challenge to social strategy and to statesmanship of these diverse cleavages is an inclusive one.

One further word of explanation is needed. The discrimination with which we are concerned consists in *the denial of equal access to public opportunity*. There are various other kinds of discrimination, such as the non-admission of members of certain groups to social or recreational clubs or to other facilities organized by private individuals for their exclusive enjoyment, where these facilities have no public reference. It is discriminatory to refuse to have social relations with any person not on intrinsic grounds but on the basis of his belonging to a particular race or ethnic group. While such behavior may be vexatious and cause much rankling and embitterment it does not lie within our province. No doubt the line between one kind of discrimination and another is hard to draw but a few examples will show what we mean by "public opportunity" and "public reference." Discrimination in our sense would include the action of the proprietors or custodians of a public hall, when they bar qualified members of a given race from speaking or performing therein. It includes the denial on similar grounds of admission to restaurants, hotels, or places of public entertainment. Obviously it includes all Jim Crow regulations or other forms of segregation. It includes restrictive covenants to keep the members of any group, defined by race, by ethnic origin, or by any descriptive term (such as "Christian") that by implication has the same significance, from residential areas or new housing developments. It includes the application of a quota system or other restrictive controls to the members of ethnic or racial groups as candidates for admission to colleges, technical schools, universities, or professional schools. It includes devices designed to impede or debar the members of such groups from professional practice or from occupational opportunities of any kind. It includes, among such devices, any bars to promotion or to membership in trade unions, or in professional associations. In sum, all impediments to *economic* opportunity, to the pursuit of a career, or generally to participation in the life of the community, when based on considerations of ethnic origin or color or presumptive race, fall within our category of discrimination.

2. THE APPROACH

Our theme is discrimination, but not directly as a subject we are seeking to learn more about, not merely as an interesting phenomenon we are curious to explore. We shall not be seeking to discover how rampant it is among this or that group or class or how far it is directed against this or that section of the community. We shall not be examining more closely the mentality that cherishes it or the interests that nourish it.

Many investigations have been and are now being undertaken to increase our knowledge and understanding of these things. Psychologists, sociologists, anthropologists, and political scientists have been giving us new information and fresh insight. Many studies are sponsored by the affected groups themselves, so that there is already a rich literature particularly on anti-Jewish discrimination as well as on the Negro-White situation. These studies in large measure provide the data we are going to use in this study. We shall be dependent on their aid throughout our work. At the same time we must add that relatively few of these valuable and indeed indispensable studies make adequate application, for those seeking guides to action, of the information they provide and that not infrequently the researches themselves would have been more effectively directed and more illuminating in their results if the issue that lies back of them, the issue of social policy, had been kept clearly in view.

Sometimes the assumption appears to be that a more precise knowledge of the facts will of itself provide the answer to our question. This attitude is to some degree characteristic even of so fine and elaborate a study, a monument in the history of the subject, as that conducted by Gunnar Myrdal and his associates. The unfortunate consequence is that generally the most scientific studies convey no message to the framers of social policy while the mass of exhortatory or advisory literature has no sure foundation in scientific knowledge.

We have examined a very considerable number of researches concerned with discrimination and discriminatory prejudice. Very few of them explore the nexus between evidence and policy, and even those that offer suggestions for action seldom tie up these suggestions with the data they present. It would seem that our scholarship needs considerable development in this respect. The recognition of this need has recently been growing. Political scientists, economists and sociologists are being forced by the demands of our times to realize that much of their research is abortive unless they draw from it the lessons it can teach. We do not take the position that the only goal of knowing is doing, of knowing better doing better, the practical things to which knowledge may be relevant. We hold that the desire to know has its own intrinsic value and its own right to exist, and that it stands high among the finally good things which redeem and ennoble human life. But much research, at least in the social sciences, is directed not so much to enlarging the system of knowledge, to making discoveries that can be incorporated into the theory of society, as to exploring particular aspects of the particular conjunctures of conditions that form and reform in the endlessly changing kaleidoscope of events. No small part of such exploration is devoted to the pathology of society, to crime and delinquency and family disorganization and prostitution and suicide and unemployment and economic disturbances and social disharmonies of various kinds. Research in these areas may happily result in new insights into the nature of society but perhaps the majority of investigations offer at least as good an opportunity to supply guidance for social strategy as to contribute fresh knowledge of theoretical import. This opportunity has been largely ignored, with the result that the investigations are listed in bibliographies, like a row of obituary notices, no longer the concern of living men.

As we have said, there is a growing revulsion against the barrenness of such research. It has been strengthened by the fact that the physicists, to whose objectivity the social scientists are always turning emulous eyes, have shown a deep interest in the social and political implications of their momentous achievement in the release of atomic energy. In our particular area one sign of the revulsion is that the Social Science Research Council has set up a Committee on Techniques for Reducing Group Hostility, headed by Professor Leonard S. Cottrell, Jr. And once our researchers go some way in exploring such "techniques" they will find they cannot stop short with the investigation of techniques as isolable formulas for specific social controls but must relate them one to another and thus commit themselves to the larger questions of social strategy.[2]

In the world of business a great deal of ingenuity is being spent on the skills requisite for efficiency in producing and in selling. Why should not the world of science, and especially of social science, develop, so far as it can, the skills requisite for the solution, and not merely the revelation, of the problems of social well-being? It is too frequently assumed that a "good" cause can rely mainly on the devotion of those who labor in its behalf. Actually a constructive purpose demands more knowledge-guided wisdom than does a destructive purpose. It is easier to stir passion than to promote understanding. There is a vast array of organizations enlisted in the cause of improving inter-group relations and they have at their command a considerable amount of money, energy, and goodwill. But little searching study has been directed to the examination of the effectiveness of their methods. A recent study by Goodwin Watson, to which later reference will be made, is one of the few exceptions. One can but wonder

2 See Appendix 2, Social Science and Social Action.

how far the leaflets and pamphlets and books poured out on
this subject, not to speak of the addresses and other exhorta-
tions, make a realistic impression on the attitudes of the
masses of people or of their leaders. Some of this work seems
finely conceived and skilfully executed, but we have little
means of testing its effect, of learning why and where it hits
the mark and why and where it misses. The Sixteenth Year-
book of the National Council for the Social Studies sums up
an elaborate review of practices employed to promote intercultural understanding by saying that "above all, the development of democratic human relations requires intensive
study and experimentation by educators and scientists to
promote know-how." Any such investigation requires the aid
of field tests of various kinds, and in spite of all the testing
devices that are available this task remains a formidable one.

Nothing is more certain than that "the facts" do not "speak
for themselves"; nor is anything more reasonable than that
those who explore the facts should be best qualified to inter-
pret them, no less for the sake of application than for the
sake of understanding.

We never learn about things simply by going forth to look
for facts. Always we learn by framing hypotheses on the basis
of what we already know or think we know and then proceeding to ask questions or conduct experiments in terms of
these hypotheses. Our hypotheses are refined and changed
and made more explicit as we gather evidence in answer to
our questions and as our questions themselves become more
relevant and more significant.

At the outset we framed our questions on the basis of the
following general hypotheses:

(1) Inter-group discrimination, of the type we have defined, is a manifestation of established social attitudes,
mainly attitudes that imply the sense of caste.

(2) These attitudes, when widely pervasive, are pre-eminently the expression of the respective indoctrinations of

the discriminating groups, stimulated by the interests of these groups as conceived by them under the influence of their indoctrinations. Under "indoctrinations" we include the notions, prejudices, and images each group entertains about the others; under "interests" we include the consciousness of advantage and disadvantage, of power and prestige and profit and the means thereto, of threats and perils, and on the underside of frustration and subjection and exclusion. It is obvious that indoctrinations and interests are closely interwoven.

(3) These attitudes can be changed not only by appropriate education and propagandization, attempting to substitute new indoctrinations for old, but also—perhaps more potently—by policies and programs that, where feasible, favorably alter the situation out of which the indoctrinations arise (for example, by extending the range of economic opportunity) or the situation the indoctrinations create (for example, by mitigating the segregation of the underneath groups).

With these considerations in mind we drew up a preliminary list of questions for our own use and that of our collaborators. This list is presented as Appendix 3.

Our present investigation is definitely one in social engineering. It is a wholly practical investigation. The researches it has pursued at first hand have been made for practical ends, following up into various areas of social conflict the leads already provided, in order to test the validity of its hypotheses and of its preliminary conclusions. If it concerns itself with psychological inquiries it is in the attempt to discover therein clues to policy. If it reviews historical materials it is in the hope that they will throw light on the difficulties of present or future action. If it concerns itself with the intricacies of social causation it is in order to learn the conditions and the probable consequences of proposed devices

for social control. In this connection we remark that the
study of the causes of things is not in itself a study of strategy
or of therapy. A social phenomenon is determined by numerous complexly interactive conditions. It does not follow that
for control of the phenomenon it is necessary to deal with
all the conditions or even to understand them all. Were it
so, social control would be an almost impossible undertaking.
Nor does it follow that if by a miracle of comprehension we
were able to grasp the whole intricate pattern of the situation
we would then have the answer to our question. It would
mean only that we were uniquely equipped to seek the answer. On the other hand we should recognize that the appropriate control of one or more factors of the many-factored
situation may suffice to bring about the desired result.
Therapy must generally go on that principle and has won
many successes that way. Our controls are mostly over things
of which our understanding is still obscure.

Our problem then may be put as follows: how far and by
what methods can we draw from the available data any conclusions respecting the policies that are most feasible and
effective and expedient for the control of inter-group discrimination? Our objective is to make some contribution
to that problem.

The available data give us much guidance on such questions as these: where and under what conditions discrimination or prejudice has increased or diminished, what groups
or types are more susceptible to or more resistant to prejudicial indoctrination and under what conditions, what kinds
of appeal for or against discrimination have been generally
made and with what results, and so forth. In such evidences
we shall look for findings on the merits of different modes
of attack, on the amenability to control of different factors,
on the weaker and stronger links in the "vicious circle" of
prejudice-discrimination-prejudice, on the role of leadership,
on the probabilities of success or failure in educational or

propagandist methods, on the efficacy of legal and political devices already in use. We shall throughout be seeking to discover what guidance can be derived from these data for the benefit of social leaders, statesmen, and organizations of various kinds engaged in combating inter-group discrimination.

What we are attempting in this work is no more than a preliminary exploration. We hope it may lead others to follow and to do a more thorough job. We hope it will at least indicate the potentialities that lie in the harnessing of scholarly investigation to social needs. We concern ourselves here only with the broader aspects, with matters of strategy and not with the numerous questions of tactics. In other words, we deal with methods rather than with techniques. But obviously the two belong together. Perhaps the first has received less consideration than the second, but both lie within the enlarging province of the student of society.

Chapter Three

The Situation

1. THE LINES OF DEMARCATION

THE RANGE of caste and of caste-like attitudes in the United States is far from being appreciated by our public opinion. It has occupied, for example, very little attention in the various books on "civics" and on "social problems," though some of them contain a rather perfunctory section on Negro-White relationships. In a multigroup society such as ours it easily happens that each group becomes acutely conscious of its own difficulties but has much less perspective on those of other groups or on the total complex of social relationships within which it plays its part. We have come to recognize that the Negro population constitutes in effect a social caste. But we do not sufficiently perceive that sentiments approximating those of caste pervade the country to such an extent as to prejudice the standing and the prospects of possibly one third of the total population.

We distinguish here between caste and class.[1] Class is a universal characteristic of human society, wherever it emerges beyond the small kin group. Social class has many determi-

[1] See the author's *Society* (New York, 1937), pp. 171–173. In the same spirit Max Weber points out (*Wirtschaft und Gesellschaft*, Pt. iii, Chap. 4) that ethnic segregation, in its full expression, evolves into a caste system.

nants, always changing with the changing conditions. Family
—the ancestral tree—may be primary, or wealth may be, or
again there may be conditions in which, though class distinctions still prevail, neither family nor wealth count for much.
But caste rests always on differences already decided at birth,
and these differences cannot be undone by native quality or
achievement, by the acquisition of wealth, or by any other
means. Caste assumes a genetic difference between human
stocks such that no merit and no excellence exhibited by
members of the groups adjudged to be genetically inferior
can ever raise them to the status enjoyed by the superior
groups. We usually limit the term "caste" to intra-communal
differences. If the members of one community regard themselves as superior, on grounds of race or ethnic origin, to
the members of another community we give this sentiment
another name. It is because within the American community
status distinctions based on race or on ethnic origin are
widespread that we are justified in speaking of our caste distinctions and our caste-like attitudes. Caste appears in its
pure form where the social barriers it creates are wholly
rigorous and unsurmountable.

The unity of American citizenship is broken by a sheer
caste line affecting some sixteen million people, by a deep
fissure line of caste affecting another five millions or more,
and by lesser fissure lines of the same order that affect, on a
rough estimate, another sixteen millions.

The caste line proper cuts off some thirteen million Negroes. Below the same barrier there are some two million
Mexicans and other Latin Americans. There are also a third
of a million Orientals, mainly Chinese and Japanese, about
370,000 American Indians, and some other groups of small
size.

The deep fissure line separates some five million Jews—
we have here no exact figures—from the rest of the people.

The minor fissure lines detach multitudes of the foreign-born. It is impossible, owing to intermarriage and other complicating conditions, to arrive at a clean-cut estimate of the numbers affected. Even if we give all Western Europeans the benefit of the doubt, there still remain Poles, Czechs, Slavs, Ruthenians, Hungarians, Greeks, and various other groups, comprising altogether around eleven millions. To these we must add some five million Italians.

Our catalogue is not complete. While it is broadly true that discrimination against the groups in question is country-wide and that regional differences in the volume of discrimination are more a function of the numbers of the affected groups concentrated in the various regions than of differences in the prevalence of caste attitudes,[2] there are nevertheless variations in the intensity of discrimination for different parts of the country. Here and there ethnic groups other than those mentioned above are in some degree exposed to it. Cultural differences, particularly those of religion, are associated with ethnic differences, as in the case of certain Roman Catholic groups, and this association may expand the area of discrimination. Furthermore, if there is a general prejudice against any group *all* the members of that group, even though some of them may hold high status in the community on other grounds, are likely to have the uneasy sense that they are not fully admitted to the membership of the community. It may then not be far from the mark to assume that from forty to fifty million people in the United States possess all the time or some of the time the feeling that they are not wholly incorporated within the American community, that in this respect they belong to minority groups, which on extrinsic grounds are subject to the fact or the danger of social or economic disparagement.

In short, the people of the United States have not adjusted themselves to the conditions of modern multigroup society,

[2] Cf. *First Report,* FEPC (Washington, D.C., 1945), p. 37.

a type of society that has had some development in nearly all countries but nowhere so much as in this country. In this vital respect they have not given realistic expression to the tradition and the social faith that constitute our historical legacy and the basis of our communal strength. Discrimination has become a feature of the national mores. The conflicts that inevitably arise between interest groups of all kinds and that are fought out in the economic and political arenas are gravely aggravated and confused by the crosscurrents of racial and ethnic issues. The tensions and embitterments thus evoked profoundly disturb the solidarity of the nation.

Some indication, though a very partial one, of these tensions is offered by the statistics of complaints filed before the Fair Employment Practice Committee and the state commissions against discrimination recently established in New York, New Jersey, Massachusetts, and Connecticut. It is evident from these statistics, in spite of their limitations, that the excluded groups reject the caste status assigned to them. In the first year and a half of the operation of the FEPC 78 per cent of all complaints were filed by Negroes.[3] Next in order came Jews—we have of course to allow for the disparity of the numbers affected—against whom occupational discrimination is more selective but still extremely prevalent. Then came Mexicans, Italians, Germans, and members of various ethnic groups. The statistics of the New York State Commission Against Discrimination are similar in this respect,[4] except that Mexicans do not play any role since they are concentrated in the Southwest and on the West Coast.

Let us now look somewhat more closely at the lines of

[3] *First Report,* FEPC, p. 37.
[4] *Annual Reports,* New York State Commission Against Discrimination, Albany, N.Y., 1946 and 1947.

discrimination that lie between these groups and the rest of the population.

(1) *The various ethnic fissure lines.* There are those who maintain that discrimination against most foreign-born groups is a waning phenomenon, that it is no longer of serious import, and that in the natural course of things it will disappear altogether. It is true that with the limits now set on immigration social prejudice against the groups concerned is no longer fed by sharp contrasts of culture and of mores. It is true that in certain urban areas members of some of these groups have an important and sometimes even a dominant position. It is true that the more educated or the more prosperous members of these groups often escape altogether from disparagement. Nevertheless these groups on the whole still suffer some social or economic handicaps in the competitive life of the United States and that fact adds a new element to the embarrassment and to the danger created by the more severe forms of discrimination.

The groups in question belong to the later immigration that began in the 1880s, was interrupted by the First World War, and was practically ended by the immigration restrictions of 1924. They were the late comers, and their members tended to occupy, for the most part, the low levels of the occupational scale. They were largely of peasant derivation. They did the hard rough work as the earlier immigrants rose in the world. Their economic inferiority, their lack of adjustment to the ways of the country, their lack of training for more remunerative pursuits, their sense of alienhood, these things conspired to create the fissure lines. They were politically inexperienced and it was easy to manipulate them, as they became citizens, for the ends of the politicians. Not infrequently they formed clusters or colonies in the less desirable areas of the larger urban communities, clinging to their old speech and their old ways in a kind of instinctive protection. Most of these ethnic groups were relatively small, had little organization, and less power. Thus the tradition of inferior status was confirmed, and still exercises considerable influence, making it harder for them to enter various avenues of advancement. For example, the author knows from his own experience that it is harder, especially in certain parts of the country, to find an appropriate position for a student with a Ph.D. degree whose name happens to be Polish or Slavic in form than to place a man, no better or not so good, whose name has an Anglo-Saxon sound.

We describe these discriminatory tendencies as lesser fissure lines because the habits and attitudes guarding them are much less rigid and less deeply entrenched than those that control other areas. Members of these groups often break through the lines of discrimination, and when they do they have relatively little difficulty in attaining social acceptance in accord with the occupational status they win. Nor do they face under such conditions any formidable barrier to inter-marriage on that level. Nevertheless the disadvantages and disparagements to which these groups on the whole are subject are very real. The derogatory names of popular usage for the members of these various peoples—"wop," "bohunk," "polack," and so forth—reflect traditional attitudes that are still by no means obsolete. The group image, the "stereo-type," still blocks the full equality of membership in the community. A well-known Italian-American has said: "We have to recognize the existence of an Italian problem; that there are specific measures that can be taken; and that the economic and political assimilation of the Italian-Americans has to be established by eliminating the old forms of dis-crimination." [5] A like statement can be made concerning all the peoples we have mentioned.

(2) *The deep fissure line.* The Jewish people occupy an

[5] Max Ascoli, "The Italian-Americans," in R. M. MacIver, ed., *Group Relations and Group Antagonisms* (New York, 1944), pp. 39–40.

anomalous position in the American community, as they do in many other countries. The discrimination they suffer has an oddly featured pattern, corresponding to the distinctive complex of prejudicial attitudes that evoked it. Unlike other group prejudices, that entertained against the Jews has a very long history, and the persistent tradition of exclusion has left its imprint not only on the Jewish people but also on the peoples which have persecuted them and driven them out, or tolerated them and segregated them, or admitted them and practised discrimination against them. The religious factor, which played a very important role in earlier days, became in the course of time inextricably interwoven with racialism and with the wanderings of the Jews from land to land as they sought escape from persecution and from their stateless condition—but our present perspective does not require the historical narrative. The treatment of the Jews in this country, as in others, has fluctuated from worse to better and from better to worse. Long past history does not determine these changes, and we must avoid the historian's fallacy that because a particular set of attitudes or of institutions has long endured it has therefore a correspondingly long life ahead. Sometimes, in this field too, length of days may be the preparation for senescence.

The unhappy history of the relations of the Jewish people and the peoples among whom they have dwelt has, however, created some special conditions that must be faced by the strategists of accommodation. Only a people possessed of great tenacity of character and remarkable skill in adapting itself to adverse conditions could have survived and overcome so signally the peculiar hazards of its lot. In the process it shaped out a system of defensive-aggressive responses that enabled its members to open up for themselves occupations disregarded by other peoples, such as the business of the trader, or subject to social or religious taboos, as was the lending of money in the Middle Ages. Thus they tended to combine a radical speculativeness in economic matters with a highly conservative socio-religious system. Their very success in this respect roused new assaults and stimulated new prejudices. Moreover, it was very natural, very "human," that in these later days a number of the intellectuals among this people should seek a way out of the experience of social frustration by becoming advocates of social revolution, and this in turn has become another source of general suspicion and animosity. The fruits of prejudice and discrimination are the seeds of fresh prejudice and further discrimination. As we shall see, this "vicious circle" is a phenomenon of high significance, and it finds no more striking illustrations than those furnished by the history of the Jewish people. The victim of discrimination, by his responses to it and his struggles against it, can scarcely, unless he has all the cunning of the serpent and all the innocence of the dove, avoid behavior that ratifies in the minds of the discriminators the discriminations they practise.

Another aspect of this state of things is that the Jewish people, having suffered severe exclusion and having been thrown back for self-defense on its own morale, has retained in an unusual way the integrity of its traditional culture. The difference between this culture and the cultures of the communities in which the Jews live is thus conspicuous. Their dietary usages and the elaborate rituals of their religion and of their social customs, penetrating into every activity of everyday life, even the particular gestures that mark a people long set apart, erect new barriers, once the habit of discrimination has been formed, to easy accommodation in the larger community. While only the orthodox portion of the Jewish people maintain the full requirements of their code, the code itself tends to identify the whole group. Culture differences in themselves need not be, and in modern society frequently are not, a ground for discrimination, but in the

special circumstances of the Jewish people they confirm, in
the minds of many, the sense of their alienage.

The Jews are highly urbanized and in the United States
are heavily concentrated in New York City, of which they
form approximately one third of the population. Occupa-
tionally they are engaged largely in trading and merchandising pursuits and in the small-unit types of manufacture.
They predominate in the clothing industry. They have very
little role in the heavy industries and, contrary to popular
ideas, are not prominent in banking or in international
finance. They are strong in the theater business, in the
movies, and in the musical world. In New York City they
are well represented in the legal profession and also in the
medical profession. They own few newspapers, but the
exceptions, in New York and Philadelphia, include papers
of the highest standing.[6]

This brief survey might seem at first glance to discount
the theory of the deep fissure line. But we began by describing the discrimination against the Jewish people as anomalous. It is exhibited, primarily, in the general exclusion of
Jews from the social life of the "upper middle class" and
from the clubs, hotels, inns, apartment houses, residential
developments and summer resorts that cater to this class.
The taboo even extends to the private wards of hospitals.
It limits the entry of Jews to various occupational avenues,
where the status factor dominates, such as banks, insurance
agencies, trust companies, and so forth. It sets obstacles to
the admission of Jews to certain types of school, college, university. There is manifestly at work a process of discrimination centering in the competitively aspiring upper middle
class, but it permeates all classes, with stronger foci among
certain religious groups whether of the Roman Catholic

[6] For the available facts see *Economic Adjustment Information Service,*
Conference on Jewish Relations (New York, 1938); and *Jews in America,* by
the editors of *Fortune* (New York, 1936).

creed or representing some form of Protestantism. Moreover, not infrequently groups that are themselves seeking to resist a status of social inferiority, such as certain Eastern European groups and occasionally a colored group, display tendencies to anti-Jewish prejudice.[7]

One consequence is a kind of social, and in degree economic, segregation of the Jewish people. Just as they have their own shops and their own schools, their own restaurants and their own hotels and their own resorts, just as they have their own charities and their own hospitals, so they have colleges in which they are largely predominant, so they have their exclusively Jewish factories and firms, so even they have a few industries that are practically their own. The economic concentration, like the educational, is evidence not so much of aptitudes and interests characteristic of the Jewish group as of the deep fissure line that separates this group from the total community. Similar phenomena are found wherever the caste principle rules. In the instance of the Jews the process is intensified on account of their extreme urbanization.

(3) *The caste line proper.* It is beyond contention that in the United States all "colored" people—and this designation must here be extended to include Chinese, Hindus, Japanese, Koreans, and Filipinos, as well as Negroes, and for fuller measure American Indians and Latin Americans—are com-

---

[7] The dominantly class or caste character of anti-Semitic prejudice is strongly suggested by the findings of various psychological researches. The following quotations are typical: "On total anti-Semitism score Republicans were higher than Democrats . . . and sorority members higher than nonmembers, all these differences being statistically significant. Anti-Semitism score was found to increase directly with amount of the father's income." D. I. Levinson and R. N. Sanford, "A Scale for the Measurement of Anti-Semitism," *Journal of Psychology,* vol. 17 (1944), pp. 339–370.

"Within the limits of our material subjects with high score on anti-Semitism were found to be characterized by two major trends. First, they exhibited a kind of conservative attitude. . . . they tended automatically to support the *status quo.* Secondly . . . [there was] a tendency to hold in high esteem one's own ethnic and social group, to keep it narrow, unmixed and pure." E. Frenkel-Brunswik and R. N. Sanford, "Some Personality Factors in Anti-Semitism," *Journal of Psychology,* vol. 20 (1945), pp. 271–291.

monly regarded as and commonly treated as constituting a
lower caste. In the drawing of this line practically no distinction is made between people of high cultural achievement or
historical eminence and those which have no such preten-
sions. We shall limit our illustration to the cases of the
Chinese, the Mexicans, and the Negroes.

Very few Chinese are admitted to the United States. The
exclusion act of 1904 completely prohibited Chinese immigration and while that act has been rescinded the number
who can enter is extremely small.[8] This, however, is a matter
of national policy with which we are not at this point concerned. What does concern us is that the Chinese who are
resident in the United States are subjected to a caste-like
discrimination, even although they have recently been made
eligible for naturalization.

The caste treatment of the Chinese is sufficiently evidenced by the fact that they have practically no occupational
opportunities except as launderers, waiters, cooks, and restau-
rateurs. Not being regarded as members of the community,
living in squalid isolation in their congested "Chinatowns,"
they are barred from any free participation in the economic
life of the country. If a few of them do find their way to
colleges or technical institutions they reach a dead end when
they are through. The vocations for which they may have
trained are effectively closed to them. A naive observer might
imagine that the American Chinese had some special affinity

[8] The Chinese Exclusion Act was repealed December 17, 1943. The number
of immigrant Chinese admitted under the quota was 44 for the year July 1,
1943 to June 30, 1944, and 91 for the year ending June 30, 1945. Filipinos
and East Indians are now also eligible for admission but other Asiatics are
still excluded. Japanese-Americans in this country are subjected to extremely
discriminatory treatment under municipal ordinances that bar them from
owning land, practising various trades and professions, and so forth. For
the facts see Milton R. Konvitz, *The Alien and the Asiatic in American Law,*
Cornell University Press, 1946.

for the laundry and restaurant businesses, in which case he would be attributing to disposition what is really due to the exigencies of caste. If any evidence were needed it should suffice to mention that under wartime conditions the barriers of occupation were lowered so that the Chinese began to find places in skilled trades both mechanical and clerical.[9]

Consider next the Mexicans. Perhaps no group offers a clearer illustration of the desolating economic and social effects of caste discrimination within the American community. A considerable portion of them are among the oldest migrants to North America—in fact many of them in New Mexico have been living there since the sixteenth century. Nevertheless they remain among the poorest and most illiterate of our citizens, and nowhere are they anything but hewers of wood and drawers of water. It can hardly be questioned that this condition is due to their debarment from the opportunities of advancement. In the border states, particularly Texas and California, they are segregated in the same manner as the Southern Negroes. In the areas of the Southwest where they form a large portion of the population they receive no adequate schooling or training and are left to live in an insanitary ostracism on deteriorated lands. They speak Spanish and are given no adequate grounding in English. They live their life apart, maintaining the old ways but without the cultural sustenance that once gave them vitality. Their children, when they go outside of the circle, exhibit the effects of the characteristic "culture clash" that besets the ambitious young of peoples which have retained in the newer environment the old traditions. Envious and frustrated, they easily fall into the ways of the gang. The sporadic

[9] Carey McWilliams, *Brothers Under the Skin* (Boston, 1943), p. 106. For an informative and sympathetic account of various racial and ethnic groups in the United States see McWilliams, *op. cit.;* or Francis J. Brown and Joseph S. Roucek, *Our Racial and National Minorities* (New York, 1937); or Donald Young, *American Minority Peoples* (New York, 1932).

and directionless "Zoot-Suit Riots" of Los Angeles in 1943 were the exhibitionist protests of Mexican youths subjected to such conditions.

As for the migratory Mexican laborers, largely recent immigrants, they form a sort of pariah labor force, moving in groups to the centers where the demand for unskilled labor is greatest. They are insulated from their fellow workers and still more from the rest of the community.[10]

By far the largest group under the color ban are the Negroes. So much so that, unlike other racially distinguished groups, they are in many areas throughout the South a majority of the inhabitants. They differ from all the other groups also in that they possess no tradition of an alien culture. Their culture is through and through American. They have been longer resident in the United States than most White groups. They are the descendants of Americans, and for that matter can count a goodly number of White Americans among their ancestors. "The American Negro is as American as a Vermont farmer." [11] The characteristic values the Negro cherishes, artistic, religious, literary, are bred within the American tradition. Indeed the less sophisticated Negroes are so thoroughly acculturated that they are apt to accept from the surrounding culture some of its anti-Negro doctrines, such as that major public concerns are "white folks' business" or that black Negroes are less to be esteemed than light-colored ones. They are on the whole less radical than other minority groups that feel the pressure of caste.[12] They have for the most part been little affected by communist appeals, in spite of the strong claims made by communists that

---

10 E. S. Bogardus, *The Mexican in the United States* (University of Southern California Press, 1934); George E. Sanchez, *Forgotten People, a Study of New Mexicans* (University of New Mexico Press, 1940); Carey McWilliams, *op. cit.*, Chap. III; Pauline R. Kibbe, *Latin Americans in Texas* (University of New Mexico Press, 1946), Chaps. 13, 14.

11 Donald Young (unpublished work).

12 Gunnar Myrdal, *An American Dilemma* (New York, 1944), vol. 1, pp. 495 ff.

they alone stand against all racial discrimination. They will
accept at need communist leadership to gain particular ends,
but they are not deeply indoctrinated.[13] In spite of their caste
condition they fight devotedly for their country. "Negroes
have been notably a loyal and patriotic group. One of their
outstanding characteristics is the singlemindedness of their
patriotism." [14]

Not only do the Negroes constitute the largest caste group
in the United States but also the caste line that marks them
off is more powerfully guarded than any other, being institutionalized in a ramifying system of segregation. The segregation in effect against the Oriental groups, the Chinese or
the Japanese, is not so rigorously invoked or so passionately
defended as that against the Negroes, whether because the
numbers of the former are relatively small or because the
sense of their racial disparity is not so strong.

The full rigor of caste has controlled the relations of
Whites and Negroes in the Southern states. With a bow to
the Fifteenth Amendment these states prescribe "separate but
equal" public services and facilities for the Negro. They are
separate but in practice never equal—indeed, were they
equal, the caste principle would already have lost its power
and the separation itself could scarcely endure. Actually the
provision made for them—made by Whites alone—in
schools, on buses and trains and everywhere else marks the
difference between the superior and the inferior caste. Take
the schools, for example. For the states of Alabama, Arkansas,
Georgia, Louisiana, Maryland, Mississippi, North Carolina,
and South Carolina, the average current expenditure in
1943–1944 per White pupil was $83.44 and per Negro pupil
$36.88. The discrepancy was least for Maryland and North
Carolina. It was greatest for Mississippi, where the figures

13 Harold F. Gosnell, *Negro Politicians* (University of Chicago Press, 1935);
S. D. Spero and A. L. Harris, *The Black Worker* (Columbia University Press,
1931).
14 *First Annual Report,* Selective Service System.

were respectively $71.65 and $11.96.[15] Even this showing is on
the average much better than that offered by earlier evidences. Negroes run businesses for Negroes, operate retail
shops for them, preach to them, teach them and give them
legal service, give them some medical service, do some insurance and banking for them—but always with a handicap,
always with a difficulty in getting adequate training for the
more technical and the more professional tasks.[16] The segregation ceases only at the point where Negroes do menial or
manual services for Whites, nursing their children, cooking
their meals, scrubbing their floors, running their errands,
hewing wood and drawing water.

The consequences of this segregation are written in our
social and economic statistics. The Negro group lives in
abject poverty, has the highest rate of illiteracy, and the
highest mortality and morbidity rates of any considerable
group. The life expectancy of the Negro, if we take the
United States as a whole, is eleven years lower than the life
expectancy of the White. The Negro suffers most from the
diseases of poverty and ignorance, from tuberculosis, syphilis,
pneumonia, rickets, pellagra, and so forth. During the last
war the rejection rate of Negroes was considerably higher
than that of Whites.[17] The White population of the areas
where Negroes are most numerous are themselves the least
advanced of the whole country, whether we take educational
or economic criteria.[18] The more thoughtful among them are

[15] The figures are taken from a Statistical Circular issued by the U.S.
Office of Education.
[16] For a detailed account see Ira De A. Reid, "The Negro in the American
Economic System," unpublished monograph for the Myrdal report, available
in Schomburg Collection, New York Public Library.
[17] *Leadership and the Negro Soldier*, Army Service Forces Manual, M5,
Washington, D.C., 1944.
[18] A ranking of the states by various indices of health, by economic criteria,
and by such cultural indices as the extent of illiteracy, the expenditure on
schooling, and the percentage of professional workers in the working population, has recently been made by Gerhard Hirschfeld and Carl W. Straw,
"Comparative Health Factors Among the States," *American Sociological*

beginning to suspect that the backwardness of the South as a whole is causally related to the operation of the caste principle.[19]

We have thus far presented, in broadest outline, the prevailing system of inter-group discrimination. Many agencies, private and public, are concerned with different aspects of it. They are attacking it on various fronts, political, economic, educational. It is the strategy of these attacks to which this study is devoted. But there is a preliminary question that calls for a brief review since any consideration of strategy must be affected by the answer to it.

2. WHICH WAY ARE WE HEADING?

Is the greater awareness of inter-group discrimination, along with the increased attention now being given to it, a response to an increase in the amount and the intensity of the phenomenon? It might of course be attributable to other conditions, such as might make the prevalence of discrimination more disintegrating and nationally perilous than before or such as might for any other reason bring it into the focus of interest. There are those, however, who claim that discrimination has actually in our days been growing more widespread and more deep-working. They bring forward a number of evidences to support their case.

One unfavorable evidence is the increasing disabilities to which alien groups are subjected, and especially those groups that remain alien because they are debarred from naturalization. The Japanese are the worst sufferers. California led the way by passing in 1913 the alien land law. Thus, besides be-

Review (February, 1946), vol. 11, pp. 42–52. On all counts the Southern states are massed at the bottom of the list.

19 For the operation of caste against the Negro see Charles S. Johnson, *Patterns of Negro Segregation* (New York, 1943); and Myrdal, *op. cit.*, Chaps. 3, 31, 32. For a clear picture of the situation see Allison Davis, Burleigh B. Gardner and Mary R. Gardner, *Deep South* (University of Chicago Press, 1941).

ing shut out from various professional vocations they were
prevented from buying land or even from leasing land except
on very short tenure. The example of California has been
followed by other Western states and the laws against in-
eligible aliens have become more stringent, so that at present
the Japanese in the United States, including even American
citizens of Japanese descent, are heavily handicapped.

There is evidence, again, of tightening restrictions on the
admission of Jews to certain professional schools and also to
leading undergraduate colleges. The Report of the New
York City Mayor's Committee on Unity stated that from
1925 to 1943 the percentage of applicants from the College
of the City of New York (which is 80 per cent Jewish) who
were admitted to medical schools throughout the country fell
from 58 per cent to 15 per cent in spite of a marked decrease
in the number of applicants. It stated also that from 1933 to
1938 the average number of Jewish students per Grade A
Medical School reporting decreased from 12.16 per cent of
the student body to 6.29. Furthermore, "in the last decade
preceding the war years the percentage of Jewish students of
the total student body admitted to undergraduate colleges
fell about 50 per cent." [20] Questions have been raised respecting the accuracy of these statistics but even when we allow
for a possible margin of error they remain formidable. The
tightening of educational discrimination is again strongly
suggested by the Decennial Census of Jewish College Students
issued November, 1947, by the B'nai B'rith Vocational Service Bureau. It shows that in the 67 medical schools reporting,
out of 89, both in 1935 and in 1946 the percentage of Jewish
students declined from 15.9 to 12.7. In the dental schools
reporting in both years the decline was from 28.2 to 18.9. In
law schools it was even greater, from 25.8 to 11.1. Since a

[20] Confidential Report, but the figures above cited have been publicly
printed. See also Dan W. Dodson, "Religious Prejudice in Colleges," *The
American Mercury* (July, 1946), vol. 63, pp. 5–13; and Frank Kingdon, "Discrimination in American Colleges," *ibid.*, vol. 61, pp. 391–399.

slightly larger percentage of Jewish students were going to college in 1946 than eleven years earlier the Bureau concludes, reasonably enough, that the figures indicate increased discrimination against Jews in professional schools.

Another evidence is the increased activity directed to the maintenance or extension of residential covenants. These devices are directed mainly against Negroes and Orientals, though in some areas they affect Jews as well. They have come into general use in the superior residential sectors, the poorer ones relying on less formal procedures to keep out the members of undesired racial or ethnic groups. With the expansion of cities and the consequent rise of ground values—and also with the increased migration of Negroes to the North and West—restrictive agreements came into vogue. They were not much in use prior to the First World War. "Even in cities like Chicago, where today the Negro ghetto is surrounded by an iron band of restrictive agreements, Negroes lived in all sectors until 1910." [21]

This close segregation of racial groups in expanding urban communities, and particularly in areas where the demands of industry bring in considerable numbers of Negro or Mexican workers, has increased inter-group tensions and disturbances. It has corralled these workers in congested, slum-like areas, has made for the economic exploitation of those who perforce live in them, and has bred an ever-smouldering resentment that sometimes flares into acts of violence. There seems little doubt that the race riots that have occurred in Detroit, Chicago, New York, Los Angeles, Boston, Philadelphia, and various other cities, though in some instances stimulated by labor jealousies, are manifestations of the dangerous tensions created by this situation.

Inter-group prejudice is universal, wherever groups are brought into contact as groups, and only a utopian can

[21] *Hemmed In,* by Robert Weaver, a pamphlet of the American Council on Race Relations, 1945.

cherish the hope that any reform of society or re-education
of man can wholly eradicate it. But prejudice of this kind is
fluctuating, is intensified or moderated by changes in the
conditions or in the stimuli to which it is responsive, not
infrequently takes new directions, and may find expression
in relatively harmless or in quite destructive outlets. Some
students of the subject accept the position that in the United
States the volume of inter-group prejudice and discrimination has been mounting. Thus Professor Allport wrote in
1944 as follows:

"Our gauges reveal that at present the pressure is danger-
ously high. Public opinion polls show that 85 per cent of
the population is ready to scapegoat some group or other (at
least they accuse them of not making a fair share of their contribution to the war effort). Labor and Jews are commonly
blamed. . . . Less than half of our population give entirely
fair-minded and unprejudiced replies to certain questions
designed to measure the extent of anti-Semitism.

"Drawing our evidence chiefly from published and unpublished opinion polls, we may estimate roughly that one-
fifth of our people are implacable Anglophobes, 5 to 10 per
cent are violently anti-Semitic, while perhaps 45 per cent or
more are mildly bigoted in the same direction. At least 40
per cent express prejudice against the Negro. The numbers
that are anti-Catholic, anti-Russian, anti-labor, anti-Prot-
estant vary, but in all cases the proportions are fairly high." [22]

For New York City, most multigroup of all cities, the
Mayor's Committee on Unity reports: "Some of the researches we are doing show that a startling amount of prejudice is the norm even in the most educated among the
population of our city." [23]

Can we conclude from such evidences that prejudice and

[22] Gordon W. Allport, "The Bigot in Our Midst," *The Commonweal*, Oct.
6, 1944.
[23] *A Blueprint on Intergroup Relations*, New York, 1946.

discrimination of group against group are growing? The question is not so easily resolved. In the first place the evidence of public opinion polls does not—as yet—enable us to make comparisons of sentiment over any length of time. They throw some light on the present situation, but even so they fall short of reflecting either the amount or the strength of prejudice. They serve by giving us a *minimum* estimate of the amount. Moreover, the questions they put are not, can hardly be, free from ambiguity of interpretation on the part of the respondents, even if we could assume both that the respondents can read their own minds and that they are completely frank in their responses. These remarks are not intended to discredit a valuable method for the assessment of public opinion but solely to point out that thus far they give little or no ground for determining whether or not intergroup prejudice is on the increase.

Again, we must distinguish changes in the actual volume of discrimination from changes in social concern about discrimination and also from changes in the attitude toward discrimination of those who suffer from it. That considerable numbers of people have become increasingly aware of the problem of discrimination and increasingly uneasy over it is manifested by the new publicity it receives, by the numerous organizations that seek to do something about it, and by the political instruments and agencies it has recently called into being.[24] That there is increasing unrest and protest and rebelliousness on the part of various groups against discrimination is also clearly evidenced. But such manifestations may be signs that a system of discrimination is losing hold, not that it is becoming more oppressive. When the

[24] Over three hundred organizations are listed in the *Directory of Agencies in Race Relations, National, State and Local,* Julius Rosenwald Fund, 1945. "Over two hundred such organizations have been established since 1943 alone" —Louis Wirth, "The Unfinished Business of American Democracy," *Annals of the American Academy of Political and Social Science* (March, 1946), vol. 244, p. 6.

conditions seem hopeless to the subjected classes they rarely indulge in vain sacrificial protests, nor do they receive much aid and sponsorship from within the classes that hold them in subjection.

In this country the patterns of discrimination are very diverse and bear on different groups in very different ways. It is quite possible that discrimination may be decreasing in some directions and maintaining itself or growing stronger in others. There is significant evidence that the caste system controlling the Negro is by no means as secure as once it was. Among the indications are the eclipse of the White primary and the greater opportunities for Negro voting in the South,[25] the stronger reaction against lynch law and the somewhat lessened impunity of White perpetrators of outrages against Negroes, the appearance of a group of liberals in the South who take a strong stand against racial oppression, the rise of organizations dedicated to racial equality (such as the Southern Conference for Human Welfare, the Southern Regional Council, and the Association of Southern Women for the Prevention of Lynchings), the degree of Negro economic betterment achieved through social security legislation and the farm security program of the Roosevelt administration, and the movement for Negro unionization being carried forward by CIO unions in the South. We note also the introduction of Negro officers into the police staff of various Southern cities. On the national scale there are again such significant evidences as the slowly increasing employment of Negro teachers, the somewhat larger opportunities opened here and there to Negro doctors, and the removal of the ban against Negro baseball players in the major leagues. There were also economic advances achieved under wartime pressures, and on the whole these have been, except at a few

[25] The Supreme Court judgment rendering White primaries unconstitutional, although evaded in various ways, is being upheld in Southern courts. Thus for the state of South Carolina Federal District Judge Waring ruled (July, 1947) that Negroes must be permitted to vote in the hitherto all-White Democratic primary.

points, maintained. Some of the newer expressions of discriminative activity, such as the developments of restrictive covenants and the resort to additional voting restrictions in some Southern states, may be explained as attempts to stem the tide of change. If we are right in the conclusion we draw later that the forces undermining the sheer caste line have a very broad base then such attempts are not likely to achieve any considerable success.

With respect to the lesser fissure lines there is too little evidence for any clean-cut conclusion as to trends. The general considerations we can adduce on the whole support the view that the situation is improving rather than deteriorating. The restriction of European immigration has probably improved the status of the groups concerned, since they are no longer associated with new supplies of cheap labor furnished by later arrivals of the same "national origin." With longer residence in the country more members of these groups rise to positions of influence or affluence. The alien character attaching to these groups wears thinner, as they become accommodated to American ways. Most of their members have become citizens, especially in recent years, and their participation in the war effort and in the testing comradeship of arms has strengthened their own sense of "belonging" and the reciprocal acceptance of them by their fellow countrymen. We should not, however, assume that the social and economic obstacles they still meet are of little account and that the process of time will level them altogether. The discrimination to which they are still subject is irksome and frustrating, even though it is qualified in various ways. Old identifications are still prevalent in majority attitudes toward these peoples. Large numbers of them still feel, and with good reason, that they are not permitted to participate fully or freely in the life of the communities in which they live.

More difficult of assessment is the situation with respect to the Jews. Here discrimination and prejudice are deep-rooted and obstinate. One evidence, if any were needed, is that the war fought against the Nazis, who were notorious for their persecution of the Jews, did not seem to evoke any strong sympathetic reaction toward the Jewish people in this country, even while there was universal condemnation of the atrocities committed against their European brethren. Indeed, the verdict of some competent observers is that conditions grew less, rather than more, favorable. The more violent forms of anti-Jewish agitation were held in some restraint, but less direct kinds of propagandism against Jews still flourished, and there was practically no evidence that prejudicial attitudes were mitigated. Without entering into the intricacies of the argument we can reasonably infer that the deep fissure line holds firm. This conclusion, particularly in view of more encouraging evidences in other areas, raises challenging questions regarding the obstacles to better relationships and the possibilities of more effective strategy for the attack upon them.

There are certain factors that cause confusion regarding the extent of anti-Jewish prejudice and discrimination. One is that the usual gauges of inter-group accommodation are not fully applicable here. For example, for other ethnic groups the rate of intermarriage or "exogamy" is a serviceable index.[26] But for the Jewish groups the statistics of intermarriage are, at first sight, quite bewildering. Thus we find in pre-Hitler Germany a remarkably high rate of intermarriage—one authority gives a rate of 51 per cent for 1915 and another gives 43.78 per cent for the crucial year of 1933.[27]

[26] Julius H. Drachsler, *Democracy and Assimilation* (New York, 1920).
[27] Arthur Ruppin, *The Jewish Fate and Future* (London, 1940), p. 108. See also Milton L. Barron, "The Incidence of Jewish Intermarriage in Europe and America," *American Sociological Review* (February, 1946), vol. 11, 6–13. A rate of 50 per cent means here that in 50 out of every 100 marriages in which one partner was a Jew the other partner was non-Jewish. The same author states that in Derby, Conn., the rate of Jewish intermarriage was zero in 1929–1930 and in 1940 was 16.67 per cent (*People Who Intermarry*, Syracuse University Press, 1946).

Whereas for New York City the rate for 1908 to 1912 is given as 2.27 [28] and for Canada for 1926 to 1931 as 4.82.[29] For the magnitude of these and various other disparities contained in the available statistics the present writer has no ready explanation. But they reveal the need for caution in using the criterion of intermarriage. We must remember that, where the distinction can be clearly drawn, religious inter-marriage is as a rule less frequent than ethnic intermar-riage.[30] We must remember that the Jewish people fall into various categories, both with respect to "country or origin," and with respect to the degree to which they retain the full Jewish faith and ritual. The rate of intermarriage varies according to the category. German Jews, like Sephardic Jews, have long shown a greater tendency to intermarriage. The amount varies according to the degree in which Jews con-stitute considerable localized subcommunities in the areas in which they live. Also, where Jews are relatively few, other conditions being favorable, there is usually more intermar-riage. Thus in Sweden, France, and Italy, the proportion of intermarriage has been very high. It varies also according to relative numbers of Roman Catholics and Protestants in the population. It varies according to the degree of pros-perity enjoyed by the group, the more prosperous being given more to intermarriage.

Back of all these phenomena there lies one primary con-dition. Every group, when it comes into a new environment or when for any reason it is relatively insulated, finds sup-port and sustenance in that which is common to its members. The more such a group is cut off from the environing com-munity the more tenaciously it clings to its group being, to its own folkways. Historically the Jewish groups everywhere have been thus cut off, in the first place because of a religious

28 Ruppin, *op. cit.*, p. 128.
29 Silcox and Fisher, *Catholics, Jews, and Protestants* (New York, 1934), p. 265.
30 Barron, *People Who Intermarry*, pp. 158 ff.

difference invested with great divisive power. Hence it has
been more imperative for them to rally to their common
cause, Judaism. Moreover, other ethnic groups have two
rallying grounds. One is their homeland, where the folk
from which they have hived off still lives—we do not say
here their *state*, for many ethnic groups do not possess, and
some have never possessed, a state of their own. The other
is the folk tradition or culture. But the Jews have only one
rallying ground: they have had no homeland, much less a
state, since A.D. 135; they have only the memory of one and
now at length, amid much contention and strife, the promise
of its partial restoration. Consequently they have more
than any other group been under the social necessity to preserve their culture, which in their case is inextricably bound
up in every aspect with their religion. This in turn has
made for reciprocal exclusiveness, on their own part as well
as on that of their community neighbors. Their obedience to
a universal human necessity has separated them from the rest
of humanity. It is a famous instance of the common rule
that man's inhumanity to man is due to man's lack of
understanding of his own humanity.

To return to our point of departure, there is a second
reason why the nature and extent of anti-Jewish attitudes is
misapprehended. The frequent use of the term "anti-
Semitism" is apt to create a false impression. We find statements of a seemingly authoritative nature to the effect that
there is little anti-Semitism in the United States. Thus the
Fortune investigation of November, 1935, reported as follows: "Anti-Semitism languished in the United States and
still languishes. Although an estimated half million people
may attend occasional anti-Semitic meetings, etc., there are
probably no more than 15,000 loyal Jew-hating group members in the whole United States. . . . Surveys of national
opinion indicate either hostility to anti-Semitic dogmas or,

what is worse from the agitators' point of view, complete indifference." [31]

It would be wrong to conclude that anti-Jewish prejudice is minimal in the United States. If we follow *Fortune*
in defining anti-Semitism as "the deliberately incited affirmative racial phobia" that leads to pogroms against the Jewish
people, the verdict it presents is accurate enough. But anti-
Semitism so defined is merely an extreme expression of a far
more pervading sentiment or attitude, and less radical expressions of it may still amount to active and insidious prejudice.
There is, moreover, no clear line to be drawn between what
is here called a "racial phobia" and the less extreme manifestations of anti-Jewish sentiment. On this point the editors
of *Fortune* are too easily satisfied. For example, a question
used in the *Fortune* investigation (October, 1935) ran: "Do
you believe that in the long run Germany will be better or
worse off if it drives out the Jews?" Fourteen per cent of
the respondents answered "Better," and 31.4 per cent took
the "Don't know" position. *Fortune* comments: " 'Don't
know' in this connection is almost certainly equivalent to
indifference and indifference is the most effective prophylactic against the pestilence of hate." Both parts of the statement are questionable. Conceivably "Don't know" might
mean a genuine unwillingness to make commitment on a
question not without some ambiguity and anyhow involving,
if impartially considered, a perplexing problem in historical
prediction. But only the sophisticated would take this point
of view. Another among various possibilities is that "Don't
know" indicates a belief that what people do to the Jews,
even the most violent and cruel treatment, will have no
significant repercussions on the country which yields to this

[31] Quoted from the pamphlet, *"Jews in America,"* published by the editors
of *Fortune*. The full report, with the same title, was published by Random
House, New York, 1936.

"race phobia." As for the optimistic belief that indifference is a safeguard against the spread of the sentiment of anti-Semitism there is the obvious reply that such indifference, revealing as it must a complete unconcern for the fate of the persecuted group, is the very soil in which the agitator sows his dragon's teeth. We note that in their definition of anti-Semitism the editors of *Fortune* speak of it as "deliberately incited." If it is incited there must be those who, not having previously been anti-Semitic, have been responsive to some incitement.[32]

Our characterization of anti-Jewish sentiment as creating a deep fissure line may be challenged further on the ground that opinion polls and other investigations report 45 or 50 per cent of the population as "mildly bigoted" in this respect, exhibiting some degree of prejudice but no serious *animus*,

---

[32] The author asked Professor Gardner Murphy for his views on the judgment of the *Fortune* editors on the import of "Don't know." His reply was as follows:

"The passage from *Fortune* puzzles me. I don't see how 'Don't know' can be equated with 'indifference,' nor how indifference can be regarded as a prophylactic against hate. Possibly the author had in mind the obvious fact that feelings for or against people may be masks for their opposites, so that the indifferent are the ones most likely to have no open or *hidden* inflammable material at all. But this would be far-fetched. More pertinent is the fact that *intense* antipathy usually arises out of a *slight* antipathy. For example, the normally distributed attitude becomes bi-modal as a result of pressure, as is shown in a number of propaganda studies.

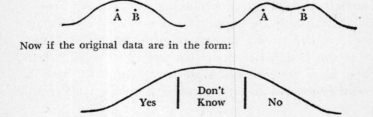

Now if the original data are in the form:

many who are near the edges of the 'Don't know' will move into the 'Yes' or 'No' regions as a result of pressure. So I think the *Fortune* statement is all wrong."

while presumably the rest of the population, apart from the small fraction of out-and-out anti-Semites, harbor no anti-Jewish prejudice at all. Is this showing consistent with the presence of a deep fissure line? We believe it is. In the first place caste differences or cleavages between group and group need not, often do not, spell active hatred on one side or on both. What they connote is difference, unbridged uncongenial difference, social aloofness, alienation. Anyone with any capacity for social observation can soon discover that this sense of uncongenial difference is prevalent in the United States, varying in its intensity. Moreover it is quite unwarranted to conclude from the responses to polls and questionnaires that about half the population are unaffected by this sentiment.[33] The usual polling devices are not well calculated to explore its range. Often those who claim to be free from it prove, on further probing, to be susceptible to it, as the author has himself discovered on various occasions. It is probably the exceptional rather than the average person who is immune to it or who has wholly rejected it.

[33] Samuel H. Flowerman and Marie Jahoda (*Commentary*, April, 1946, pp. 82–86) point out that the polls on anti-Semitism cannot be accepted as accurate guides, but at least they strongly support the conclusion that over 50 per cent of the population, in addition to the 5 to 10 per cent who are violently anti-Semitic, are disposed to "some degree of anti-Semitism."

Chapter Four

Balances and Circles

1. BALANCES

FOR REASONS already given we do not undertake any elaborate
analysis of the ramifying intricacy of causes from which
emerge the processes and features of inter-group discrimination. But there are certain type figures that characterize many
otherwise very different situations and the nature of which
we must clearly grasp if our programs of action are to be
well founded. Unless we understand these configurations we
shall be insensitive to the probable effects on other aspects of
a situation, of a policy directed at one aspect in particular.
Reformers often sin by disregard of the repercussions of
legislative measures designed to check behavior that in their
judgment offends the common weal. Often they make no
realistic attempt to foresee the counterbehavior of those
whose activities they seek to control or guide. Often they
fail to see that the one factor they would control is so closely
interwoven with others that their efforts may disturb without
ameliorating, may merely divert into other channels the
tendencies they seek to arrest. The history of moralistic regulation and of laws to suppress crime is full of illustrations.
The prohibition experiment is still recent enough to be an
object lesson. We do not imply that the reasonable anticipa-

tion of some untoward consequences is an adequate ground
for refusing to take action. It may, for example, be desirable
to regulate prices under certain conditions although it is
certain to stimulate black market operations. The point is
that only by reckoning these probabilities and weighing
them against the direct benefits expected to accrue from action can an intelligent policy be formulated or carried out.

The configurations of causality to which attention needs
particularly to be called belong to two major types. One
presents a *balance* of forces, the other a kind of *circle* or
roundabout. Both types signify ways in which the complex
interplay of forces maintains the situations to which the
forces belong. The first type stresses the opposition of forces;
the second, the interlocking of forces. We shall first distinguish some forms of balance or equilibrium.

The Tense Equilibrium. Here the given situation is characterized by sharp opposition and, on one side or on both,
strong emotional stress. One side is politically and socially
dominant; the other is filled with resentment and bitterness.
The dominant side acts repressively while the other offers
whatever resistance is in its power, depending on its numbers,
its degree of organization, and so forth. No accommodation,
no compromise, is possible. The suppressed group would re-
volt if it had the means; the upper group may be strong
enough to be merely contemptuous or, in the more tense
condition, it may live in fear lest the lower group get "out
of hand."

This situation is marked by outbreaks of violence. These
may take the form of lynchings, pogroms, and other terror-
istic outrages on the part of the upper group. In some circumstances the lower group resorts to more clandestine
violence, sometimes, as in Russia under the later Czars, to
counterterrorism. Where the lower group is numerous there
may be street fighting and riots. These clashes take place in
an atmosphere highly charged with passion and hatred.

The tense equilibrium is punctuated by these outbreaks. They are set off at any moment by some *precipitant,* which may be fortuitous or designed. An assertion of rights by members of the lower group, a transgression of the limits set to it by the upper group, any act that offends the presumption of superiority, or any measure of desperation or revenge, is sufficient to create a commotion and an outburst of violence. The precipitant reveals the forms of tension at the same time that it raises the tension level. Sometimes members of the upper group deliberately manufacture precipitants: for example, by spreading a false rumor, as in the case of a relatively recent Jewish massacre in Poland where a boy was instructed to tell a story of having been kidnapped by Jews as a preliminary to his ritual sacrifice. The fabrication under the auspices of the Russian (Czarist) secret police of the *Protocols of the Elders of Zion* is an example of a particularly elaborate variety of precipitant. Since the precipitant often imperils a movement toward the reduction of discrimination and may be deliberately injected for this purpose it is important that leaders and policy-makers should be awake to this danger, so as to be immediately ready to prevent its injection or to thwart its operation.

So long as the tense equilibrium endures there is little hope of effective betterment of the relations between the opposing groups. The immediate task is to control, so far as possible, the precipitants that at short intervals generate fresh tension and new clashes. Otherwise nothing short of a revolution will drastically change the situation. The dominant group, if so minded, can control the activities of its more fanatical or sadistic members who provoke acts of violence. Thus the tension will be abated and more constructive measures can be introduced, allying themselves with the processes of economic and social developments that make for greater cooperation between the opposed groups.

On occasions and in places in which tension runs high the

immediate need is for the skilful application of *anti-precipitants,* so as to ward off or counter the incentives and provocations to violence.[1] These anti-precipitants may take various forms according to the situation—the exposure of an agitator, the appeal of a leader, the swift intervention of legal processes, the authoritative denial of a false rumor, the skilful handling of a riot situation by the police authorities, and so forth.[2] The anti-precipitant need not, however, be something expressly designed to meet a need. It may be an event favorable to the subject group. A quick change in economic conditions may turn the situation, or the death of a mob leader, or the necessities arising out of war, where the need for skilled man power blunts the resistance to the demands of the disparaged groups for occupational opportunities. The anti-precipitant attacks the weak spot in the discrimination front. Just as the precipitant reveals the focus of tension and heightens it, so the anti-precipitant reveals the margin of resistance and lowers the tension.

The Precarious Equilibrium. By this designation we refer to a type of situation that portends imminent change *in one direction only.* In this respect it differs from the "tense equilibrium." The physical counterpart is an overhanging mass that may at any time descend in an avalanche or a rock perched on a cliff that a strong push will hurl below. Under such conditions the immediate issue is solely that of the maintenance or downfall of the *status quo,* and the mode of its downfall is clearly indicated. The situation is so loaded that any disturbance may serve as a precipitant. In the tense equilibrium a precipitant, according to its kind, may turn

[1] On *precipitants* and *anti-precipitants* see the author's *Social Causation* (Boston, 1944).

[2] See, for example, the Police Training Bulletin of the California Department of Justice, *A Guide to Race Relations for Police Officers,* by David McEntire and Robert B. Powers (California State Printing Office, 1946). Another excellent manual is that prepared by Joseph D. Lohman with the cooperation of the Division of Police of the Chicago Park District, *The Police and Minority Groups* (Chicago, 1946).

the situation in one or other of two opposite directions. Here the precipitant can act in only one way.

Sometimes a situation that superficially may appear quite stable turns out to be, on closer examination, one of precarious equilibrium. This, for example, may be the case with the phenomenon long known as the "Solid South," the domination of Southern politics by a single party so close-knit that while rival candidates may fight it out in the primary they do not let their differences affect their party loyalty when it is over. On this principle, and on the various devices by which voting is hedged about with restrictions, has depended the standpat front of Southern conservatism. But recently a series of changes have been undermining the system. The division between liberals and conservatives has become sharper, and this division threatens conventions based on the assumption that such differences are quite secondary matters. For this and other reasons, later to be discussed, we agree with Myrdal that the situation is "highly unstable," and that "the Southern conservative position on Negro franchise is politically untenable for any length of time." [3]

Two subtypes of the precarious equilibrium should be distinguished. In one variety the collapse of the given equilibrium is merely a question of time. The forces maintaining it are barely able to resist the assaulting forces and the latter are being recruited whereas the former are not. In the physical example the erosive action of wind and rain must at length undermine the balanced rock. We can find examples also in the social sphere. When industrial development advances a feudal class system becomes precarious and is bound sooner or later to collapse. When changing conditions undermine the basis of an old power system the social structure it sustains will sooner or later fall. The fall may be hastened by a sudden blow, a revolutionary uprising for example, but it will come in any event.

[3] Myrdal, *op. cit.*, vol. I, p. 518.

Sometimes, however, a question arises. We have before us the collapse of a system. It is easy, in the light of the fact, to conclude that the collapse was inevitable. Many historians think that the assassination of the Archduke Francis Ferdinand in 1914, the precipitant of the war that destroyed the old "balance of power" system and the "Hundred Years' Peace," merely hastened a clash that was bound to come sooner or later. The inference may be right or wrong—there is no way to confirm it. In other words, it is *possible* that the precarious equilibrium of world peace in the period ending in 1914 might have continued and in time have been reinforced. If so, it would belong to our second subtype. This has reference to the situation in which, while the alternatives immediately presented are either the breakdown of the *status quo* in one clearly indicated direction or its maintenance, the possibility remains open that the prospective change may be not only postponed but averted. Take, for example, the situation in which inter-group tension has increased to the point where a "race riot" is threatened. A precipitant may set it off at any moment, but skilful control on the part of authorities or civic leaders may be able to prevent it. The tension then dies down and no riot takes place.

Here two points of strategic importance emerge. One is that in the second subtype the role of the precipitant is far more significant than in the first. In the second the blocking of the precipitant or the introduction of an anti-precipitant may be of primary importance for the future development of the situation. The riot, the war, the revolution, the *coup d'état*, or whatever it be, may not take place, and as conditions change thereafter a new and different order may be built up and the precarious equilibrium may cease to exist. The second point is that in the uncertainty of human affairs it is often merely a matter of conjecture whether or not the loaded situation must at length yield to its bias. If the impending change is one that would defeat our hopes it is there-

fore unwise to assume its inevitability, to accept it as "the
wave of the future." That is a sure way to make it inevitable,
by stalling the more constructive forces. We should never
accept the position that the riot, the lynching outrage, the
war, is inevitable, however impressive or triumphant the
forces of destruction may seem to be. The balance of forces
may be changed. The tensions that portend a violent explo-
sion may already have reached their height and the more
constructive factors may be capable of new developments.

The Indifferent Equilibrium. This designation is taken
from Myrdal.[4] It refers to a type of situation that is in important respects the antithesis of that signified by "the tense
equilibrium." There is, say, a state of discrimination or
segregation, but the conditions and sentiments that maintain it are offset by conditions and sentiments that, if given
expression, would reject it. There is here no sharp clash of
extremes, no heightened opposition of animosities. Or the
situation may be one in which discrimination is actually
minimal, but the prejudice that induces it may be stimulated
with relative ease if those who are so minded are given a
free field.

It is a situation in which a precipitant can quickly change
the balance, toward or away from discriminatory practices.
In this type of situation an act of leadership can be highly
effective. Myrdal gives the following example: "Northern
White workers are often said to start with a feeling of strange-
ness and suspicion against Negroes. If they meet a firm policy
from the employer they change, usually quickly." [5] The
reason is that the first introduction of Negroes is opposed
by the strong inertia of workmen who, lacking experience of
collaboration with colored people, are full of prejudicial
"stereotypes" concerning their capacities. The White workers soon discover that the Negro is a better man and a better

4 *An American Dilemma,* Chap. 17.
5 *Op. cit.,* I, p. 304.

comr.. ..an they had imagined, so that, once admitted, the Negro ... a good chance to hold his job. This argument is supporte.. by considerable evidence from the history of the Negro's role in the industry of the North, and receives further confirmation from the records of cases settled by the FEPC and by the recently established commissions set up in some states to administer antidiscrimination laws. There are, on the other hand, situations where the fear of Negro competition is strong enough to resist the influences of side-by-side collaboration. We do not imply that the experience of working together has always a happy result. Our point is that there are many cases in which it has succeeded, and that these cases exemplify the condition designated the "indifferent equilibrium." The same principle applies in relevant situations where the employer and not the worker opposes the introduction of workers on racial or ethnic grounds, and where the precipitant factor may be governmental pressure or some immediate economic consideration. Thus, for example, "reluctant Eastern manufacturers of highly involved war mechanisms through experience discarded their belief that Negro workers could not acquire the requisite skills." [6]

When on the other hand the danger is that of the entry of discrimination the immediate objective of wise policy should be to ward off precipitants and the longer-run objective to strengthen constructive tendencies, through education, through leadership, through institutional devices, and through the encouragement of the appropriate socio-psychological processes. These various means should be applied—without neglecting the adverse elements—and applied particularly to the indifferent or ambivalent sector. In this type of situation there is likely to be a large percentage falling into the latter category. The consequences of indifference can be shown up in various ways and the self-contradictions of ambivalence brought to the light. We have already

[6] *First Report,* FEPC (Washington, D.C., 1945), p. 3.

pointed out the fallacy of regarding indifference as a safeguard against the encroachments of sharp prejudice. Myrdal's
whole work is a study of the ambivalence of American attitudes with respect to discrimination. He gives as an example
the prevailing attitude regarding the education of Negroes.
Strategy can take advantage of the conflicts of ideology to
which the discriminating groups are here exposed.

The indifferent equilibrium may be centered in the economic area or in the ideological area. We may find it specifically in the habits of action or in the habits of thought—
though the two can never be separated. In the American
scene, as Myrdal points out, it is exhibited notably in the
swaying balance between the traditions and sophistications
that uphold racial discrimination and the ideologies cher-
ished as peculiarly American, the ideologies that reject caste
and privilege, that ask for "a free field and no favor," that
proclaim men "born free and equal" and regard the United
States as the home of democracy and progress.

The Moving Equilibrium. The type of situation here indicated is one that has accommodated itself to certain definite
trends without breach of continuity or serious disturbance.
The trends may, from our point of view, be favorable or unfavorable, and they may advance rather rapidly or with relative slowness. If and when, for example, the United States
justified the description of being a "melting pot" it would
signify a moving equilibrium making for the absorption into
full citizenship of the members of various ethnic groups.
Similarly a process of change in which the line of caste grew
gradually thinner between White and Negro would fall into
this category. In the longer retrospect we may discover a
moving equilibrium even where at the present time we discover nothing but clashes and disturbances. Under favorable
conditions the tense equilibrium may change into the moving
equilibrium.

In the area of inter-group relations the moving equilibrium

is likely to be found under two antithetical sets of conditions. One is where tradition and custom strongly control a whole community, and where the dominant mores are not greatly disturbed by technological change or by external forces. Here processes of accommodation may occur, though the movement may be so slow as to be imperceptible. Alien groups may be absorbed gradually but so effectively that they completely lose their alien character—as has happened, for example, in China for some Jewish groups. The other set of conditions that admits a moving equilibrium is that of a mobile democratic society, where rather rapid change is the rule and not the exception. If the democratic mores are strong enough they too are favorable to processes of inter-group accommodation. The history of the United States, especially in its westward expansion, has afforded many illustrations.

2. CIRCLES

The patterns we have so far been describing have all been characterized by their polarity. Each situation was presented as a balance, stable or unstable, of opposing forces. We now turn to patterns of causation in which a series of conditions or forces sustain, confirm, and generate one another. Each of the conditions so interacts with the other conditions as to promote and perpetuate them and thus the whole system they together constitute. These patterns exhibit something more than the interdependence of factors that obtains in every established system. To take the simplest possible case, if you begin with condition *a* it sets in motion condition *b*, and *b* in turn keeps *a* going. The system, in other words, embodies the principle of circularity.

The circular pattern is often associated with an equilibrium pattern. Indeed, as we shall presently see, the most

significant schemes of social relationship present us with
this combination. For the study of discrimination it is of
great importance to understand how the two types of pattern
combine.

There are many kinds of circular pattern and they can be
classified in diverse ways. Since our interest lies in the social
conditions that maintain either discrimination or the absence
of discrimination we shall confine our analysis mainly to
the particular kinds that are relevant to our theme.

Let us begin with a few simple instances of the causal
circle. A rumor spreads through a community that a particular bank is insolvent. There is a run on the bank. Since
no bank can immediately liquidate its resources—apart from
outside help—so as to honor all the claims upon it, the bank
closes down. The rumor is self-confirming. There are many
other situations in which the mistrust of an institution under-
mines the strength of the institution so as to confirm the
mistrust. An institution exists only where men believe that
it exists. It exists in the acceptance of its existence. Its strength
is the strength of the belief in it. If, for example, men accept
with conviction an organization called the United Nations
it will be as strong as the conviction is wide-based and will
fulfil its functions with corresponding success. If they do
not believe in it it will possess only a nominal and futile
existence. Hence the kind of circle we may name *the self-
fulfilling postulate,* working, according to its kind, for better
or for worse.

Another and very similar kind of simple circularity we
shall name *the self-fulfilling anticipation.* This type realizes
itself in the behavior of an individual or a group without
reference to institutional relationships. A good student, for
example, is afraid of failing in an examination. He grows
nervous, loses his poise, does himself less than justice, and
consequently fails. The fearful anticipation of the outcome
of behavior, of accident, of loss, of ill health, of some mis-

carriage of plans, frequently brings to pass the things men fear. Authorities on the subject tell us, for example, that the fear of a lack of virility causes impotence. Worry about anything digs the channel along which is borne the evil our imagination projects. On the other hand the confident anticipation of success is frequently a factor in its attainment.

The self-fulfilling postulate, it should be noted, is a phenomenon of group psychology, whereas the self-fulfilling anticipation works itself out in the experience of the individual. We should further observe that neither kind is fully circular. The conclusion of the process is not the reassertion of the initial postulate or anticipation. The scheme they exhibit is as follows:

(1) $P(x) \rightarrow$ behavior based on $P(x) \rightarrow x$
(Postulate that bank is insolvent $\rightarrow$ run on bank $\rightarrow$ insolvency of bank)

(2) $A(x) \rightarrow$ behavior affected by $A(x) \rightarrow x$
(Fear of failure $\rightarrow$ loss of nerve $\rightarrow$ failure)

The true circle has instead this form:

$x \rightarrow$ behavior based on or affected by $x \rightarrow x$

The end is again the beginning, the reassertion, possibly in a strengthened form, of the beginning. Once set in motion the process goes on and on of its own momentum. Thus it becomes:

$x \rightarrow B(x) \rightarrow x \rightarrow B(x) \rightarrow x \rightarrow b(x)$ ......

To take an example, the process of international armament may run as follows:

armament in country $A \rightarrow$ fear in country $B \rightarrow$ armament in country $B \rightarrow$ fear in country $A \rightarrow$ armament in country A, and so on *ad infinitum*—or *ad bellum*

Here is a very simple example in the field of our own interest. Myrdal in his study of anti-Negro discrimination speaks of "the self-perpetuating color bar" and concludes that "discrimination breeds discrimination." In schematic form we have:

discrimination → sequel of discrimination → discrimination

It is easy to illustrate the process here indicated. For example, a group suffering from discrimination becomes disaffected or rebellious, and the evidences of disaffection become in turn a ground for discrimination. Thus:

discrimination → disaffection → discrimination

Similar formulas may be applied to other consequences of discrimination. We may, again, insert various intermediate terms in the circle, for example:

discrimination → lower income level → lower standard of living → lower education → lower earning capacity → discrimination

It should be observed that in the second of these two examples the causal sequence has a somewhat different character from that exhibited in the first. Strictly speaking, we cannot call it discriminatory to pay lower wages for inferior capacity. The initial discrimination that may be responsible for this inferiority of skill or of education works out thus its own justification—in the eyes of those who discriminate. Looking at the consequences of their discriminatory treatment they find in them a plausible justification of the discrimination that produces them. *This procedure is one of the important ways in which the circle of discrimination is sustained.* If we turn now to the first example we may raise the question whether it is discriminatory to block the economic opportunities of a group because they—or, rather, some of them— are rebellious or malcontent. However we decide we must in any event admit that the denial of economic opportunity, on grounds other than economic efficiency, is an expression of group policy, not an operation of economic law.

The examples we have just given bring out an important

aspect of the "vicious circle" of discrimination.[7] Besides the vicious circle as a pattern of causation there is *the vicious circle argument* as a mode of reasoning. Its peculiar property is that it takes the existence of one link in the circle as independently given, as a fact of nature or even as ordained by God, and concludes from that premise that the next link, the behavior predicated on the earlier link, is not prejudicial or discriminatory but a rational and proper response to the inferior capacities or qualities of the group subjected to it. Those who put forward the argument wilfully or blindly ignore the sector of the circle that lies on the other side of the evidences to which they appeal. They refuse to recognize that the conditions on which they base their argument arise out of, or are themselves sustained by, a prior process of discrimination.[8]

The vicious circle argument is extremely common and plays a large role not only in the rationale of prejudice and discrimination, soothing the doubts and removing the scruples of the discriminator, but also in the maintenance of the practices and institutions of discrimination. It enters strongly into the attitude complex that forms part of and controls the vicious circle. All of us are in some measure and in some relationships exposed to its influence. It is the same argument that was used so long ago by so great a thinker as Aristotle, when he justified slavery on the ground that the slave was an "animate tool," fit only for servile tasks. It is used very freely, especially in the South, to support the segregation of the Negro. He is, they say, lazy, unenterprising,

[7] The phrase "vicious circle" is convenient to distinguish causal complexes of a circular type when they sustain social situations we adjudge to be undesirable. It is of course a purely subjective designation, dependent on our particular value scheme. When we approve the prevailing order of things we are likely to find "beneficent circles," such as those that were adduced by the believers in *laissez faire*. When we disapprove we look for "vicious circles."

[8] Those interested in the principles of logic should observe that our "vicious circle argument" is a different fallacy from the "vicious circle," or circular reasoning, to which textbooks on logic call attention.

shiftless, dirty, immoral. Divine providence ordained him
to his place. Those who would make him the equal of the
White or give him equal opportunity have never lived among
Negroes, do not know the facts. The Negro owes all he now
enjoys to the civilization built by White men. The difference
of conditions is not reckoned in the count nor is the test
accepted that would show how far conditions are responsible
for whatever truth the allegations may contain, the test of
equal opportunity at every stage. A similar argument, in a
less extreme form, is directed at all ethnic or racial groups
that are denied equal opportunity. The Jews, for example,
are subversive, unscrupulous, racketeers, black market agents,
secretive, aloof, unassimilable. Their ways and their manners
are alien and unpleasant. They are not good citizens. The
story is an old one, forever repeated. Since it confirms the
privilege and status and pride of the discriminating group
and since there are, in the nature of things, always *some* evidences it can exhibit it has an immense plausibility.

The argument is popular with the educated no less than
with the uneducated. Not long ago a cultured lady, defending
her anti-Semitic attitude, said to me: "Well, why don't they
behave like other people?" "Would you behave like other
people," I asked her, "if you had been born in a ghetto or
had lived from your childhood in a society where you constantly met with exclusion or frustration? If they don't behave
like other people your anti-Semitism is one of the reasons
why they don't." A similar attitude is frequently displayed
by the well-to-do in their comments on the behavior of the
poor. Why are they so untidy, so vulgar, so mean? Obviously
they belong to an inferior class. The undesirable results
become the justification of the undesirable conditions.[9]

We suggest in passing that a thorough understanding of
the vicious circle argument is an essential objective of any

[9] Any indictment of a *whole* people or ethnic group or of a whole social
class is likely to involve the vicious circle argument.

educational campaign against inter-group prejudice and discrimination. The importance of this type of education will become more evident as we proceed with the analysis of the causal circle of discrimination.

The primary circle can now be presented as follows:

discrimination $\rightarrow$ conditions of life confirmed or imposed by discrimination $\rightarrow$ discrimination

In symbolic form the circle proceeds:

$$D^1 \rightarrow C^1 \rightarrow D^2 \rightarrow C^2 \rightarrow D^3 \rightarrow C^3 \text{ etc.,}$$

where D stands for discrimination and C for the sequent conditions relevant to it. The situation here symbolized is one of progressive discrimination. Where discrimination is established and relatively constant, we have a circle in a stricter sense, as follows:

$$D \rightarrow C \rightarrow D \rightarrow C \rightarrow D \rightarrow C \text{ etc.}$$

This situation occurs in countries where a traditional caste system prevails. It is more or less exemplified by the position of the Negroes as it has been maintained in most Southern states, or of some ethnic groups where their economic life has been channeled within a limited occupational range, or of the Jewish people where they have been confined to ghettos.

Now let us consider more closely the manner in which the conditions that are confirmed or imposed by discrimination operate to sustain it. The discriminating group starts with an advantage. It has greater power, socially and politically, and usually it has a superior economic position. Thus it is enabled to discriminate. By discriminating it cuts the other group off from economic and social opportunities. The subordination of the lower group gives the upper group a new consciousness of its superiority. This psychological reinforcement of discrimination is in turn ratified by the factual evidences of inferiority that accompany the lack of opportunity, by the mean and miserable state of those who live and breed in poverty, who suffer constant frustration, who have no incentive to improve their lot, and who feel themselves to be outcasts of society. Thus discrimination evokes both attitudes and modes of life favorable to its perpetuation, not only in the upper group but, to a considerable extent, in the lower group as well. A total *upper caste complex* congenial to discrimination, a complex of attitudes, interests, modes of living, and habits of power is developed and institutionalized, having as its counterpart a *lower caste complex* of modes of living, habits of subservience, and corresponding attitudes.

It would make our symbolic representation too elaborate if we sought to include in it all the causal interactions we have here indicated. We shall therefore be content to give an abbreviated expression of it, as follows:

$$D \rightarrow \begin{matrix} U \\ \updownarrow \\ L \end{matrix} \rightarrow D$$

where U stands for upper caste complex and L for lower caste complex. As will presently appear, we do not imply that all the conditions involved in the relationships of the upper and the lower caste inevitably confirm a system of discrimination once established. If that were so the vicious circle could never be broken.

3. THE PRINCIPLE OF THE VICIOUS CIRCLE

The circular pattern of causation, as above described, is pre-eminently the mechanism maintaining all caste systems, all systems based on the superiority of one racial or ethnic group over another, and more generally all social arrangements of superordination and subordination that limit the opportunities of one class for the advantage of another.

There are many variations of the pattern but in broad terms we may distinguish the following:

(1) the form exemplified by the Hindu caste system, where the supremacy of the upper castes is conveyed through mystical-magical myths that pervade the whole society;

(2) the form exemplified by the feudal system of estates, where the supremacy of the upper castes is assured by oligarchical institutions, under which economic power and political power are fused and vested in a social hierarchy;

(3) the form currently exhibited in the United States of America, where there is no all-pervading myth to sanction it and where the larger institutional structure gives it no warrant, so that it depends mainly on the economic advantage and on the social prestige of the various groups occupying the more dominant positions, and on the variant derivative myths they can rally for its support.

It is the last-mentioned form to which alone our analysis will be directed. It differs from the others in that it is more unstable, more exposed to the assault of counterforces generated within the community. Under these conditions the principle of the vicious circle, if its operation is properly understood, has, from the standpoint of the policy-maker who seeks to combat discrimination, its favorable as well as its unfavorable aspects. This point needs more examination than it has hitherto received.

Gunnar Myrdal states, for example, that in this type of situation "a rise in any single one of the Negro variables will tend to raise all the other Negro variables and thus, indirectly as well as directly, result in a cumulatively enforced attack upon white prejudice." [10] Again, distinguishing three "bundles of interdependent causative factors" in the vicious circle, (1) the economic level, (2) standards of intelligence, ambition, education, morals, and so forth, and (3) discrimination itself, he claims that "a primary change, induced or planned," affecting any one of the three, "will bring changes

[10] *Op. cit.,* vol. II, pp. 1066–1067.

in the other two and, through mutual interaction, move the whole system along in one direction or the other." [11] A favorable change, in other words, will react favorably on the whole system, and presumably an unfavorable change will do the reverse.

Such statements must be carefully interpreted or they will mislead. They tell only one side of the story. The circle, vicious or beneficent, is the dynamic interadjustment of the "outer" and the "inner" conditions of human living, of man's attitudes to the opportunities, obstacles, and necessities he meets. Each "variable" in the situation is sustained by the other variables. Now if one is changed there will be the pull and push of the others to bring it back into line. There will also be the counterinfluence of the changed condition on all the rest—but it is still merely one against many. Without the aid of forces lying outside the vicious circle it is unlikely to maintain itself in the transition to readjustment. Indeed, if one "variable" in the lower caste complex is changed "upwards," there will be not only the drag of the other variables in this complex but also the whole pressure against the change of the upper caste complex, the resistance of which may be intensified in reaction against it. If, for example, the Negro has new occupational avenues opened to him as a result of a war emergency the advance may easily be lost when the emergency ends. The old traditions and myths reassert themselves; the old modes and standards of living of the majority of Negroes, the old inferiority of Negro education and training, the old conditioning to lower wages, all exercise their downward pull; and the return of sharper competition increases the prejudice and the discriminatory attitudes of those who feel that their interests are threatened.[12]

11 *Ibid.*, vol. I, p. 208.
12 Myrdal, *op. cit.*, vol. II, p. 1068, refers to the increase of prejudice that may be evoked by the *prospect* of a higher plane of living for the Negroes, but distinguishes this response from an opposite response of decreased prejudice after the prospect is realized. For reasons suggested above this analysis seems inadequate.

The problem, then, is that of maintaining and stabilizing an advance in one "variable" against the downward drag of all the rest. The immediate determinant of the advance may itself be transient, the seizure of a favorable occasion, as in the war emergency, but the occasion passes and the discriminatory influences reassert themselves. Then the advance—the rise in the wages or the occupational status of the disadvantaged groups, the new statute prohibiting occupational discrimination, or whatever it be—is beset by all the forces of the "vicious circle." Hence we must revise the proposition that an upward change anywhere in the lower caste complex will tend to raise all the other conditions within it. Instead we should say that *a favorable change in any one of the distinctive conditions will, if it can be held constant long enough, tend to raise the other conditions and to bring about a readjustment of the whole system in conformity with the favorable change.* By "long enough" we denote the period within which the requisite habituations and reconditionings, the responses of the group to the altered condition, are formed and established. Thus the receipt of higher wages must last long enough to be translated into a higher standard of living and to evoke the attitudes and expectations congenial to it. When we say that the advance must be "held constant" we mean that the forces that brought it into being must continue in operation, aided by whatever new forces the change may evoke, in sufficient strength to resist the assaults of resurgent opposing forces. Such assaults are indirect as well as direct. If, for example, a new statute against discrimination has been set up there is the danger that it will be evaded or even nullified even though it is most unlikely that it will be actually repealed.

The proposition we have just formulated can furnish important lessons for the policy-maker. They will concern us later but we shall in passing mention briefly some of them. We have shown that without powerful support a breach of the vicious circle at a single point is precarious and likely to be short-lived. One obvious conclusion is that where feasible the attack on the vicious circle should be made not at one point only but at several. There is no single front that alone is the predetermined way to victory. Each "variable" supports and is supported by all the rest. We should not scorn the educational attack because we are devoted to the economic one nor deny the importance of the political front because we are committed to the battle against prejudice.

This conclusion, however, does not imply that all approaches are equally available or equally effective under all conditions. We have to ask what changes can be brought about, at one stroke, by concerted well-directed action and what changes can be achieved only by slower processes. We have to ask what kinds of advance can best be stabilized and held against the opposing forces. We have to ask what are the weakest points in the resistance of the "upper caste complex" and what are the factors most susceptible to change in the "lower caste complex." We have to consider what agencies, legal, economic, social, are best qualified to assure the retention of gains once made. Just as a general must plan his campaign in the fullest knowledge of the disposition and nature of the enemy's forces and must be ready to adapt his own strategy to the changing situation, so should the fight against discrimination be planned.

The necessity to sustain over a period of some length an advance once made does suggest, however, a particular merit attaching to gains that are registered in a tangible form or else have an institutional embodiment. When new occupations are once opened to a disprivileged group, when its members are admitted to a trade union that previously had barred them, when the policy of equal wages without respect of race is accepted, when a law against discrimination is passed, these are specific advances manifest to everyone, advances that cannot be covertly rescinded, that are in some measure protected by the usages and forms they bring into being, and that constitute definite landmarks from which further advances may be made. In the direct struggle against prejudice, intolerance, and racial and ethnic myths we achieve no such clear indications of our progress. The reduction of prejudice is hard to measure and the revival of prejudicial myths comes subtly and insidiously. It does not follow that the educational front is any less important than the economic or the political front. Without liberation from the spirit of intolerance, without a widespread recognition of the moral rights of others, without the consciousness of the social evils and national perils that spring from the discrimination of group against group, the dynamic for the achievement and the maintenance of institutional or economic advances is lacking. The inference is rather that institutional and economic reforms are necessary to *consolidate* victory on any front. Furthermore, reforms of this character, because of the social apparatus they set up and because of the new habituations and changed modes of living they initiate, are themselves highly effective agencies for the development of the social attitudes congenial to their preservation.

The abbreviated and schematic presentation we have given of the principle of circular causation may convey the impression that its operation is much more simple than is actually the case. The complexity of interaction must be recognized before we can effectively relate the principle to the strategy of control. We shall therefore return in conclusion to our general formula:

$$D \rightarrow \updownarrow \rightarrow D$$

with U above and L below the central symbol.

in order to indicate somewhat more fully the nature of the complexes we have designated as "upper caste" and "lower caste" respectively. Taking as our example the Negro-White situation in the Southern states, we shall limit our amplification to two major aspects of all such complexes, the economic and the socio-psychological. It should of course be understood that various other aspects are involved, and that the aspects selected are characterized only in the broadest terms. With these limitations in mind we have drawn up the Table that follows.

TABLE 1

SOME ASPECTS OF UPPER CASTE AND LOWER CASTE COMPLEXES AS EXHIBITED IN THE NEGRO-WHITE SITUATION IN THE SOUTHERN STATES

UPPER CASTE COMPLEX	LOWER CASTE COMPLEX
Economic Aspects	*Economic Aspects*
Superior economic power. Higher standards of living. Economic privileges secured by policies of discrimination, denial of economic and social opportunity to the Negro, and devices of various kinds to prevent the advance of Negroes in social status.	Lower standards of living, physically exhibited in mean insanitary habitations, slum-like character of segregated areas, etc. Economic life mostly canalized into menial, unskilled, and semiskilled occupations. Economic insecurity. Lack of adequate educational provision.
Deviant Feature Economic position of "poor whites."	
Socio-Psychological Aspects Anti-Negro ideologies of racial superiority. Corresponding conceptions of "good" and "bad" Negroes. Attitudes requiring "social distance" between Whites and Negroes. Fear of Negro restiveness. General antipathy to social change.	*Socio-Psychological Aspects* Habituations to mode of living on low economic level. Disregard for mores of dominant Whites. Sense of frustration manifested in apathy, irresponsibility, etc. *or* in resort to magico-religious consolations, *or* in active discontent, rebelliousness, and demand for social reform.
Deviant Feature Increasing importance of groups resisting current ideologies and favoring betterment of Negro status.	

Our characterizations are purely typological. There are many variations of circumstance and still more of attitude on both sides of the caste line. We have noted in the Table two strongly deviant features. The total situation is far from being static, and there are forces within it that combat the principle of the "vicious circle." On the Negro side the divergences of attitude are so marked that we have had to include even in so summary a table three very diverse sub-types of psychological response to upper caste control. When the third subtype, that of articulate protest, is prominent it marks a situation of transition or of unstable equilibrium. Where the barriers are too strong to be assaulted the sense of frustration breeds some kind of accommodation, which may be expressed either in inertia, in the "laziness" and irresponsibility of which the upper caste is apt to accuse the lower, or in some mystical or highly emotional transference, in religious fervor, in the ecstasy of ritual or the dance, in sex orgies, and so forth. The assertive drives that are not thus "sublimated" are redirected to the achievement of dominance within the subject group itself, thus creating a class hierarchy that becomes an obstacle to a united front against upper caste domination. Strongly conflicting attitudes and policies con-sequently develop within the lower caste.[13]

We conclude with one or two general observations on strategy that seem to be borne out by a study of the operation of the "vicious circle." In the first place it makes against the hypothesis of a single or even a prepotent factor the control of which is requisite and alone necessary for victory over the forces of discrimination. There is, for example, a school that gives this priority to the economic factor, whether under-stood in a Marxist sense or in some other. This viewpoint appears to ignore the closely interwoven system of causes that maintains the division between the upper and the

---

13 See, for example, John Dollard, *Caste and Class in a Southern Town,* *passim* and particularly pp. 174, 424; Hortense Powdermaker, *After Freedom* (New York, 1939), Pt. IV. Cf. the author's *The Web of Government* (New York, 1947), pp. 283–287.

lower castes.[14] It is expedient, rather, to search without pre-possession for the vulnerable links in the "vicious circle." We shall find that not all the "variables" in the low status complex are equally susceptible to attack, and that under different conditions one or another of them will offer the most favorable opportunity. It may well be, as our later argument will show, that the economic front is of major importance, but that decision gives no ground for the neglect of the other fronts or for the anticipation of complete success by an attack on that front alone. Any strategy is precarious that is committed in advance and under all circumstances to a predetermined plan of campaign.

Finally, the single front conception is often associated with the belief that the enemy forces can be overthrown by a single master blow, whereas our analysis of the complex interdependence of factors gives some justification for a policy of gradual broad-based change, resolutely pursued, in which each new-won ground becomes a rallying point for the next advance, as against a drastic attempt to abolish the whole system at one revolutionary stroke, ignoring alike the perils of failure and the repercussions of an immature success. What can be revolutionized by political dictate, at least so long as any freedom still endures, is no more than the legal form imposed by authority on the life of the community. Of signal importance as the form may be—and we shall give it due recognition at a later stage—it cannot serve any high purpose unless it meets adequate responsiveness in the attitudes of the people. Otherwise it becomes the corrupting instrument of power. The experience of the Southern states during the ruinous fiasco of "reconstruction" after the Civil War is a case in point. New institutions can indeed have an educating influence but if they are suddenly thrust on a people unprepared for them the new state of that people becomes worse, not better, than the old. The processes of education

[14] Cf. Myrdal, *op. cit.*, vol. II, p. 1069.

and of habituation must work through to a new consensus,
the "vicious circle" must be broken at several points, not at
one alone, if a "beneficent circle" is to take its place.

4. SOME LESSONS FROM THE VICIOUS CIRCLE

Besides the more special inferences we have already drawn
there are certain broad lessons we can derive or reinforce
from a study of the causal chain called the "vicious circle."
In the first place such study should broaden and correct ideas
about the nature of prejudice. Prejudice is not a simple thing.
It is not a mere expression of human blindness and bias.
Prejudice, so to speak, is not altogether prejudice. It has a
rational element combined with an irrational one. The irrational element is often sustained by a response to observed
behavior that might be accounted fair and proper if the observation were not so selective or if the observed behavior
were the whole evidence. The proportion of the two ingredients, the rational and the irrational, will vary according to
the kind and degree of prejudice.

It is true—let us say it "without prejudice"—that some
Negroes are dirty and careless and immoral and lazy. It is
true that some Eastern Europeans who have migrated to
these shores are rude, uncultivated, venal, with narrow interests. It is true that some Jews are vulgar, ostentatious,
ready to advance themselves by illicit or underhand methods;
and that some Jewish groups are clannish and socially inbred.
Nor is it an effective answer to charge that the members of
the dominant groups display equally undesirable or unpleasant attributes. No headway can be made by that kind of
"you're no better."

When, however, we have admitted these things—though
avoiding the gross exaggerations, generalizations, and distortions of them that are the concomitants of prejudice—we

have not weakened but rather have strengthened the case against discrimination. This is the lesson of the "vicious circle." We should not discriminate against Negroes because some of them are shiftless and irresponsible. Nor against Bohemians or Italians because some of them are uncouth and their votes can be cheaply bought. Nor against Jews because some of them are prominent in the black markets, and so forth. Instead we should seek to comprehend that our very discrimination disposes them to these ways, and that *the more severe the discrimination the more evidence it will itself provide to justify its own perpetuation.* In other words, if we dislike the traits we condemn we should know that the best contribution we can make toward their removal is to cease our discriminating. Whereas if we continue to discriminate we are doing all in our power to fasten them on the groups in question and on our own community.

Where groups are held in the grip of the "vicious circle" it would be wiser to admire the strength and courage of those who have broken "their birth's invidious bar" than to condemn those who failed to do so. America has given so many examples of the former that its history is itself a strong argument against the theory that peoples and ethnic groups are by nature divided into the permanently inferior and the permanently superior.

There is a lesson here also for the subject groups. It does them no good roundly to condemn the groups which discriminate against them or to regard themselves as angels of light victimized by the powers of darkness. They too, like their oppressors, have their own share of human weaknesses and vices. There is no reason to assume that if they in turn were on top they would be more discerning or less arrogant than the groups that now occupy that position. Equally they too have their role to play in the struggle against discrimination. The "vicious circle" constricts them but it does not wholly control them. It makes their role a harder one, but all the more necessary. They have always the power of organization. It is imperative that they learn how to use it aright. And they must use it not only to break through the exclusive prerogatives and selfish dominations of the other side but also to promote in their own ranks those attitudes and those responsibilities that will make their full entrance into the life of the community an easier transition and a more obvious contribution to the welfare of the whole.

Again, our perception of the operation of the "vicious circle" offers a new slant on the nature of group attributes. Every group has its distinctive characteristics, responsive to the conditions under which it lives. When the conditions change the ways of the group undergo a process of change. It is a false philosophy that denies the differences between groups, and it is a misguided program that in the name of our common humanity seeks to instil the belief that these differences are either negligible or nonexistent. Genuine cultural differences exist all about us, and all men set store on their own culture. To minimize these differences is no solution of the problem of inter-group relations, and the teaching that propounds it is rejected by the discerning student. We have reports from our psychological colleagues that bring out the boomerang effects of such teaching.[15] The first commandment of the multigroup society is that we learn to get along with others who are culturally different, in various respects, from ourselves. That commandment is not fulfilled by the denial of differences.

Nevertheless—and here is where the principle of the "vicious circle" is so revealing—we need not assume that these cultural differences, in so far as they exist *within* the effective range of a community, will become cultural walls separating group from group. More especially we need not fear the persistence in the excluded groups of those traits on

15 Special statements prepared for the author by Dr. L. Joseph Stone and Dr. Gardner Murphy.

which the discriminators base their argument in favor of discrimination. Discrimination itself proves to be the major factor among the conditions to which these traits are a response. When this factor is removed true social integration becomes for the first time possible, an integration that differs as much from a juxtaposition of separate cultural enclaves as it does from a system of enforced "assimilation."

Finally, we can use the principle of circular interaction as a starting point for the refutation of certain too narrow explanations of the nature of inter-group prejudice. When we say "too narrow" we mean that they fail to do justice to the intricately interwoven social strands in the causal complex. Prejudice is not the expression of the native reaction of individuals to the actual attributes of other individuals or of whole groups. It is stimulated in a variety of ways by social conditioning. It is responsive to the changing relations of group to group. The principle of the "vicious circle" shows how group prejudice is maintained, not how it comes into being. It takes the mores of prejudice as a datum. When the circle is in full operation it provides a rationale for discrimination that was not present in the formative stage. The fruits of discrimination, since they offer partial evidences to support discrimination, give some plausibility to the theory that prejudice is less prejudicial than it is, in other words, that it is initiated as well as sustained as a response to unpleasant or undesirable attributes possessed by those against whom it is directed. It is a doctrine very comforting to the discriminators, but it is wholly without foundation. We have pointed out, for example, that when there were only a few Japanese on the Pacific Coast there was no prejudice against them and that in countries where there are few Negroes there is not operative the kind of prejudice that develops where they are present in large numbers. What has changed is not the qualities of the Japanese or the Negroes but their relation to the other groups in the community, with the consequent evocation of certain interests and motivations in the other groups.

Similar considerations can be brought to bear against the antithetical type of psychological theory, which explains prejudice as an outlet for aggressive drives or regards the group subject to it as the victim of some kind of emotional transference or as the "scapegoat" of the dominant group. Psychological analysis has done valuable service in showing how aggressive tendencies that are balked in one direction seek a vent in another, and how the frustration of these tendencies builds up anger and irritation that heightens prejudice and strengthens the need for some kind of outlet. But that is only part of the story. These impulses do not move in a social vacuum. There are many deviations they may take. A man may "compensate" for his frustrations by the way he behaves within his family or in his business or in his community, and in any of these directions the "compensation" may assume any one of a variety of expressions. There is nothing in the sheerly psychological context to tell why a particular group becomes the object of discrimination, or why that object changes from time to time. To solve these questions we must seek the relation between the sociological and the psychological conditions.

Here is a large theme that lies beyond our scope. What concerns us is a tentative conclusion regarding policy. Since policy measures can hardly hope to change the basic drives of human beings whereas they have some potency over social institutions and economic conditions the concentration of effort should be directed to the latter rather than to the former aspects of the discrimination complex. We doubt, for example, whether any serious gain can be made by highlighting the "scapegoat" element in discriminatory treatment. It need by no means be left out of the reckoning, but any advantage to be derived from the exposure of it will be at best quite subsidiary to a strategy the main assault of which must be delivered against less elusive and more controllable factors.

Chapter Five

On Strategy in General

1. THE DEFINITION OF OBJECTIVES

THE REST of this work will be devoted entirely to questions of strategy, applied to the various fronts on which the war against discrimination must be fought. But there are some broad considerations that apply to all fronts, and it may be well to make these serve as a background to the more specific discussions that are to follow.

To put the broadest first, it is the task of strategy to recruit and organize the strength on its side in the manner that will be most effective for assault and then to seek out and strike at the weakest points of resistance in the enemy lines. All this is so elementary that it might seem scarcely worth the mention. But too often, where social goals are concerned, men give little thought to the kind of preparation without which they would not dream of conducting any enterprise of business or of sport.

It is generally agreed by those who are engaged in combating inter-group discrimination that there is in the American community a vast amount of goodwill and responsiveness for the cause they champion, though it makes little impact on the actual situation. It is implicit in the American tradition and the American creed. It is manifest in the attachment to the principle of freedom of opportunity. It is witnessed by the readiness of organizations of the largest scope, religious organizations, educational organizations, civic organizations, to sponsor and support movements directed against discrimination. It is seen in the fact that the Northern states that have recently passed antidiscrimination laws met relatively little opposition in carrying these measures through, since the legislators were well aware of the political hazards of opposition, arising not solely from the resentment of the groups subject to discrimination but also from the considerable public sentiment on their side. However, this public sentiment is for the most part unfocused and undirected. It is generally uninformed and it is shot through with contradictions. We shall as we proceed examine some of the issues of strategy raised by this situation.

In passing, however, let us refer to the simple truth that one reason, here as elsewhere, for the lack of cohesion and drive behind public support is the detachment of sentiment from activity congenial to the sentiment. Unless sentiment is hitched to action it dissipates itself and is easily routed by active interests enlisted on the other side. There is a moral here both for the organizations that oppose inter-group discrimination and for the mass of individuals whose sympathies are favorable.

Hence there is a good psychological justification for those practical appeals that explain to the average well-disposed person just what things *he* or *she* can effectively do. It is not merely that the doing of these things helps the cause but also that it gives a new vitality to the cause itself. The clear straightforward suggestions contained in Lillian E. Smith's *There Are Things To Do,* ranging from the rejection of "nigger jokes" to the search for Negro friendships, constitute a good example of this kind of appeal.[1] Miss Smith's sugges-

1 Pamphlet reprinted from *South Today* (Winter, 1942–1943), Clayton, Georgia. See also the present author's chapter, "What We All Can Do," in R. M. MacIver, ed., *Unity and Difference in American Life* (New York, 1946).

tions have particular relevance to the relations of Whites, especially Southern Whites, to Negroes, but in every situation there are activities of similar character that turn sentiment into service.

Nevertheless it is not to be expected that the large majority of well-disposed individuals will sustain any program of action so long as they remain detached from appropriate group allegiance. Hence the need for effective organization, which must at the same time work directly for its cause and create in its members a lively sense of the significance of belonging. The two ends, that of creating the dynamic of the group and that of forwarding the objectives of the organization, are so closely bound together as to be almost inseparable. We shall later be concerned with the question of group dynamic and shall here confine ourselves to some comments on the formulation of objectives.

In the first place it seems of little avail to proclaim and promote principles as such, no matter how eloquently they are enunciated or how widely they are broadcast or how much prestige attaches to those who are enlisted as their sponsors. Principles must be translated into programs of action and programs must be harnessed to well-considered ways and means for driving through to results. It would be invidious to mention instances but some organizations in this field may be relying too exclusively on the promulgation of inter-group harmony, goodwill, and brotherhood. Without clear objectives principles accomplish little.

During the last war the military commands had to combat racial discrimination and prejudice in the armed forces. They did so because these conditions prevented the adequate utilization of man power for military purposes. They went straight to the mark by the explicit training of officers and others, putting before them the objective of soldierly solidarity necessitated by the common cause. Officers and men were instructed to look on Negroes as persons like other

persons, to regard their problems as the human problems of
a group faced with particular difficulties of its own, to realize
that Negroes are cut to no one pattern of response any more
than other men. The bulletins and special orders issued on
this subject are well worth the study of civilian leaders.[2]
Officers were carefully instructed to treat Negroes without
discrimination, to elicit their skills and to provide them with
equal opportunity to develop their skills, and to avoid all
catchwords and derogatory epithets that have a racial implication. So far at least as the formulation of the problem went,
the clear wartime objective overrode the subterfuges and
evasions, the hesitations and doubts, that so often dim the
objective of interracial harmony in times of peace. It is true
that military practice fell sadly short of the aims so admirably
formulated. But the clear assertion of specific standards had
its impact. And the peacetime leader can draw the lesson that
he too must formulate clear objectives based on a study of
the conditions and must pursue them with singleness of purpose, letting no ulterior considerations interfere either with
the realism of his approach or the idealism of his mission.

Effective strategy must seek out positions, not merely proclaim principles. Nobody is hurt and nobody is much bene-
fited by raising in the void the war cries of fair play and evenhanded justice and opportunity for all. Nor does it avail
much to follow up these slogans by general prescriptions such
as more education, mutual understanding, a better deal for
minorities, community participation, and so forth. The program maker must get down to the everyday issues of ways
and means. To do so he must understand the practical difficulties experienced by the disprivileged group and the particular conditions under which they live. He must know what
Alexander Leighton calls "the governing of man," as is ad-

---

[2] We select, as a particularly good example, *Guide to the Command of
Negro Personnel*, Navpapers—15092, Bureau of Naval Personnel, Washington,
D.C., 1944.

mirably illustrated in the book so entitled.[3] He must learn
to translate principle into strategy and to implement strategy
through appropriate tactics. Nor must he fall into the error
prevalent in some scholarly quarters, that "tactics" means a
neat set of ready techniques, foolproof devices that guarantee
results. Tactics is the opportunistic application of strategy to
the immediate situation, as it is sympathetically and knowl-
edgeably comprehended by the policy maker.

We have included in the purposes of strategy the searching
out of the weak points in the opposing line. Here is a theme
that should be given constant study by those enlisted against
discrimination. There are always weak points in the line,
and it is simply common sense to direct the assault against
them. Take for example the resistance to the advancement of
the Negro. We shall later present evidence to show that
Whites on the whole are considerably more concerned to
maintain the lower social status of the Negro than to deny
him a greater measure of economic opportunity. The opposition to his training for better economic jobs and to his admission to them is, except among some particular interest groups,
definitely less obdurate, and has already been dented in
various places. There are not a few industries in which he has
attained better wages and somewhat better positions, including the automobile industry, the iron and steel industries,
and the trades of the longshoremen, stevedores, and seamen.[4]
Even within the South there has been some degree of recognition of the principle of equal pay for equal work. In Kentucky the Department of Public Instruction fixed the salaries,
effective in 1945, for Negro teachers at the same level as those
for White teachers. Advances along this line do not encounter
the emotional block that guards the system of social segregation. There is, for example, an obvious equity in equal pay

[3] *The Governing of Man* (a study of the Colorado River War Relocation
Center at Poston, Arizona. Princeton University Press, 1945).

[4] Myrdal, *op. cit.*, vol. II, pp. 1097–1122. For recent developments see Chap.
VI, §2.

for equal work—it is not in conflict even with the myth of racial superiority. Nevertheless in the longer run economic gains will make for higher status.

There are other reasons why resistance on the economic front is less determined and less unified than on the social front, as will appear when we deal specifically with that subject. It will also become evident that the weak points of the enemy line must be explored afresh for every situation, for every group, and for every change in circumstances.

There is, however, one general weakness that attaches in the United States to the whole line of inter-group discrimination. It might be called an ideological weakness. It is the contradiction of valuations that besets those who believe in racial or ethnic superiority, since that belief is incompatible with the spirit and practice of democracy, with the denial of rank and preordained privilege, with the belief in the common man, and with the mores of free enterprise—all of which are included in the American tradition and presumed to be incorporated in the American way of life. This conflict is the central theme of the whole elaborate study of Negro-White relations contained in Gunnar Myrdal's *American Dilemma*. It is, this writer says, "the ever-raging conflict between, on the one hand, the valuations preserved on the general plane which we shall call the 'American Creed,' where the American thinks, talks, and acts under the influence of high national and Christian precepts, and, on the other hand, the valuations on specific planes of individual and group living, where personal and local interests; economic, social and sexual jealousies; considerations of community prestige and conformity; group prejudice against particular persons or types of people; and all sorts of miscellaneous wants, impulses, and habits dominate his outlook." [5] To him "the Negro problem is primarily a moral issue of conflicting valuations." [6]

[5] *Op. cit.*, vol. I, p. xliii.
[6] *Ibid.*, vol. I, p. xlvi.

We are confronted with a sort of moral schizophrenia. From this point of view the major objective of strategy is to impress the contradiction on the minds and hearts of men, to show them that their highest values are flouted by their prejudiced pursuit of immediate and superficial advantages, to pierce through the disguises and subterfuges by which they "rationalize" their inconsistent behavior, and to rally the latent spiritual forces that will revitalize the creed and help to overthrow the institutions and the attitudes that deny it or defy it.

There can be no doubt that the American system and doctrine of democracy are utterly inconsistent with intergroup discrimination. Nor can there be any question concerning the need to bring this issue into the open or concerning the desirability of mustering the moral forces that make and bind the community. Indeed, without the dynamic of these forces no social cause can triumph. We therefore agree with Myrdal that it is an essential of strategy to evoke the powerful spiritual aid that inheres in the living conception of human brotherhood and in the democratic creed that the value of personality is not to be measured or bounded by distinctions of color or ethnic origin. At the same time we must distinguish between the broad support of moral forces by which a cause is sustained and the particular methods by which that cause is advanced. Without morale an army is worthless, but morale alone does not show the road to victory. Moral forces become effective when they are enlisted on the side of economic, political, and social ends. We should remember also that inconsistency is a charge that does not bite deep, as the history of every religion makes clear. Most men seem to get along on some kind of compromise with their creeds, and they are adept enough at makeshift adjustments in the ordinary business of living. It is well to expose their rationalizations but nevertheless they have great capacity for finding new ones. They may have some uneasiness on this score, but often it is not potent enough to make them change their ways. Furthermore, it by no means follows that this uneasiness will of itself make for greater tolerance and be a stage on the road to understanding. Guilt feelings are uncomfortable, and they may be got rid of by a harder and blinder defensiveness, supported by new justifications, so that the spirit of discrimination is not diminished but rather intensified.

We mention these commonplaces not to confute the position of Myrdal—we shall in due course bring out, from a somewhat different approach, the great importance of what we shall broadly call the educational front—but only to raise a caution against the assumption that a moral or spiritual assault alone will carry through the opposing line.

This conclusion is in harmony with our next suggestion regarding strategy in general. It is that there are great advantages in attacking at points where, if success can be achieved, the gain can afterwards be stabilized. The great difficulty of the direct attack on prejudice is that there is no assurance that the ground won can be maintained. Prejudice is volatile and is always changing its locus. It is fluctuating and subject to all kinds of ebb and flow. It is driven out here only to reappear there. Hence the attack on it should wherever possible be associated with specific programs of institutional and economic change such as can register any advances made in the moral or ideological area. An institution once established tends to perpetuate itself. It affects men's habits and in time their attitudes. It creates an interest in its own maintenance. A law on the statute book has a good expectation of life. It is harder to repeal a law than to pass it in the first instance. Law cannot move far in advance of the dominant public opinion but it can ratify and fortify every expression of that opinion. The laws against discrimination already in being in a few states, while they will accomplish more or less according to the responsiveness of the public, will certainly endure and will give a new background and a new security to the antidiscrimination forces. Similarly, if the struggle against prejudice is recorded in the opening of new economic opportunities for those hitherto excluded or in a raising of their wage level these concrete advances give new arms, new bases—and new morale—to the forces that have achieved them.

For these reasons we are in general agreement with the judgment of Dr. Goodwin Watson as stated in his survey of the methods and programs of organizations working for the improvement of inter-group relations: "One of our most fundamental hypotheses, growing out of this survey, is that it is more important to attack segregation than it is to attack prejudice." [7] The argument is twofold. On the one hand the impact on discriminatory attitudes of participation in common tasks is likely to be greater than the direct assault on these attitudes through educational methods. On the other hand, "if we try to change people's feelings while the caste barriers remain tacitly accepted, the habits built around these barriers will silently undo anything we accomplish." [8] In the discussion centering round the presentation of the report in question President Charles S. Johnson of Fisk University, a distinguished Negro student of the subject, commented favorably on this conclusion.

In our own formulation we do not place the attack on segregation first, at least so far as the South is concerned. What comes first must depend on the changing situation. But the general principle holds, that any attack must seek to advance into ground that, once taken, can be stabilized as a new position for further attacks. The difficulty of the struggle against prejudice *as such* is that it does not offer this advantage.

[7] *Methods of Improving Community Co-operation:* Report of the Planning Survey to the Commission on Community Inter-relations of the American Jewish Congress (1945), now published under the title *Action for Unity* (New York, 1947).
[8] *Ibid.*

Furthermore, the scale as well as the direction of the attack must be carefully considered or otherwise energies and resources will be dissipated and spent in vain. In the first place, it is obvious that where discrimination is widespread and where prejudice has a strong hold on the community we cannot expect early results from an educational process that is concerned mainly with the "conversion" of individuals. The process is too slow and the strong contagion of community sentiment is always at work to undo its effects. As one investigator says, "I do not see any hope for control of the mass phenomenon by reconditioning the individual." [9] In any event, strategy is not devoted to such slow and precarious procedures. Rather, in the matter of re-education, it will seek to enlist and influence the men of leadership, the men with prestige, the men who hold key positions in industry, in the trade unions, in the churches, and in the community. There is another question of scale that is of the greatest importance. Some forms of discrimination cannot be effectively attacked by local controls; they require statewide, regional, or possibly even national programs. Many cities in the United States now have "committees on unity." These can do excellent work, but some of the problems they must face can be met only by their sponsoring statewide policies.

One reason why this is so lies in the impact of a system of discrimination on the nondiscriminators. If, for example, in an area where social discrimination against a particular group is rife one hotel, inn, restaurant, or resort breaks the taboo and refuses to discriminate the consequent influx of those who are elsewhere excluded may give it a clientele drawn mainly from that particular group. (We know personally of cases where this has occurred.) The former clients resent the change and go elsewhere. The establishment comes to be regarded as one that caters to this particular group. By reject-

9 John Dollard, "Acquisition of New Social Habits," in Ralph Linton, *The Science of Man* (New York, 1945), p. 463.

ing the principle of segregation it finds itself segregated.
Such segregation may become almost absolute when an institution opens its doors freely to Negroes in an area where they
are present in considerable numbers. It tends to be strongly
marked, if not so complete, when Jews are welcomed to a
summer resort hotel in areas where exclusion is "fashionable."

Even where this result might not happen the fear of it acts
as a deterrent on those who are themselves disinclined to
discriminate, especially when they run establishments that
depend on the patronage of the upper middle class. Though
we have no specific evidence to offer we believe that other
classes are not so "sensitive" on this score. There are indeed
some indications that in housing developments the fear of
the effect of a policy of nondiscrimination is often much
exaggerated.[10] However this may be we must acknowledge
that both the genuine repercussions of nondiscrimination
on a local scale and still more the fears that they engender
make it desirable, sometimes even necessary, that programs
directed against discrimination include an area wide enough
to negate or at least greatly reduce the danger.

A similar problem occurs in the educational field, for educational institutions, like others, are somewhat at the mercy
of the prevailing fashions and taboos. A school, college, or
university that singly abandons whatever system of limitation
it has adopted, in an area where there is a considerable number of the group who are victims of discrimination, will tend
to become distinctively associated or even identified with the
group in question. Thus in New York City Brooklyn College
is 75 per cent Jewish and City College 80 per cent. It is reasonable to conclude that any college within this area that has
high standing or prestige would move strongly in the same
direction if it, all by itself, took a vigorous stand against any
degree whatever of discrimination or, what might amount to
the same thing, against any policy designed to draw a con-

10 See below, pp. 256–260.

siderable proportion of its student body from outside of the
area in question. The college that thus freely opened its doors
would lose prestige with the prejudiced majority, who would
send their sons and daughters elsewhere. Even the unprejudiced would hesitate before sending their sons or daughters
to a college where they would be a religious and social minority and where they would "lose caste" with the members of
their own group, nor would these sons and daughters themselves be likely to approve the choice.

So long as discrimination is widespread in the community
there is no entirely successful solution of this problem. The
onus cannot be placed on the single institution that under
these conditions seeks to maintain some kind of balance. Still
less can it be put on the group which because of restrictions
elsewhere floods such opportunities as may be available to it.
The only promising way out is through a program that is
statewide. The program should not seek to interfere with
general educational policies, nor should it be based on the
invidious assumption that a state board can decide in the
case of individual complainants the expert question whether
they were as well qualified for admission as successful applicants, but should rest on the broad principle that there are
reliable statistical evidences as to whether an educational
institution is seriously barring entrance to the qualified
members of particular groups. If schools and colleges
throughout the state could be led to abandon such severe
and irrational restrictions as exclude altogether the qualified
students of the group in question or else limit them to a
negligible quota, all the worst evils and pressures of the
present situation would be removed. It is of course an entirely specious plea, when made on behalf of these excluding
institutions, that they admit Jewish students in proportion
to their numbers in the particular areas where the institutions are located. They do not follow this policy for other
groups nor does it have any relevance except as a device of

discrimination. If the suggested change were brought about then the fears that beset nondiscrimination would be in large measure removed. And we might cherish the hope that in the longer run, with the removal both of pressures and of fears, the whole tendency to discrimination in educational institutions, where it is so alien to the essential cause for which they stand, would dwindle away.

2. STRATEGY FOR MINORITY GROUPS

So far we have been viewing questions of strategy from the standpoint of organizations of any kind the purpose of which is to combat discrimination. But we must include some considerations on the strategy of the minority groups themselves and of the agencies that represent them.

In the first place, there are some groups subject to discrimination that face peculiar problems of integration into the general life of the community. For reasons already suggested the Jews fall particularly into this category. Not only is their religion essentially exclusive to themselves but the customs and rituals associated with it are very pervasive and make their daily practices, their festivals, and their weekly calendar very divergent from those of the majority of the community. Even though these requirements are not regularly observed by a proportion of the Jewish people that fact does not alter the tendency to regard all Jews as having an alien outlook and an alien mode of life. For this reason, and others, Jewish people should develop and in their public relations should stress the *cultural* attitudes and ways of living that they share with the rest of the community. Otherwise they are driven to the position of a cultural enclave around which prejudice will continue forever to surge. It is for the same reason very important that the Jewish group as a whole participate, in spite of obstacles, in the common affairs of citizens, instead of confining their attention to the welfare of their own group. Many Jews have done signal service in this respect, but the tradition of aloofness and exclusive clannishness still is strong. Although Gentiles are largely responsible for what aloofness exists the more the Jewish people can give evidence against it the better will be the chances for the dissipation of the prejudice from which they suffer.

Again, we raise the question of the manner in which subjected groups should carry on their campaign for equal rights. What, in particular, is the efficacy of radical programs, especially when vigorously put forward under the banners of these groups themselves? We have no ready answer to this question and can submit only some tentative considerations. There is much division of opinion on the subject, some maintaining that aggressive uncompromising belligerency not only receives greater public attention but also does more for the cause than milder or more conciliatory methods. Others regard it as too dangerous, as liable to arouse more obstinate opposition, as having a boomerang effect on the group that uses it. There is need for some genuine research here, for the subject has not been carefully investigated.

When we speak of radical demands we are thinking, for example, of the position taken by the Negro following that adheres to such organs as *The People's Voice*. They call for the full establishment of equal rights everywhere for Negroes and denounce in the strongest terms the entire system that denies these rights. They call for coercive measures against discrimination and discriminators. We may perhaps include in the same category the more clamant utterances, sometimes spread out in large-scale advertising, of left wing Jewish sections and the attempts of some members of these sections to bring legal action against certain organizations that they charge with practising discrimination against them.

It is beyond doubt that these radical demands and utterances do bring into the spotlight the issues they raise, and that they disturb the complacency of many people who otherwise would be glad to let things remain as they are. For a long time there was a kind of conspiracy of silence in the United States over the issue of caste and the discrimination that goes with it. Sociologists, political scientists, and publicists deemed it scarcely worth mention or perhaps thought it preferable not to ventilate the theme. Churchmen and moralists largely passed it by. Politicians were loathe to make any reference to it. But ringing denunciations and extremist demands force it into the open. They make headlines. They reveal the resentments that hitherto smouldered underneath. They cast doubts on the system that can breed such resentments. No longer can the subject be ignored.

But whether they dispose the public to an attitude more favorable to the cause they champion is another matter. There are situations in which historical evidence strongly suggests that drastic action on the part of the suppressed has good chances of success. One such situation is that of a people struggling for self-government. Not infrequently even a small people ruled by an alien government with much more powerful resources than its own has, by obstinate unyielding intransigence, won its way at length to freedom. It is true also that any minority group possessed of some lever of power, whether economic or political, can often, in our modern world of interdependence, gain its ends by the aggressive assertion of its claims. Neither of these situations, however, resembles that with which we are here concerned—although it is possible that the Negro may some day develop his voting power into a lever of the kind we have in mind. Until this condition is attained, whether for the Negro or any other group, it is doubtful that drastic demands or extremist actions will bring the desired results. The subject, as we have said, needs to be investigated and until this is done we can offer only such general considerations as the following.

At the outset aggressive or all out demands in the name of a disprivileged group lacking any leverage of power may be beneficial to its cause, simply because it awakens the people and their leaders to the seriousness of the problem. Persistence in such methods, however, is likely to heighten hostility and prejudice, since the demands they make have no support in the prevailing usages and could not possibly be met until there is a considerable change in the mores. The sense of cleavage is intensified. The aggressive front evokes an opposing aggressive front. The moderate elements, usually a majority of the whole, will react unfavorably. Many potential allies are discouraged, especially as they find themselves denounced as enemies or traitors to the cause. The forces already engaged in fighting discrimination are divided. Those who cannot go all the way with the left wing demands can find no basis for common action. The radical group develops a closed and exclusive ideology. The strength of the whole forward movement is broken—a phenomenon similar to that which has been witnessed in Germany, Spain, and other countries when left wing extremism grew strong. It is not without significance that the demand for the sweeping abolition of racial and ethnic inequalities is voiced by those identified with the communist postion and that communist support is given to Negro and other groups which advocate the more revolutionary programs. This fact, in a country like the United States, is itself influential in stirring opposition and prejudicing the whole cause that is thus supported.

Our argument here applies only to situations in which we have to reckon with ingrained habits and attitudes and social usages that sustain a system of discrimination. Nor does it have anything to say against the unequivocal assertion of the goal of complete equality, nor is it opposed to drastic or spectacular *action* for *moderate* demands—such as the Negro "March on Washington"—but only against programs that loudly insist on the immediate implementation of outright (even if intrinsically rational) demands. The underlying reason is that no reform in this area can succeed unless it makes alliance with changing custom. Any successful advance against discrimination must be preceded, accompanied, or followed by appropriate adaptations of men's attitudes. Here is the advantage of the gradual forward movement—which, however, should be no less decisive and no more timorous than the more extreme assault. If the advance is step by step, men can accommodate themselves to new relations. For example, the opposition of White workers to the presence of Negro workers usually diminishes as they learn to work side by side. In time such an arrangement comes to seem perfectly natural and reasonable. Thus the way is prepared for a new forward movement, such as the admission of Negroes to positions of responsibility, as foremen and as executive officers. Whereas peremptory proposals for ungraduated change meet violent resistance, so that even if they could be carried into effect they would not admit the operation of the healing processes of adaptation. In fact they could not be implemented except by coercive measures on so large a scale that they would mean either a greater cleavage or a more universal bondage. To succeed it is necessary to follow the lines of socio-economic change, to take advantage of the opportunities they offer, and to press steadily toward the greater goal.

One more question of general strategy comes up for consideration here, because while it is of high concern to all who fight against discrimination it calls for particular discretion on the part of the groups that are immediately involved. The question is how best to deal with the purveyors of group prejudice, with rabble rousers, and with organizations such as the Silver Shirts, the Columbians, the Ku Klux Klan following, or even the more "respectable" agencies that propagate group hatred and group antagonism. These elements aggravate the situation in two ways. In the first place they are *excitants,* turning latent into active hostility, blowing active hostility up to fever heat, and directing, where they can, the universal human emotion for the "we-group" into a burning hatred for the "they-group." In the second place they are *precipitants,* provoking clashes, race riots, lynchings, and all manner of disturbances and thereby in turn fomenting new tensions and new antagonisms.

There has been much controversy on the proper methods to meet this menace.[11] How far, in particular, should legal sanction be invoked? How far should legislative controls be sought in addition to the legal processes already available? Should legal tolerance be extended to those who advocate intolerance? Should free speech be permitted to people who are out to destroy freedom, including freedom of speech? Should the criminal libel laws be broadened or amended to include the calumniation of racial or ethnic or religious groups? Should, for example, anti-Semitic publications be made subject to prosecution and to suppression? The appeal for such measures is a natural response on the part of those who deeply deplore the harm wrought by these fomenters of hate and especially on the part of the groups they insult and traduce.

Nevertheless there are strong reasons why the resort to law and coercion should be taken sparingly and with much circumspection. An adequate exposition of these reasons would take us beyond the scope of this survey. In brief, there are two main grounds on which the argument rests. One is that the legal-judicial mechanism for dealing with this issue is ill-equipped to draw the line between fair and proper comment and the malicious libel of a group. The most damaging attacks on a minority group are not so likely to be those that

11 See, for example, the symposium on "Legislation and Social Action" in *Report of the Plenary Session,* National Community Relations Advisory Council (New York, 1946), pp. 17–25.

use the explicit terms on which an indictment could be based
as those that in smooth and specious language suggest insidious doubts and fears. Nor can the law deal with the in-
variable response to the prohibition of free utterance, the
underground whisperings and rumors that are the more difficult to counteract because they move so quietly and surrepti-
tiously below the surface of society.

Moreover, the mechanism is double-edged, and can readily
be applied against the upholders of liberty of thought and
speech. When we outlaw any doctrine, no matter how de-
testable we think it, we give to the prosecutor and the judge
a discretionary power that can easily become the wedge of
tyranny cutting into the first of all liberties.

The other ground is that legal action is apt to give, by the
publicity associated with it, an undue importance and notoriety to the scandal monger or rabble rouser. In our age of
mass communication through press, radio, and moving picture, legal prosecution of such persons multiplies a thousand-
fold the attention paid to their utterances. But even before
the days of the newsreel and the broadcast there was much
experience to give point to the warning. Any cause, whether
high or low, good or bad, has news value when associated
with a public trial. The prophet of a great cause or the unscrupulous ignoramus can thus alike win recognition. A
famous historical instance was that of the trial in England in
1877 of Charles Bradlaugh and Annie Besant for republish-
ing an old book by an obscure author dealing with the principle of birth control. The republication had been selling
some 700 copies per annum previously, but in the three
months between arrest and trial the sales rose to 125,000
copies. And the following year witnessed the beginning of
the long descent of the birth rate in England.[12]

Our viewpoint is affirmed by various researches into the
nature and effects of publicity. There have been, for example,

[12] J. A. Field, *Essays in Population* (Chicago, 1931), Chap. VII.

a number of studies on the effects of the rebuttal of false rumors through exposure of their falsehood. A well-conducted test of this sort was sponsored by U. S. Army authorities, in which rumors were mentioned over a radio program, followed by a refutation giving the actual facts. The conclusion reached was that it was better not to repeat rumors at all. "For every rumor spiked by the program twenty-seven rumors were planted! . . . Never repeat a rumor *even to deny* it. . . . When you repeat a rumor you are spreading the rumor." [13]

In the fight against discrimination it is essential to state the truth that is perverted by false reports. The Army bulletin just cited holds that in this situation the preferable method is first to give the facts and then to point out that ugly rumors are falsifying them, but without retailing the particular rumors themselves. There may be exceptions to this rule, and the treatment of rumors should certainly be handled differently according to the nature of the audience, according to the temper of public opinion, and according to the degree of exposure of the offended group to untoward consequences from the broadcasting of the rumor.

One general lesson is that the foes of prejudice and discrimination should avoid bringing to the focus of public attention the hatemonger and all his works. He is often an exhibitionist who thrives on exposure. He is always a sensationalist who courts publicity. The press and the other agencies of communication can greatly help by refusing to gratify these seekers after notoriety, by not featuring their gestures and their outpourings. A good illustration of the effect of such treatment is what happened to Gerald Smith on a mission to Pittsburgh. In that city he received no free advertising from the press, and his campaign proved a dud. Whereas in Detroit and in St. Louis he met with vehement

13 *Leadership and the Negro Soldier*, Army Service Forces Manual (October, 1944), p. 63.

resistance, in St. Louis being opposed by a group of veterans and in Detroit being met by large-scale picketing, creating much clamor and giving him a corresponding importance.[14]

For these two reasons we agree with the position of the American Civil Liberties Union, itself a staunch defender of the rights of minority groups, that in general laws and city ordinances which would coercively suppress the expression of racial and religious prejudice are dangerous and likely to be detrimental. Only in the clearest cases of outright libel, and then only with the greatest discretion if at all, and in cases of definite incitement to violence, should the law be invoked, especially by the groups that are the victims of such assaults. The words of Justice Holmes, quoted by the Union, are in point. "I think that we should be eternally vigilant against attempts to check the expression of opinions that we loathe and believe to be fraught with death, unless they so imminently threaten immediate interference with the lawful and pressing purposes of the law that an immediate check is required to save the country." [15] In all other cases we should resort to seemingly slower but more deep-working methods for the healing of group antagonisms, a subject to which we shall later devote some space.

3. THE ARMING OF LEADERSHIP

There is one aspect of strategy to which, on account of its great and undeveloped potentialities, we devote a separate section. It is the role of leadership, the question of its evoca-

[14] Cf. S. A. Fineberg, "Checkmate for Rabble Rousers," *Commentary*, September, 1946.

[15] See, for example, the pamphlets issued by the American Civil Liberties Union in 1946, "The Case Against Legal Restraints on Racial Libels and Anonymous Publications," and "What Do You Mean, Free Speech?"—though we do not entirely agree with some minor points of the argument in the second of these two pamphlets.

tion, of the special services it can render, and of the manner
in which it must be trained and sustained to render these
services. It has been remarked by some observers of the
American scene that in the United States leadership is particularly influential in social policy.[16] If this be so, then
leadership is nowhere more important than in the battle
against discrimination. For, as we shall have occasion to
show later on, the factor of social prestige is a powerful motive for discriminatory treatment, since such treatment implies the lower worth and maintains the lower status of the
groups subjected to it. In a society that is open enough to
admit rather freely the competitive quest for status there is
a peculiar temptation to use group discrimination as a safeguard against the imputation of inferiority. It gives the
magic of unearned merit to the dominant groups.[17] Here
then is one of the main reasons why leadership counts for
so much. The association of prestige with group discrimination is discounted when the higher prestige-bearers, as leaders, reject it.

Considerations of social status are bound up with all group
discrimination, whether the ostensible ground be race, ethnic
derivation, religion, cultural difference, class distinction, occupational category, or any other. The racial discrimination
of the Southern states, for example, is dominated by the
White desire to retain the position of an upper caste and by
the fear lest this higher status be invaded and confounded
should the Negroes be afforded rights and opportunities.
Status, with all that it conveys, is everywhere of moment to
human beings. If they lose it, they fear that everything is lost.
One corollary is that we should not denounce the South for
doing what all human beings, according to their situation,
do. The only understanding attitude is one that recognizes
their plight but seeks to show that the position they adopt

16 Cf. Myrdal, *op. cit.*, Chap. 34.
17 See the author's *Society*.

is outmoded, untenable, detrimental to their own well-being, and fraught with national peril. They are the victims of a heritage that belongs to the past, and their only future is to be sought through courageous adjustment of action and of attitude to the demands of the present. The same lesson, according to their different circumstances, must somehow be impressed on other discriminatory groups. Everywhere the quest for status and perhaps most of all, in our competitive society, the clinging fears of inferiority lie behind the processes and institutions of discrimination.

There are, however, some types of discrimination for which the prestige factor has a special significance. It is so, as we have already suggested, with anti-Jewish discrimination. As John Dollard remarks: "Anti-Semitism, perhaps of an indirect kind, is a matter of fact among the social leaders of America." One cannot, for instance, frequent any "country club" without listening on occasion to the inevitable "latest one about the Jew who . . ." The laughter that follows rings with the overtones of in-group complacency, just as clearly as ever did the Pharisee's prayer, when he thanked God that he was not as other men. It is a way of asserting prestige, and even the person who thinks it unfair and prejudicial may hesitate not to join in it lest he too seem to fail before the shibboleths of the tribe. Hence the counterattack of prestige leaders is so salutary. No doubt it is this consideration that led Mr. Dollard to add that "perhaps the most positive mechanism, if it could be managed, would be the example and influence of the leaders at the top of our society." [18]

Some outstanding leaders have been lending their influence to this cause. It helped when Pope Pius XI, referring to the language of the Mass that calls Abraham "our patriarch and ancestor," declared that "anti-Semitism is not compatible with the sublime reality of this text. . . . We are spiritually Semites." It helped when General Eisenhower opened the

[18] John Dollard, *op. cit.*, pp. 462–463.

drive of the United Jewish Appeal for the relief of European
Jews and declared that mutual confidence between groups
was a primary world need. It helped when Eric A. Johnston,
then President of the American Chamber of Commerce,
spoke forcefully of group superiority as "the myth that
threatens America." It helps when anyone who has a considerable following puts his influence on the side of inter-
group equality, whether he be the President of the United
States appealing against discrimination in the name of the
American creed or Frank Sinatra telling his adolescent ad-
mirers that differences of race or color should never allow
them to forget that all citizens of America have equal rights.
The impression, however, made by occasional utterances of
this kind is short-lived, especially as they are usually couched
in general terms. Example is more important than precept,
and leadership in specific action against discrimination makes
a deeper mark than the noblest words. Above all, we need
leadership operative in this field more than the occasional
aid, valuable as it is, of leaders who devote their energies to
other fields.

Besides the efficacy of prestige there is another reason why
the evocation of leadership is crucial for the control of inter-
group discrimination. The utterances to which we have al-
luded, the adherence to the same cause of churchmen of many
faiths, the strong sympathies of educationalists, the success of
novels that portray the effects on personality and on social
relations of racial and ethnic discrimination, and various
other evidences indicate the presence of a large volume of
opinion and sentiment opposed to the antidemocratic processes of group subordination or segregation. But this potential support is not marshalled and much of it remains
inarticulate. It cannot be focused and made to bear effectively on policy except through leadership. Furthermore, the
large majority of the public is enrolled in organizations—
particularly the churches but also some political, civic, and

social organizations—that profess principles directly contradicted by the relegation of racial or ethnic groups to an inferior status among their fellow men or fellow citizens. It is the task of leadership to drive home this contradiction by enlisting their followers to accept and to work on behalf of the practical demands of the faiths they profess to espouse.

It should be obvious, in the light of what has already been said, that the existing leadership of these organizations has had relatively little success in this direction and needs to be trained and armed if it is to achieve greater results. There are departments and committees associated with these organizations, such as the department on inter-group relations of the Federal Council of Churches, that devote themselves steadily to this task. There are also such general associations as the Bureau for Intercultural Education, the National Conference of Christians and Jews, the Council Against Intolerance in America, and the American Council on Race Relations, and several others, offering stimulation, information, and other aids to the leaders in question. But however valuable the services of these bodies may be it must be acknowledged that the mobilization of the available forces is still inadequate.

This defect reveals itself in the frequent discrepancy between public profession and private behavior, a discrepancy brought out by various psychological and sociological investigations.[19] There is a resort to all kinds of subterfuges and "rationalizations," in order to admit practices completely at odds with principles. As Myrdal suggests, one function of the leader here is to bring persistently to bear on these issues the values or principles "kept in the shadow of inattention." [20]

The discrepancy referred to is nowhere more flagrantly exhibited than in the realm of religion, and consequently the potential contribution of leadership in this realm must be

[19] See, for example, Myrdal, *op. cit.*, II, pp. 1139 ff.
[20] Myrdal, *op. cit.*, II, p. 1028.

rated very highly. The well-armed leader, if he had more regard for his cause than for the plaudits of his audience, would know how to confront his followers with their responsibilities, to bring their evasions to the light, to evoke in them first a sense of uneasiness and then some recognition of the injury they are doing to their own values, in such a persuasive manner that many of them would be more inclined to seek a way of reconciliation than to reject his teaching altogether.

An instance or two out of many may be cited here to illustrate the manner in which a fatal contradiction often besets the ministry of the Christian Churches. In a session at Columbus, Ohio, March 6, 1946, the Federal Council of Churches went on record—the session was addressed by President Truman—as opposing racial segregation, rejecting it as "the pattern of American race relations," and calling on constituent churches to act in accordance with the resolution. The actual response showed the vacillation and hesitancy that prevails and *therefore* the opportunity for strong leadership. In November, 1946, the North Carolina Baptist Convention meeting at Asheville passed a resolution declaring that racial segregation in churches was a denial of the tenets of Christianity. Next day the Convention backtracked, rescinding the resolution.

Here is clear evidence of the ambivalence that prevails in the churches. We may set the action and reaction of the North Carolina Baptists alongside the resolution passed at the Georgia Baptist Convention about the same time. This resolution called on "all Christian people of Georgia, particularly Baptists," to oppose "with every ounce of energy" the groups that uphold race superiority, and proclaimed that "no man shall be discriminated against because of race, creed, or color." But this was a declaration of principle, not a program of action: and the principle is denied by the caste structure of the Baptist Churches of Georgia and flouted by the daily behavior of the vast majority of their members. Nevertheless all these manifestations witness to a stir of uneasiness, a sharper sense of the flagrant contradiction between faith and conduct, a restive wish to mitigate it in some way. It is precisely this situation that provides the opportunity for the strong leader. The churches of the United States, and especially the grossly offending churches of the South, await the leader who can turn uneasiness into determination and vacillation into forward action.

In the rest of the country there are signs of the same ambivalence that is so unmistakable in the South. Marian Anderson is awarded the Bok prize as the most distinguished resident of Philadelphia, but she would not be acceptable as a guest in many of the restaurants of that city. A Negro graduates at West Point to the cheers of his fellow cadets but when he enters the service he meets again the system of segregation. Such contrasts everywhere abound, and we need leaders to capitalize on them.

In all situations where there is ambivalence and uncertainty of direction the resolution displayed by the leader is of crucial importance. In the economic area there occur various situations of this order, particularly the situation we have already described as the "indifferent equilibrium." Many instances are given in the able pamphlet prepared by John A. Davis on "How Management Can Integrate Negroes in War Industries." [21] The general hypothesis on which resolute action is based in these instances is that, unless the mores of the community are violently in opposition, the experience of working side by side with Negroes leads to an habituation on the part of the White workers that weakens the initial opposition. This hypothesis was confirmed in the cases cited, such as that of the Winchester Repeating Arms Company,

[21] New York State War Council's Committee on Discrimination in Employment, 1942; see also the pamphlet issued under the same auspices in 1945, *The Negro Integrated,* by Nicholas S. Falcone.

New Haven, Connecticut, which found that, once the decision was carried into effect to employ Negroes in all capacities for which they showed fitness, the policy proved workable, so much so that some of the chief opponents became its stoutest defenders. The pamphlet carried this testimony: "All persons who have dealt with this problem, including the personnel managers and government officials interviewed, agreed that nothing is so important as a firm position on the part of management."

Similar testimony is conveyed and appropriately illustrated in a confidential OWI Report.

It may be objected that the cases here cited fell within the range of war industry, when the powers of government, acting through the civil or the military arm, were much extended and when the authority of government was much enhanced by the patriotic ardor of the country. No doubt this fact gave assurance to executives who acted with firmness, but it would in no way account for the later success of the policy, for the change of attitude brought about by habituation. It is on this prospect that the policy is based, and we have shown in another connection that it can be successfully applied in peacetime industry. There have been instances where the attempt to introduce Negro workers has failed, leading to strikes, but not infrequently this result has occurred where the workers belonged to a trade union, as in the railroad industry, which had a set tradition of exclusion or else where the executives failed to act with promptitude and assurance or did not bring to bear the pressures at their command. Apart from such situations the prognosis, according to the available testimony, points strongly to the success of resolute leadership in this area.

In the North many important business corporations employ Negroes side by side with Whites, and on their clerical staffs as well as elsewhere. Among firms that pursue this policy are the Western Electric, Sperry Gyroscope Company,

Bell Telephone Laboratories, Consolidated Edison, Eastman Kodak, International Harvester, and Chase National Bank. The general verdict is that Negro workers are as good as other workers, that when they have the same training and the same opportunity they do quite as satisfactory a job, that like all other workers they have their own difficulties and that a particular one in some cases is, as might indeed have been expected, a "persecution complex." There is also much testimony to the effect that management has an often needless fear of introducing Negro workers and that personnel directors in this respect often display more timidity than insight, more discretion than courage.[22]

The argument is relevant to action by trade union leaders no less than by business executives. Indeed the former are in some respects in a more favorable position for affirmative action. They are closer to the workers and can use persuasion along with firmness. A well-established trade union leader has great authority with which to influence the officers of locals as well as the rank and file. He has often a considerable freedom in the development of policy. Through his influence over the locals he can prepare the way for a change of program, and it must be remembered that the local union agent is generally a key man in the local labor situation. Moreover, in some industries union policy has become dominant over employer policy. The worker is frequently more dependent on the good will of his union than on that of his employer. Hence the union can generally afford to display firmness in dealing with recalcitrant members. An example of how it is done is offered by the sheet of instructions issued in a training course given by the National Maritime Union. It is entitled: "What to do when a seamen refuses to sail with a Negro brother." The NMU stands against racial or ethnic discrimination, and the instructions proceed: call a meeting; show up the arguments of the other side; appeal to the con-

22 Cf. Nicholas S. Falcone, *op. cit.*, pp. 3–10.

stitution of the NMU; ask the objectors if they believe in the constitution; when they answer, as always, "yes," point to the clause against discrimination; if they still object tell them they can get off the ship.

There is finally another and very different kind of leadership that might possibly play a decisive role. It is the leadership that establishes a *cultural style,* in this instance the style in accordance with which people think about other groups within the greater community. There is a style or pattern of thought congenial to every society and to every age, a style always in process of change or development. Into this broader pattern numerous special patterns are inwoven, thought modes or folkways that dominate the minds of men. These include the thought modes that sustain the processes of discrimination. They make people resistant or impervious to contrary indoctrination—a theme we reserve for further discussion. Hence there is need for a kind of flank attack on these thought modes, and this must come not from the political or economic leader nor directly from the intellectual leader but from the creative artist who subtly transmutes old styles into new. The opportunity for this service comes particularly when the old style is out of keeping with primary needs or demands of the new age, as is group discrimination in the multigroup society.

While other forms of creative art may render great services we may anticipate that, in our age of mass communication, the most effective medium will be that of the written word, particularly in the form of the novel, aided as it is likely to be by the moving picture. The opportunity provided by the situation of the Negro has already been utilized with considerable success, and there is a still greater opportunity awaiting the understanding novelist who can convey his or her message in the style of the times. In our age the denunciatory style is generally futile. The exhortatory style falls flat. The sentimental style, once so successfully practised by writers like Harriet Beecher Stowe, is outmoded. But writers who have the gift of sympathetic realism can move masses of people. The vivid work of Lillian E. Smith in *Strange Fruit* and the admirably toned appeal of Margaret Halsey, *Color Blind,* point in this direction. We are thinking, however, of a still broader depiction that might bring home the tragic futility and waste of the anti-group movements and anti-group attitudes that pervade the country—the distortion of aims and aspirations, the frustration and embitterment of youth, the skewing of all intrinsic values, the thousand untoward consequences of the whole system of racial and ethnic discrimination. For this purpose, though there are accompanying perils, the novelist has an advantage over the non-fiction writer, since he can present his theme in the warm colors of human experience, selecting and shaping his materials to his design, thus giving them unity and artistic concentration, so that the reader is moved to new sympathies and possibly to new comprehensions.

The time is ripe for this kind of creative appeal. In the summer of 1947 two novels at or near the top of the bestseller list, *Gentleman's Agreement* by Laura Hobson and *Kingsblood Royal* by Sinclair Lewis, were addressed to the issues of ethnic or racial discrimination. These issues have also become the theme of Broadway plays and have even entered into the conservative area of the movies. Such productions are portents of the changing situation, but even the best of them is still far from sounding the depths of the problem they depict.

Chapter Six

The Economic Front

1. ADVANTAGES OF THE ECONOMIC ATTACK

BY THE economic front we mean the area in which the struggle against economic discrimination is waged. In the rest of this work we shall concern ourselves mainly with three forms of discrimination, the economic, the political, and the educational. These present the major fronts on which the war against ethnic and racial disprivilege must be won. The final issue may be one of social *status,* but the superior status of one race or ethnic group over another is bulwarked by the more specific forms of discrimination we have mentioned. For social discrimination is very dependent, at least in our kind of society, on economic, political, and educational advantages, and it crumbles away when its props are removed.

It is idle to ask which of these three fronts is the most important. There are those who give high priority to one or another. Some claim the struggle must be won or lost on the economic front. Others make a similar claim for the educational front. In some quarters there is a tendency to minimize the political front while others see no victory except in a political revolution. Such claims are ill-advised. They are an offense to good strategy. It may indeed be perfectly true that *if* all discrimination could be abolished in *any* of the major areas of the conflict the whole system would in effect come to an end. But so sweeping a gain could never be achieved on one front alone. Any great advance in the economic area requires also an advance in the other areas. Education must prepare the way for it and political institutions must support and stabilize it. The social and moral forces that attack economic discrimination are active in the assault on other kinds of discrimination as well. A victory on one front weakens the enemy on every other.

The more we study the lines of attack on a particular front the more are we impressed by the opportunities they offer. Each front has its own advantages, and the task of strategy is to discover where they lie and to exploit them accordingly. First, then, we shall point out wherein lies the peculiar importance of the attack on economic discrimination. In succeeding chapters we shall seek to do equal justice to the other areas of the great battlefield.

The evidences at hand reveal the following strategic advantages in favor of the attack on economic discrimination.

(1) *The resistance to the demand for economic opportunity is less deeply entrenched than the resistance to various other kinds of equality, being determined more by short-run promptings of economic interest than by the ingrained indoctrinations of social prejudice.*

Economic interest is a powerful stimulant of racial and ethnic prejudice. We find, for example, that when there are very few representatives of a particular ethnic or racial group in a community there tends to be a minimum of opposition to or resentment of their presence, whether on economic or on social grounds. But if the group grows larger and economically more important its members become thought of as competitors in the economic struggle, as holding jobs or pre-empting positions that otherwise would fall to members of the dominant group. The attitude of the dominant group is colored by such considerations. At one period or another this process could have been observed working against the Irish in Massachusetts, against the Poles in Detroit, against the Mexicans in California, and against the Japanese on the Pacific Coast. Everywhere the fear of economic competition enters into the complex of conditions that evoke inter-group discrimination. It is particularly prominent in the feelings of White workers in the industrial crafts when Negroes begin to seek admission to them and it lies back of the policy of exclusion practised by so many labor unions.

Other economic categories also fear the competition of the "out-group" or else covet their economic acquisitions, such as the prosperous farms or the business undertakings the latter may have developed. As soon as prejudice gains a hold certain interests, such as dealers in real estate and owners of the more "desirable" residential properties, seek economic protection in a concerted policy of discrimination. The members of the "out-group" are relegated to an inferior status, and many professions set up bars against their admission, both by refusing them access, or at least equal access, to the necessary training and by making it hard or even impossible for them to obtain the registration, certification, or other credentials required for professional practice. Even should the member of the disprivileged group transcend all these difficulties he is likely to find that prejudice confines his professional practice to his own racial or ethnic circle, and in some fields, such as, for example, engineering, this limitation will mean that an Oriental or a Negro has no outlet of any kind for his services.

As for the more mechanical or more menial occupations, it is generally the worker, and not the employer, who resists the admission of the lower "caste," the Negro, the Mexican, and the Oriental. Here the employer has usually no direct economic motive for discrimination and is likely to be deterred from opening his doors to any qualified workers only

by fear of the reaction of the workers or the workers' union.
Sometimes, however, the employer is prone to a prejudicial
undervaluation of the labor qualities of the disprivileged
groups, of their efficiency, or of their "reliability." In special
areas, where personal or intimate service is implied, employers discriminate against "out-groups" for fear of offending the customer or else because they think that by their
"lily-white" policies they give a higher "tone" to their establishments. Thus Negroes, sometimes Jews, and occasionally
members of other ethnic groups are discriminated against as
waiters in higher-class restaurants, hotels, and clubs, as stew-
ards or attendants in airplanes, as operators in beauty parlors,
as salespeople in "elite" dressmaking and millinery shops,
department stores, and so forth. This particular form of
prejudice is peculiarly irrational, since the very people who
maintain it often have no objection to employing Negro
cooks in their own households and having their children
cared for by Negro nursemaids. It is clear that much prejudice of this type is mainly a matter of usage.[1]

Our brief survey to this point indicates the variety of conditions and of motivations that make against the economic
opportunities of subordinated groups. Our argument is, however, that the opposing forces are less strongly entrenched
here and less well-armed than in some other areas. *An interesting and valuable field of research would be the assessment
or measurement of the strength of the resistance of dominant
groups to the demands of subject groups for different kinds of
equality.* Since adequate studies are not available we must
fall back on general indications. Thus the testimony of many
observers is to the effect that Negro claims to greater eco-

[1] We find, for example, that in the more deeply prejudiced South there
is not the same sharp-cut residential segregation that characterizes Northern
cities. In coastal cities such as Galveston, Mobile, and Charleston, S.C., White
and Negro habitations stand side by side, in the same blocks. Again, there
are such anomalies of usage as the fact that the White man gets shaved by
Negro barbers in Savannah and by White barbers in Atlanta.

nomic opportunity do not arouse the same vehemence of
opposition that meets claims to greater equality of social
status—or anything resembling the bitter resentment and
violent reaction that overwhelms any suggestion in favor of
the last of all equalities, that involving freedom of intermarriage.[2]

We should not on this account underestimate the often
stout resistance to equality of economic opportunity. The
strategic conclusion is that the same amount of well-directed
effort is likely to have a greater impact on this barrier to
equality than on others. We should furthermore observe that
within the economic area some positions are more strongly
guarded than others. The indications suggest the following
ranking, in which we move downward from the least to the
greatest resistance:

(a) Access to unskilled jobs;
(b) Access to semiskilled industrial and domestic jobs;
(c) Equal pay for equal work—even in the South this
    principle is often formally accepted;
(d) Access to training, technical or professional education
    for skilled and professional positions;
(e) Access to promotion or upgrading, involving positions
    of responsibility;
(f) Such access where it involves economic relations giving
    Negroes or members of other disprivileged groups
    some control or authority over Whites or members of
    the more privileged groups;
(g) Access to professional or administrative opportunities
    that are not limited to service within the disprivileged
    group itself.

While resistance is met all along the economic front it
tends to yield, as we have already seen, when a resolute policy
is adopted by employers, governmental officials, and other
authorities. To add another to the examples already given
we may take the successful action of Henry Ford when he put

2 Cf. Myrdal, *op. cit.*, vol. I, pp. 60–67.

into operation his program of hiring Negroes in proportion
to their population ratio in Detroit, without any segregation
in the workshops. The initial opposition soon weakened and
the program worked.[3] There was somewhat greater opposition
to promotion, but this too was modified, especially during
the war.

We have seen that the verdict of men of practical experience is favorable to resolute attacks on the barriers to economic opportunity. And it is not difficult to discover the
reasons why this mode of attack holds so much promise. In
the first place there is an easy appeal against the prejudice
that rejects the economic capacity of the disprivileged groups.
The test is the actual trial of their qualities. The proof of
the pudding is the eating of it. Prejudice can deny these
qualities but it has no ground for refusing people the chance
to show whether they do or do not possess them. The test is
simple and quite objective. Fitness is judged by the performance of function, given the requisite training. When prejudice deals in intangibles it is hard to refute, but when it makes
claims that are controverted by simple arithmetic there is no
line of retreat.

When the gates of economic opportunity are opened to
hitherto excluded groups the prospect is generally good that
the initial opposition will gradually be modified or even disappear altogether. We observe in passing, however, that the
strategy of admission must be implemented through appropriate tactics organizing inter-group relationships within the
factory or the office. There are various degrees and stages of
interadjustment. If complete acceptance is the final goal there
are certainly intermediate processes involving partial acceptance, acceptance with reservations, the working cooperation
of groups that still retain some "social distance." Hence the
amount of mixing or separation between the members of the
different groups and the conditions under which interper-

3 Myrdal, *op. cit.*, vol. II, pp. 1121–1122.

sonal relationships are carried on as well as the layout of the workbenches or the office desks, the arrangements made in the plant restaurant, the recreation facilities, the toilets, and so forth, are of high importance. No general rules can be laid down, since situations are so variable, and only intensive research on the ground can give adequate guidance. Such research, if undertaken by skilled investigators who have established themselves in the economy of the plant, can render valuable service.[4]

Another important consideration is that the belief in economic opportunity is invincibly dear to the average American. It is rooted in the ethos of American society. Economic opportunity is commonly regarded as the most obvious, the most elementary, of human rights. It is frequently blocked by economic interest, but when the issue is brought into the open, while various excuses may be offered to mitigate the offense, scarcely anyone will be found to justify the denial of it. Economic opportunity is held to be one of the great bulwarks of the established order, one of the essentials of the "American way of life." Moreover, the denial of economic opportunity is not only contrary to the tenor of the Bill of Rights but has been specifically and on several occasions declared unconstitutional by the Supreme Court of the United States. Thus in *Truax* v. *Raich* it was laid down: "The right to work for a living in the common occupations of the community is of the essence of that personal freedom and opportunity which it was the purpose of the Fourteenth Amendment to secure." [5] And again in *New Negro Alliance* v. *Sanitary Grocery Co.:* "Race discrimination by an employer may reasonably be deemed more unfair and less excusable than discrimination against workers on the ground of union affiliation." [6]

[4] See Everett C. Hughes, "The Knitting of Racial Groups in Industry," *American Sociological Review* (October, 1946), vol. 11, pp. 512–519.

[5] 239 U.S. 33.

[6] 303 U.S. 552.

Finally, although particular interests, seeking to protect themselves against competition or to maintain some monopoly of labor control, are antagonistic to the economic opportunity of the excluded groups, there are powerful economic forces working on the other side. It is normally the interest of the employer to enlarge the potential supply of labor. It is certainly not to his advantage to exclude any group from this kind of economic opportunity. In this instance it so happens that one important complex of private economic motivations is in harmony with a primary condition of universal economic welfare. But this brings us to our second major argument.

(2) *Discrimination is always economically wasteful. It inflicts serious injury on the economic well-being of the whole community. This truth can be driven home to the consciousness of the people and thereby the attack on the economic front can be advanced.*

It is not possible to reckon the financial cost of discrimination—its consequences ramify too far into the national life. Economists have made estimates: in the United States so many billions of dollars per annum. But such calculations are entirely precarious. Even if we could reckon the direct costs—which is very doubtful—we cannot assess the indirect costs, including the losses involved in the illiteracy, lack of training, lack of incentive, frustration of capacity, unrest, social tension, malnutrition, disease, and criminality that are the fruits of the system. Economic analysis can tell us that the costs are great, far heavier than we generally realize, but it cannot reckon just how grievous the price is that we pay.

The economic backwardness of areas where discrimination operates on a large scale, and especially where its extreme form, segregation, prevails, is not a fact of nature or an "act of God" but in large measure the inevitable penalty of this offense against humanity. The obvious costs of segregation, the duplication of facilities of all kinds, schools, waiting rooms, railroad coaches, churches, theaters, hospitals, and so forth—providing at a greater total expense a graded inferiority of service—are a relatively small part of the whole burden. Even so, they are serious enough.[7] Segregation means that a secondary, economically needless, and socially wasteful equipment and service of poorer quality must be provided for one section of the people. At this price it denies them the opportunity to enhance and to participate in the welfare of the community. At this price it deprives the community of the greater services this section could render. At this price it breeds disease and poverty, inefficiency and frustration. In these respects the Southern states, and the Southwestern states where the Mexicans are numerous, lag behind all the rest. In every community all things are bound in incessant reaction. The Southern White segregates the Negro but he cannot segregate himself from the consequences of segregation. The infection crosses the dividing line to plague those who have set it up.

In the South every little town and rural district has to maintain two schools where one would suffice and where one would be economically and educationally much more advantageous. Some of the funds that might have gone into a better school for all are diverted to supply inferior equipment and inferior teaching—since the Negro teacher not only receives much lower pay as a rule but is debarred from adequate training—for the lower caste. The wasteful duplication extends to technical and professional education and to such institutions of higher education as the Negro can secure. The State of Missouri, for example, in order to maintain its policy of segregation, had to set up a separate law school for a handful of Negro students. In January, 1948, the United States Supreme Court ruled that "equal education facilities" must be provided for Negroes as promptly as for Whites, and under this ruling the Supreme Court of Oklahoma has or-

[7] Cf. Louis Wirth, "The Price of Prejudice," *Survey Graphic*, January, 1947.

dered that a separate law school be set up in that state on the petition of one Negro young woman. In this and in all instances of segregated service not only is the separate provision an additional cost but the result of the additional cost is a liability and not an asset in the balance sheet of economic welfare.

Discrimination inherently acts as a barrier to economic progress. It would not be difficult to show the working of this law throughout human history. We could go back to the Classical Greeks and show that this most ingenious and enterprising of peoples, building their economy on slave labor and regarding industry and the manual crafts as degrading occupations, made no advance in industrial techniques or in economic organization comparable to their advance in other respects. Instead, the internal class and caste divisions of the Greek states brought on endless strife and, according to Thucydides, the greatest of Greek historians, led to the downfall of Greece. We could turn to Rome and learn why, after she had conquered vast areas and diverted much of their wealth to her own use, her economic position grew weaker instead of stronger. According to leading thinkers and statesmen of Rome her economy was ruined by the growth of the caste system, under which the farms formerly cultivated by freemen were merged into large estates organized on a slave basis. We could show how the caste system of medieval society, under which the land was worked by serfs tied to the soil, was directly associated with the poverty of the people and particularly with the tardy development of agriculture and cattle raising. Passing over many other instances, we could show how the caste system maintained in the Spanish and Portuguese empires of Latin America wrought long-enduring economic ruin in these lands.

The other side of the exhibit would be the greater economic advancement of the areas and the peoples that opened the avenues of opportunity more freely to all classes. The

contrast is sufficiently. clear within our own country, where
the caste-dominated states of the Union have the lowest
standard of living and the lowest rating by every economic
index.

The testimony of history is corroborated by a simple piece
of economic analysis. Discrimination limits economic opportunity and therefore cuts down productivity. Discrimination
limits the economic utility of what is produced, for the flow
of production to the groups that need it most is artificially
reduced. The groups subject to discrimination are kept at
a needlessly low economic level. Their incentive to produce
is discouraged at the same time that their ability to produce
is balked. They cannot make their potential contribution to
the welfare of the community. The market for the productivity of others is narrowed because of their lack of purchas-
ing power. As Eric Johnston expressed it, "Intolerance is a
species of boycott and any business or job boycott is a cancer
in the economic body of the nation." The presence of a dis-
satisfied lower caste reacts on the attitudes and activities of
the upper caste. It breeds in them a sense of insecurity that
makes them blindly devoted to the established system and
stubbornly resistant of new developments. Their leadership
becomes consecrated to reaction. Every stimulus to progress
is blunted because the conditions of progress spell danger to
the establishment. Thus in various ways a system of discrimination puts brakes on economic advancement, and in its
more extreme manifestations it makes for a stationary or
even regressive economy.

(3) *The economic impact of discrimination is more cramp-
ing, is more bitterly resented, and causes a greater feeling of
futility and frustration than do its other impacts on the
subject group.*

It is the consensus of many observers that those who suffer
from discrimination are generally more concerned about
economic opportunity than they are about admission to the

social status and the other privileges of the dominant class. This conclusion is supported by various researches dealing particularly with Negro-White relationships. Several of these researches find an inverse relation between the Negro estimate and the White estimate of what things matter most. One study, for example, sums up the matter as follows:

Whereas the Negro says his greatest problem is jobs, Whites consider his problem to be fully as much one of social discrimination. . . . Negroes are twice as inclined to mention job opportunities (61 per cent) as segregation, Jim Crow rules, and social ostracism (27 per cent).[8]

More broadly, Myrdal claims that in the estimate of the gravity of discriminations "the Negro's own rank order is just about parallel, but inverse, to that of the White man." [9] He is most wrought up about economic opportunity, is relatively less concerned about social discrimination, and has generally no impulse whatever to attack the inner citadel of racial distinction, that which holds the line against miscegenation.

There may be extraneous considerations that prompt the Negro to mention economic opportunity more prominently than the social equities. Nevertheless it is well to accept the lead of the people who are under the yoke and learn from them where it is most galling, especially since by a happy coincidence Whites are less reluctant to make concessions in economic than in social relationships while a significant minority of them admit in this respect the justice of the Negro claim.[10] Moreover, there are strong reasons why the

[8] "The Color Line in Industry," a "personal and confidential" report of the Public Opinion Index for Industry, Opinion Research Corporation, Princeton, N.J., April, 1944. Quoted by permission of the Opinion Research Corporation.

[9] Myrdal, op. cit., vol. I, p. 61.

[10] Further evidence is given in some OWI reports, particularly "The Negroes' Role in the War: a Study of White and Colored Opinions," Memorandum No. 59, Surveys Division, Bureau of Special Services, July 8, 1943.

victims of discrimination should feel most aggrieved over its economic aspects. The members of any group readily accept the view that given an equal economic chance they can work out for themselves all the requirements of successful living. Economic disadvantage is to them the primary handicap. It may be particularly so in American society. "Economic increase is identified with moral improvement by a large middle section of our society." [11] On the other hand, low economic status is commonly associated with inefficiency as well as insufficiency, with every kind of inferiority no less than with material scarcity.

Apart altogether from such social valuations there can be little doubt that economic discrimination has a more paralyzing effect than any other kind on the aspirations and ambitions of the subject group. The members of such a group can without too great impediment pursue their various aims even if they are shut out from the homes and the clubs and the residential areas and the resorts of the social elite. Their pride is affected, their status may be diminished, but if they are freely admitted to any vocation on the same terms as other men they are not balked from the satisfaction of their major needs. Moreover, even when the objective of the discriminating group is social exclusiveness rather than economic advantage it employs economic discrimination as a potent means to this end. For example, we suggested that anti-Jewish sentiment was primarily motivated by a sense of social distance, but one of its essential devices is the denial to Jewish persons of access to the more prestigeful occupations and positions of responsibility. Likewise the debarment of Negroes from many occupational opportunities is motivated by the desire to keep them on a lower social level. The same principle operates all along the line. Indeed it is a reasonable inference that economic discrimination is a mainstay of social exclusiveness. Were it deprived of its economic controls social dis-

11 W. Lloyd Warner, Robert J. Havighurst, and Martin H. Loeb, *Who Shall Be Educated* (New York, 1944), p. 155.

crimination would in most instances be much more weakly
defended. This point is strengthened when we relate it to
the final strategic advantage we present on behalf of a sustained attack on the economic front.

(4) *Economic objectives offer highly promising ways of
breaking into the whole "vicious circle" of discrimination.*
Our further conclusion is a corollary from the other three.
The reader is referred back to our discussion of the "vicious
circle" in Chapter Four. For reasons already given the economic factor is generally the most open to attack as well as
the most vulnerable. Any gain in the economic sector is particularly visible and is therefore reflected in the attitudes of
the dominant group. The strong association of inferiority
with lack of economic success can no longer be brought to
bear as before. The economic gain almost automatically pre-
pares the way for other gains. It brings more social power
with it, more command over the means to social advancement.

One qualification, however, must be introduced. The
strategic significance of economic betterment depends on
the situation and on the previous economic level of the subject group. Against some kinds of social prejudice economic
advancement would avail nothing but might rather have the
opposite effect. We would not expect, for example, that any
improvement in the general economic prosperity of the mass
of the Jewish population in the United States would have a
mollifying influence on anti-Semitism. Nor would we expect
that a rise in the economic welfare of the Pacific Coast Japanese would by itself lessen the prejudice to which they are
exposed. The qualification is in accord with our main argument that discrimination is a complex thing and cannot be
successfully combatted on one front alone, no matter how
many advantages that front may offer. But where groups are
manifestly in an inferior economic condition, are not marked
off by any great cultural apartness, and are at the same time

treated as ethnically or racially inferior there can be no more effective or accessible means of breaking the chain of discrimination that binds them than by attacking the weaker economic links in it. The American Negroes clearly fall into this category. So, in different degrees, do various other groups, including the ethnic groups of the later immigration.

Let us confine our attention mainly to the groups that are in the above-mentioned category. Let us consider the kind of economic clamp that holds them down and ask how economic strategy, given sufficient support, can be applied to loosen or break it.

Economic conditions are always changing. Nothing is more familiar to us than the incessant ups and downs of the "economic cycle." Because of the working of the "vicious circle" the groups subject to economic discrimination do not share proportionately with the rest of the population in times of prosperity and they suffer disproportionately in times of depression. Let us first establish these two principles and then we shall quickly see what kind of strategy must be brought to bear in order to correct these gross disparities.

(a) *The principle of disproportionate loss.* We find, for example, that when unemployment increases a larger percentage of Negroes than of Whites lose their jobs. This tendency was exhibited in the depression of the thirties, when Negroes in the South lost ground both in agriculture and in industry. "Undoubtedly the proportion of unemployed among Negro workers in the South increased more than that among White workers during the Great Depression, even if there are no reliable statistics available to prove it." [12] There are data for particular groups that establish the fact beyond question. "During the thirties," Dr. Northrup tells us, "Negroes in the South suffered disproportionately from the depression in the building industry. In each of the six crafts

12 Myrdal, *op. cit.,* vol. I, p. 289.

the proportion of Negroes declined." [13] Jobs previously assigned to Negroes were taken over by Whites in every area of employment the latter were willing to enter. When employers begin reducing their payrolls the Negroes, the foreign-born, the less advantaged groups of every kind, are more likely to be fired. The higher-prestige groups are resentful and cause trouble if their members are dismissed when the necessity for reduction can be directed against the others. These others are the marginal employees, the labor reserve, hired when the demand for labor is keen, discharged first when it slackens.

In different parts of the country various groups fall into this category. In places like Detroit, for example, the Mexicans are in this position, and to some extent the Poles and other East Europeans. [14] On the Pacific Coast the Orientals suffer from it. The fiercer the competition for jobs the worse, relatively to the rest, becomes the competitive position of the socially disadvantaged. The prejudice against them, accentuated by economic motives, becomes more intensive. Their social disadvantage and their economic handicap increase together.

The same phenomenon manifests itself in a variety of ways. Thus, where a socially disadvantaged group and a dominant group mix in the same locality or residential area and there is increasing inadequacy of or pressure on the facilities they share in common, tensions and antagonisms grow, to the particular detriment of the disadvantaged group. If, for example, the children of the two groups have inadequate educational or recreational facilities, insufficient schools or cramped playgrounds, lack of opportunities for their cultural development, lack of outlets for their free energies,

---

[13] *Organized Labor and the Negro* (New York, 1944), p. 21.
[14] Norman D. Humphrey, "Employment Patterns of Mexicans in Detroit," *Monthly Labor Review*, Bureau of Labor Statistics, Washington, D.C., November, 1945.

there is generally an embitterment of group relations. This tendency has been repeatedly observed in the congested areas of New York, Chicago, and other cities. Under such conditions, we remark in passing, it may not avail much to preach goodwill and mutual respect. The children will respond more quickly if they are given ampler space for their ball games, in which they can turn their contentiousness into healthy rivalries.[15] In so concluding we are not slighting the great role that education can play, as will appear when we take up that theme.

(b) *The principle of the less than proportionate gain.* In times of economic expansion there is some lessening of the competitive pressure against the disprivileged groups. When business is really booming or when for any reason, such as a state of war, there is a shortage of labor the prejudice against them does not prevent the fuller employment of their services. Clearly in such times there is more opportunity for aggressive strategy. In times of depression the struggle against discrimination must be largely a defensive one, an effort to hold such ground as has previously been won. In more prosperous times the positive economic advantages of nondiscrimination can be more powerfully presented and can be effectively linked with the eternal principles of justice, with the social and moral considerations that civilized man has always associated with the law of nature or the law of God.

So much is this the case that many competent judges hold the opinion that only in prosperous times can any serious advance be registered. "Representatives of labor, management, government, and private agencies have been unanimous in pointing out that a high level of employment is almost a necessary condition to any permanent improvement

15 That is why local organizations that seek to make provision for these needs, such as the Good Neighbor Federation working in East Harlem, New York City, are to be commended.

in race relations." [16] In particular, it has been frequently
claimed that to improve the status of the Southern Negro it
is necessary to improve the economic standards of the South.

Taken broadly enough, the proposition that economic
progress is favorable to the betterment of inter-group relations has strong support on its side. Let us note, however,
two qualifications. In the first place our proposition is relevant to the conditions of a socio-capitalist economy with its
recurrent ups and downs and asserts that the ups provide
the strategic opportunity for the attack on discriminatory
policies. It does not follow that there is less discrimination in
areas or in countries where there is a higher economic level
than in those on a lower economic level. Too many variables
are involved to justify so sweeping an assertion. Historical
and anthropological evidences show that discrimination may
increase at the same time that wealth increases—even although discrimination is itself a factor militating against
economic welfare.

In the second place the upward trend of business activity
does not automatically promote the cause of the disprivileged.
Even if directly or indirectly some economic benefit accrues
to them from the greater prosperity of the times their *relative* position will be worse, not better, unless other than
economic forces work on their behalf. This is the principle of the less than proportionate gain. They will be more
fully employed than before, but only in the lowest categories
of employment. Many members of the dominant groups will
pass to more lucrative or more responsible jobs and allow the
disprivileged to enter where they quit. There will still be
important economic interests barring their advancement,
and the entrenchments of status and power, of inertia and
prejudice, will still resist their aspirations.

A brief comparison of the economic lot of the Negroes

[16] President Charles S. Johnson, addressing the Annual Institute of Race
Relations of the American Missionary Association, Fisk University, July, 1946.

in the First and in the Second World War respectively should bring home the lesson. In both periods there was of course an extraordinary demand for labor of every kind and grade. Nevertheless in the period of the First World War, regardless of the country's need, the federal government and the dominant groups alike refused to make concessions to the demand of the Negroes for economic opportunity. The only specific agency set up for this end, the office of the Director of Negro Economics in the Department of Labor, was completely ineffective. The Department of Labor itself, like the other departments of government, maintained a rigid color line. The percentage of Negroes in various governmental departments actually declined.[17] The protests of the Negroes themselves were conveniently disposed of as due to foul plots on the part of enemy agitators seeking to sabotage the war effort.

When the United States became embroiled in the Second World War the situation had changed significantly. The Negroes themselves were better organized. The National Urban League, which had existed since 1910, was now a much stronger body and had learned something about strategy. The National Association for the Advancement of Colored People, the National Negro Congress, the Negro Youth Congress, were all actively in the field. The Negroes had now their labor organizations, their participation in the CIO unions, and such labor leaders as A. Philip Randolph. They had their own press to maintain and spread the consciousness of their needs. In the Northern states the Negro voter was gaining importance. In every respect Negro leadership and Negro organization were more effective than in 1916. The Negroes could bring greater pressure to bear on government, and on industry through government. At the same time there was now a part of the public that had been aroused to the

[17] Leon A. Ransom, "Combatting Discrimination in the Employment of Negroes," *Journal of Negro Education* (1943), vol. 12, p. 408.

importance and urgency of the issue. The first consequence
of these changes was seen in various proclamations of policy,
headed by that of the National Defense Advisory Commission, that in the defense program (as it was before Pearl
Harbor) no discrimination on account of race, creed, or
color, should be admitted. Nevertheless the evidence shows
that these proclamations would have remained for the most
part pious gestures if strategic steps had not been taken by
the Negro organizations and their supporters throughout
the country.[18]

We shall not here recite the story. We merely point out
that discrimination remained practically undiminished after
the proclamations, including one from the President, were
issued, that the rapidly growing aircraft industry was particularly conspicuous for its rigidly discriminatory policies, and
that the government itself continued to be a notable offender
against its own pledges. There can scarcely be any doubt
that this state of affairs would have continued had it not
been for certain measures of which we shall say something
in the next chapter. In the end there was a real difference
between the degree of economic opportunity afforded to the
Negro during the Second World War and his complete de-
privation of economic opportunity during the First. Even
so it might be hazardous to maintain that he made an economic gain proportionate to that made by the White population. But assuredly, had it not been for the strategy of the
protesting forces, he would again have offered a clear illustration of the principle of the less than proportionate gain.

Let us now sum up the argument. We have seen that the
disprivileged groups are generally the victims of fluctuating
economic conditions, that if things are allowed to follow
their "normal" course they do not reap the benefits of better
times while they bear the heavier brunt of times of depression. We have seen that economic disadvantage carries with

18 Ransom, *op. cit.*

it, especially in our own civilization, the imputation of social inferiority and thus tends to confirm prejudice and discrimination which in turn perpetuate economic disadvantage. We have also seen that economic discrimination is in important respects more vulnerable to direct attack than other forms of discrimination. The conclusion is clear. When ethnic or racial groups are disparaged and treated as social inferiors, and when these groups, like the Negroes, occupy a position of distinct economic subordination, any strategy that seeks to break the "vicious circle" in which they are held must undertake a vigorous concentration on the economic front.

2. STRATEGY OF ECONOMIC ADVANCE

It is obvious from what we have already said that there are two sides to the strategy of the economic front. In times of economic depression the major problem is generally to maintain an advance already made. At other times the question is how most effectively to achieve new advances. In the former situation the guiding consideration is that the longer a gain is held the easier it is to hold. In the latter the first consideration of strategy is to search out the points of least resistance and break through them. There are times, however, when both considerations are equally relevant. Such a time began with the end of the Second World War. There has been on the one hand the need to preserve wartime gains. On the other, since the war was not immediately followed by a depression, or even by the "recession" so freely predicted, there has been the opportunity to make further gains.

The foreboding that the end of wartime pressures would wipe out the occupational advances registered by disprivileged groups, and particularly by Negroes, has not been realized in the immediate postwar years. The continuing high level of employment has been a major factor, while the increasing alertness and somewhat better organization of the antidiscriminatory forces have played their part. These present advantages give no assurance that a subsequent depression will not bring a serious reaction, but it has certain encouraging aspects. Short as the period of relative stabilization has been it has enabled these groups somewhat to entrench their position since it confirms the habituations that are so important in matters depending on social attitudes and strengthens the expectations that give momentum to their demand for recognition. It increases the courage and self-confidence of these groups themselves. This latter fact is evidenced in various ways, as for example in the appeal and protestation presented to the United Nations by the National Association for the Advancement of Colored People. There has thus been a chance for the disprivileged groups, and for the organizations devoted to their cause, to prepare themselves better to resist a future reaction.

A review of the situation in 1947 brought out the following facts.[19] In that year the occupational distribution of Negroes retained generally the pattern established during the war, with here and there some distinct gains since the end of the war and very few losses. The wartime shift from the low-status, dead-alley employments (so far as Negroes are concerned) of farming, domestic service, and common labor was not reversed but on the contrary has been appreciably extended. "Approximately 7 out of 10 Negroes employed in 1940 were in these occupations, whereas in 1944 and in 1947 the proportion was only slightly more than 5 out of 10." In the traditional occupation of agriculture the proportion of all employed Negroes is given as 34 per cent in 1940, 21.6 per cent in 1944, and 17.3 per cent in 1947. No less significant was the shift in the employment pattern of Negro women.

[19] Seymour L. Wolfbein, "Post-War Trends in Negro Employment," *Monthly Labor Review*, Bureau of Labor Statistics, December, 1947. The figures and quotations in the paragraphs that immediately follow are taken from that report.

In 1940 over 70 per cent of them, outside of farms, were engaged in domestic service, while in 1944, as also in 1947, the percentage was below 50. Negro women were entering into fields of employment, in factory and office, in restaurants and beauty parlors, that gave or promised an advance in occupational status.

These changes meant, of course, that Negro labor was breaking some of the bounds that had denied it the first condition of economic opportunity. In industrial and clerical employments there were chances of advancement and of relative economic liberation. "Approximately 1 out of 3 nonfarm workers during the war was engaged either as a craftsman or operative as against 1 out of 5 in 1940." And here we come to the most significant feature of the 1947 figures. Although the wartime shift was mainly in the munitions industries the new distribution of Negro labor thereby established was not reversed in 1947 but instead was more fully developed. Nothing could more effectively illustrate our argument that the practice of nondiscrimination in any area, if only it can be maintained over some length of time without serious challenge, sets up tendencies and attitudes favorable to its persistence, just as the practice of discrimination reinforces the conditions that sustain it. The period under consideration is still relatively short, and the gains made by the Negro would still be thoroughly endangered by the onset of a serious depression. Nevertheless a change is in progress that holds genuine promise.

It should be noted that these Negro gains have not been registered proportionately over the whole range of industry. Some industries, such as many of the building trades, have been particularly exclusive. Moreover, though new doors were opening to Negroes, there was no lessening of the intention to keep them on the bottom floor. In fact the proportion of Negroes employed as craftsmen and foremen fell from the 1944 level. Again, there are certain occupations of a higher grade, in the managerial sector, in which, although Negroes registered rather high gains in percentage terms, the numbers concerned are so small that the advance made scarcely any inroad into White preserves. In another sector, the professional and semiprofessional, the change has actually been retrograde from the initial low level obtaining in 1940.

In the economic area there is great unevenness of discrimination. There are numerous local and regional differences. There are differences between the policies of neighboring plants in the same industry. Everywhere there are inconsistencies. Take, for example, the situation in the trade unions. Some bar colored workers altogether, some segregate them in Jim Crow "auxiliaries," some freely admit them. Some proclaim a policy of nondiscrimination but fail to practise it; some go all out against discrimination. The economic opportunities of the Negro, to take only the group subject to the extremity of discrimination, vary considerably with the type of occupation, the locality, the policy of the union, the attitude of the employer, and the laws of the particular state.[20]

It follows that the strategy of economic advance must be flexible and opportunistic, in the sense that it must adapt itself to conditions that are everywhere variant and always changing. *Its object must be to move through the points of least resistance to new positions, from which again it must seek out new points of least resistance.*

This strategy is in accord with the processes through which economic gains have actually been registered by subject groups in their own struggles for social equality. But the processes can be accelerated with the enlistment on their side of important social forces and influential social organizations. We shall offer some examples, drawn from the situa-

[20] See, for example, Ira de A. Reid, *The Negro in the American Economic System* (in Schomburg Collection); Charles S. Johnson, *Patterns of Negro Segregation* (New York, 1943); and Richard Sterner, *The Negro's Share* (New York, 1943).

tion of the Negroes in the United States, first to illustrate
the nature of the processes and then to show how competent
strategy can take advantage of them.

While the Negro is everywhere heavily handicapped as an
"economic man" he has been able at various points to win
through to some measure of occupational opportunity.
There are, for example, occupations where work is arduous
and calls for endurance more than for specific training. Into
these the Negro readily found a way. In some such occupations working conditions improved and for one reason or
another relatively good wages came to be paid. In various
industries where such conditions prevail the Negro has
somewhat improved his economic condition. Into this category come the jobs of the stevedore and longshoreman and
certain jobs in the iron and steel industries, in railroad maintenance, and in the packing industries. Everywhere, but
especially in the North, Negroes strengthened their position
in the longshoreman's trade.[21] In the iron and steel industries
they came to occupy a larger percentage of relatively skilled
jobs than they hold in other industries, and generally they
make in these industries better wages than do other Negro
wage earners.[22] In Minnesota more Negroes are employed
in the packing plants than in any other occupation except
railroading.[23] In railroad occupations, where the old-estab-
lished Brotherhoods pursue policies of rigid exclusiveness,
Negroes have long been associated with the service and
maintenance departments, while they have a more precarious
hold, owing to the opposition of the corresponding unions,
in the occupations of brakeman and fireman.

In some other directions the Negro has made modest advances. He is making some progress in the distributive trades
and particularly in retail merchandising. In the three or four

21 Myrdal, *op. cit.*, vol. II, p. 1097.
22 Myrdal, *op. cit.*, vol. II, p. 1116.
23 *The Negro Worker in Minnesota*, Report of the Governor's Interracial
Commission, March, 1945.

states that have passed laws against occupational discrimination he is slowly finding wider opportunities than before. But he still finds it almost impossible to attain entrepreneurial or managerial rank. And in the professions the little headway he makes is, apart from the artistic field, almost wholly within the area of his own caste.

Such industrial gains may seem small enough, and it may be pointed out that many of these occupations have onerous, menial, or unpleasant characteristics that render them unattractive to White workers. It is true that employment in such capacities has been a line of least resistance. The point is, however, that not only do the conditions of employment improve but also they admit of advances to new positions. These industrial employments differ in the latter respect from the blind alley jobs of caretakers, elevator operators, watchmen, janitors, domestic servants, club attendants, pick-and-shovel men, street cleaners, and so forth. Only when Negroes have a strong foothold in an occupation can they hope for the next advance, that of upgrading. In spite of considerable opposition some upgrading has occurred in these industries. Advancing through the line of least resistance the Negroes have begun to crack the next line of resistance.

Let us consider the situation in those new industries that depend on technological advance. Before traditions of exclusion come to be established the Negro may here find an opportunity of admission that later on may be lost. It is therefore highly important that a concerted effort be made to secure the introduction of Negroes at an early stage and that steps be taken to provide for Negroes whatever special training the new industries demand. If the initial resistance can thus be overcome the future pattern of employment may be changed. It may mean also that the labor unions of the new industries will be receptive to Negro members from the start. The history of some of our great new industries can teach us valuable lessons in strategy. Take, for example, the aircraft industry. Here the initial policy of management was highly exclusionist. There were excellent economic reasons for the employment of Negroes, and beyond these, during the war, there were primary considerations of national welfare. Under these pressures the resistance was in many respects broken down, and plant after plant modified its policies. The story is a complicated one and cannot be given here.[24] The CIO unions in the field freely accepted Negro members. The United Automobile Workers favored their upgrading. The more resistant machinists' unions yielded where the pressure was strong enough and above all where management took a strong stand, as in the Boeing plant at Wichita, the Curtiss-Wright shops in St. Louis, and the Pratt and Whitney works in Kansas City.

The automobile industry offers another example. As this great new occupational field came to be opened up Negro workers at first were limited to heavy unskilled jobs, and particularly the dirtiest and least agreeable of these.[25] Some important developments have taken place, however, and these have been due mainly to two factors. One was the resolute action taken by Henry Ford, who instituted the policy of hiring Negroes in proportion to their population ratio in the city of Detroit. There was considerable opposition from White workers but the company's clear formulation of an equitable hiring program could not be effectively resisted and the opposition gradually dwindled.[26] Ford refused to admit segregation in workshops, and this policy worked so well that the social segregation of the Negroes in the restaurants, in the everyday relations of the workers, in turn diminished. There was still much difficulty over up-

[24] For a short account see Robert C. Weaver, *Negro Labor* (New York, 1946), Chap. VII.

[25] Robert W. Dunn, *Labor and Automobiles* (New York, 1929), pp. 68–69.

[26] Myrdal, *op. cit.*, vol. II, p. 1121. There is no implication in our statement above that Ford's particular formula is at all a desirable one for general application.

grading, and here is where the second factor came in. The
UAW-CIO unions were opposed to discrimination but both
management and the unions moved slowly over the issue of
promotion. It was not till the conversion of the industry to
war production in 1941 that the unions took a strong lead.[27]
The upshot has been a considerable advancement of the
economic opportunity of the Negro.

The instance just cited leads us to the consideration of
another mode of advance through the less resistant to the
more resistant positions. On the whole the Negro has improved his standing and increased his membership in the
trade unions. He can make extremely important use of such
standing as he has already obtained in the field of organized
labor. In the first place, wherever union membership is already open to him he should learn the great advantage to
be derived from as large a Negro enrollment as possible. Some
Negro workers are slow to learn this lesson and a failure of
Negro support for unions fighting on their side has more
than once had unfortunate consequences. The union is an
effective means for the stabilization of any advantage the
Negro may achieve no less than an agency through which he
may reach new achievements. The fact that some half a
million Negroes are enrolled in trade unions in the South
means in itself a weakening of the caste system because it
establishes a solidarity *across* the color line. The union is an
educational force both for Whites and for Negroes; the Tex-
tile Workers' Union in the South has done good service in
this respect. Already, although segregated locals remain the
rule, the unions in the South are probing for ways to break
the customs of segregation that hamper Negro and White
workers from making common cause, even from meeting
together for that purpose. Advances from the positions thus
gained are accessible. It would, for example, have a powerful

[27] Herbert R. Northrup, *Organized Labor and the Negro* (New York, 1944),
pp. 199–203.

effect if the Southern trade unions proceeded to set up leadership centers to develop strategy for the common interests of White and Negro workers.

In general the future of Negro unionism holds much promise. The unions from which Negroes are now excluded are mainly the old-line craft unions. Some of these, like the first Brotherhood of Locomotive Engineers and the Order of Railroad Conductors, were originally fraternal benefit organizations and thus were not inclined to extend their range to colored workers. Their policy was followed by many of the later-established "brotherhoods," and some of these have remained bitter and persistent enemies of Negro opportunity. On the other hand the industrial unions, the majority of which are included in the CIO though some very important ones adhere to the AFL, have been in practice as well as in principle thoroughly opposed to discrimination and have often taken a decisive stand against it.[28] Since technological change favors the expansion of industrial unionism we may reasonably expect that the Negroes will become more and more incorporated in the trade union structure. From this vantage point they can put increasing pressure on the resistant unions. Some of the latter now admit Negro "auxiliaries"—these can be merged into the primary unions. Segregated locals can be replaced by mixed locals, to the great advantage of Negro labor. The discriminating craft unions no longer work as separate crafts but within large industrial systems. They may have more and more to accept a common policy rejecting discrimination, when that policy is promoted and is approved by the management. We have already referred to an instance of this sort, when machinists' unions engaged in the aircraft industry during the war reluctantly accepted the conditions of nondiscrimination established for the whole plant.[29] Other considerations play a part. For

28 Northrup, *op. cit.*, Chap. I; Weaver, *op. cit.*, Chaps. XII, XIII.
29 Weaver, *op. cit.*, p. 128.

example, it is against the interest of union members to exclude Negro workers from their unions when these workers may otherwise compete against them at lower than union rates.

All in all, the prospects of Negro unionization are distinctly favorable, although certain sheltered crafts, particularly in the building trades and in the operating sections of the transportation systems, may be able to maintain their exclusionist policies.

We pass to another area that offers a particularly simple illustration of our principle of strategy. The Negro who wants to become a skilled worker is often faced with a "vicious" dilemma. Unless he trains for the occupation he is not qualified to enter on it; if he does train he is barred from entrance. In this situation he may be advised to give up his ambition rather than have it frustrated after years of training. But, though it may sometimes work hardship on the individual who finds his effort was all in vain, the line of strategy requires that the training be accepted and that as much advantage as possible be taken of that decision. It is easier to find access to training than to gain admission to the skilled occupation. Over that point of less resistance the Negro must advance. He must have at least as good a training as the White worker. Given that, the next advance becomes possible. Those who have the welfare of the Negro at heart should devote their efforts to securing that the training he receives is no longer, as it has so often been, inferior to that available to the rest of the population.

What applies to specific training applies to the whole business of education. The Negro has never had the educational facilities of the White and in the Southern states the provision for his education is deplorably poor and inefficient. This difference has been one of the most potent devices for hamstringing the economic competence of the Negro as well as for keeping him in a lower social status. "By depriving

the Negroes of adequate educational facilities and by contributing only a minimum of educational opportunity, the
Whites constantly subordinate the Negroes." [30]

Various other illustrations of our principle could be
offered, but we shall limit ourselves to one more. In our
modern civilization government has become the greatest of
all employers of labor—labor of every kind from ditch-
digging to the most specialized type of executive or professional function. Now the government of this country is
under a special obligation not to discriminate against race or
nationality group, against color or creed. Discrimination
violates the spirit of the Fourteenth and Fifteenth Amendments. It is contrary to the claims our country makes in the
name of democracy. It is contrary to the policy proclaimed by
the Federal Government on many occasions. It is repudiated
by statutes of many of the states and by special antidiscrimination measures in several. We may therefore assume that the
obligation of government not to discriminate in the recruit-
ment and in the promotion of its own employees is more
binding than that of the private employer, and that the campaign against governmental discrimination has strategic advantages not present elsewhere. It is true that within the area
of the Federal Government there is a bloc dedicated to the
principle of discrimination, but when the issue is brought
into the open that bloc, however powerful, is bound to be
a minority. Hence it is sound policy to bring as much pressure as possible to bear on the government, bringing out
evidences of discrimination and demanding reform. Where
entry to an occupation is elsewhere barred to colored people
the first breach in that resistance might well be achieved in
the governmental sector. The policy is applicable to every
range of government, from the federal to the local.

The opportunity is certainly great. There is still a marked

[30] Warner, Havighurst, and Loeb, *op. cit.*, p. 137.

lag between principle and performance. In the period following the presidency of Theodore Roosevelt the Government of the United States set a worse example, so far as
Negroes were concerned, than in the preceding half-century.
All but the humblest positions in the federal services were
in effect closed to Negroes.[31] The Civil Service code did not
accept the implications of the Fourteenth Amendment, since
it barred discrimination only on grounds of religion or of
political affiliation. Not until recently, with the defeat of a
Georgia congressman who was chairman of the Subcommittee
on Appropriations for the Department of Labor, did the
United States Employment Service cease to have a segregated file for Negroes in its Washington office. It is still most
obviously true that the Federal Government is "abridging
the privileges or immunities of citizens." In this land dedicated to democracy American Negroes are not free to sit in
the restaurants of the Senate and the House.

There has, nevertheless, been a considerable improvement
in the admission of Negroes to jobs and offices under the
Federal Government, showing that concerted efforts in this
direction have good chances of success. These efforts were
made mostly during the Second World War. "In 1938, less
than 8.5 per cent of the federal employees were colored and
90 per cent of the Negroes were in subclerical capacities.
By November, 1942, about 17 per cent of the federal workers
in Washington were Negroes, and almost half of the colored
employees were in clerical and professional capacities." [32]
A few governmental agencies, particularly the OPA, set a
fine example. But at this point we reach a theme that belongs
to our next chapter.

[31] L. J. W. Hayes, *The Negro Federal Government Worker* (Washington,
D.C., 1941).
[32] Robert C. Weaver, *op. cit.,* p. 137.

Chapter Seven

The Political Front

1. THE ROLE OF GOVERNMENT

IN THE matter of inter-group discrimination there is much misunderstanding of what government can or cannot do, should or should not do. The author has listened to a public address at a meeting of an important organization devoted to the struggle against discrimination, where a prominent speaker decried any resort to government or any intervention on the part of government. On the other hand there are those who believe that government can and should abolish discrimination just as government has abolished slavery. Both positions are falsely dogmatic and quite unrealistic. Government cannot abolish discrimination—certainly not in any country in which the people retain any rudiments of liberty. For government cannot abolish prejudice, and so long as the prejudice between group and group endures, it will be expressed through some degree or kind of discrimination. Nevertheless government is a most important agency for the achievement of better and fairer relationships between groups. Those who take the opposite stand make the elementary error of identifying government with coercion.

It is true that coercion is a dangerous recourse. It is true that reliance on coercion in matters that depend on the attitudes of men is generally shortsighted and displays an impatience that is the close ally of stupidity. There is in some quarters a too facile assumption that all social evils can be removed by passing laws against them. Unless there is wide support for laws that seek to control such evils they will fail of success under democratic conditions. Discrimination cannot be defeated by law alone. It takes subtle forms against which coercion cannot prevail. Coercion is far too blunt an instrument. If it has to be employed to any considerable extent it stirs resentment that in turn accentuates the prejudice against which the law is directed.

There is the further consideration that in certain areas of discrimination the executive or the judicial agency is simply unqualified to pass on *individual* cases. There is, for example, considerable discrimination in the admission to various colleges. But it is highly questionable that the way to deal with it is to vest a political commission with the power to decide whether or not this particular candidate or that was rejected because of bias. The judgment of relative qualifications in this field is one requiring expert knowledge, and here discretion must be left to the selecting authority. It is easier to determine whether, of the relatively small number of applicants for a particular factory or office job at a given moment, a complainant was rejected on discriminatory grounds in spite of his superior qualifications—though even here it would be unwise to conclude on a single instance or two, instead of on clear evidence of a continuous policy.

There are still stronger reasons why government should not attempt to put *legal* restraints on what may be deemed defamatory statements against ethnic, racial, or religious groups. No legal distinction can be drawn between honest (if misguided) expressions of opinion and statements deliberately designed to calumniate a group. Legal prosecution of this sort attracts much public attention and gives wide circulation to the "libellous" opinions. The resort to this weapon is unlikely to encourage more favorable attitudes toward the group in question and may very well have the opposite effect. Moreover, the more serious kinds of propaganda against particular groups can easily evade any legal criterion. It is insidious suggestion rather than forthright calumny that works the deeper mischief. Hence, while definite incitements to injurious *actions* against groups may properly be taken under the cognizance of the law, mere expressions of unfavorable opinion should not be dealt with in this way. There is above all a danger that the power of government over the realm of opinion—the final stronghold of democracy—will be ominously extended and abused. It is, by the way, significant that the attempts made in this country to ban group defamation by law have all been unsuccessful. Thus the New Jersey statute of 1935 aimed against the anti-Semitic propaganda of the German Bund was ineffective and was presently held unconstitutional. The Massachusetts statute of 1942 brought no convictions. The Rhode Island statute of 1944 was vetoed by the acting Governor. The arguments against *direct* legal action apply equally to the denial of mailing rights to publications that make prejudicial statements about groups.

These considerations, however, do not mean that government has no proper role to play in the struggle against discrimination. Far from it. Law is not mere coercion, and government is vastly more than an instrument of coercion. Government establishes civil rights—and these may be unequal as between group and group or if formally equal they may be substantially unequal. Government administers justice, but the scales of justice may be weighted in favor of some groups and against others. Government renders many and varied services to its citizens, but it may show partiality in the performance of them. Government provides funds for various ends of social welfare, but they may be allocated or distributed unequally or without due regard for the conditions and needs of different groups. Government grants privileges, through licenses, certificates, passports, and so forth, but it may confer them in a discriminatory fashion. Government sets up standards, standards of health requirements, of safety, of minimum wages, of maximum rates, and so forth, and here is a great province in which it can assure essential benefits to disprivileged groups. Government provides employment on the largest scale, and we have already seen how it can in this respect render great service—or disservice—to those groups that are disadvantaged with respect to occupational opportunity.

Moreover, government itself, by means of the legal code, sets the broad conditions within which discrimination operates. According to the nature of the code the different groups within the population possess in equal or in unequal measure the fundamental conditions of opportunity. "The chief device of social segregation in the South is the law," says one author well qualified to speak on the subject.[1] The law and the courts of law became the guardians of the system of Negro segregation. Beginning with miscegenation statutes the codes of a number of states proceeded to Jim Crow statutes and more recently have institutionalized residential segregation.[2]

Hence we should realize that no small part of the service government can render consists not in the imposition of coercive restraints on a free people but in the restraint of coercion itself, and in the first place in the removal of the barriers to opportunity that are themselves coercive. The law may be the enemy of discrimination or on the other hand its strongest ally. We must not forget that while eighteen states in the Union have in varying degree prohibited discrimination—or segregation—twenty states have in varying

---

[1] Ira de A. Reid, "Southern Ways," *Survey Graphic*, January, 1947, p. 39.
[2] Charles S. Mangum, Jr., *The Legal Status of the Negro* (University of North Carolina Press, 1940).

degree made it compulsory.[3] In a number of states the law fences it round with a whole system of compulsions. Thus in Georgia, as Professor Reid points out, the law forbids white taxi drivers to carry colored passengers, forbids restaurants to serve wine or beer to both white and colored patrons, forbids white and colored from frequenting the same public park, forbids the burial of white and colored in the same cemetery. Thus the law bars the processes of accommodation that might modify the principle of segregation. The law hardens custom and stands as guardian against change. How then can we deny the importance of the political front?

There is another important consideration. Disprivileged groups are disprivileged not only in the treatment they receive but also in their relative inability to gain influence or representation in the councils of government. If their political standing were bettered they would be in a stronger position to resist discrimination. If they were more effective in the polling booths they would not only win greater respect from those who understand power more than they understand humanity but would also be able to make government more responsive to their needs. This point, as we shall see, is well illustrated by the changing status of the Negro. But to achieve greater political effectiveness requires leadership, organization, and resources. And here is another reason why the political front is one of major importance.

Before we leave this theme we might observe that even when the legal code sustains discrimination and before the time is ripe for its revision its rigor can be modified and its regulations can be reinterpreted provided there is a growing movement in favor of the disadvantaged group. We can find not a few illustrations in the marginal states of the South. Thus in the rural areas of Kentucky, where there are relatively small Negro groups, school superintendents some-

[3] Milton R. Konvitz, *The Constitution and Civil Rights* (Columbia University Press, 1947), p. 132.

times connive at their admission to White schools. In the same state educational segregation is sometimes evaded by the technical device of calling instruction classes "work units" and in one important school for professional training Negroes are "unofficially" admitted and are given "unofficial" diplomas. Through these and other devices the law is undergoing a process of erosion.

Obstructive law has often loopholes through which liberty can thrust a wedge. A large-scale instance of this process has occurred throughout Latin America. The system of slavery therein established admitted the ancient principle of manumission, under which a slave might buy his liberty or receive it as the reward for exceptional service or merit. Social custom and religious doctrine supported the practice, with the consequence that manumission became a common procedure and the slave little more than a debtor who could attain his full liberty by instalments.[4] Thus a legal loophole gave, under favoring conditions, an entirely different status to the slave, so that slavery at length disappeared and at the end of the process no caste barrier distinguished the freedman from his former master. In the United States, on the other hand, the principle of manumission was rendered difficult legally and was socially discouraged. The caste difference held firm, and emancipation was powerless to remove it.

2. POLITICAL MEASURES AGAINST ECONOMIC DISCRIMINATION

In recent years a much-debated question has been whether political regulations forbidding discrimination against particular groups on the part of employers, trade unions, institutions for professional training, and other organizations con-

[4] Frank Tannenbaum, "The Destiny of the Negro in the Western Hemisphere," *Political Science Quarterly* (March, 1946), vol. 61, pp. 1–41.

trolling the admission to occupational opportunity, are in
the public interest and can be effectively administered. The
controversy was stimulated by the setting up of the wartime
Fair Employment Practice Committee and the subsequent
enactment of antidiscrimination laws in New York, New
Jersey, Massachusetts, and Connecticut. Sufficient evidence
has already accumulated to justify certain conclusions. In
the first place, these measures have put some check on the
tendency to occupational discrimination and have in a considerable number of instances, and mostly without friction
or undesirable later repercussions, improved the occupational chances of members of groups subject to discrimination. Secondly, these measures, where they have been or are
in force, have given the groups in question a new sense of
their rights as citizens, have helped to make them feel they
belong in the same community with their fellow men, removing something of the alienation that balked their participation. They have learned that government is on their
side and that they have a resource against prejudice, the
appeal to a governmental committee or commission that will
seek to deal fairly by them. The contribution these measures
have thus made to the solidarity of American citizenship may
in the longer run prove to be their greatest service. Thirdly,
they have given a central rallying point to the forces working
against discrimination, have revealed some of the particular
modes and conditions under which discrimination operates,
and have provided a secure institutional basis from which to
launch further advances.

It is of primary importance to realize that whatever results
such measures have thus far achieved have not depended on
the resort to direct coercion. The FEPC was not invested
with the power to enforce its decisions and while it could
report to the President concerning violations of the contractual obligation in war work contracts that fact, in view
of the political situation, had no strongly deterrent effect.

The state laws against discrimination have of course punitive sanctions but these have remained entirely in the background. The 1946 Report of the New York State Commission Against Discrimination said that although 752 complaints were investigated and 567 disposed of during the year in no instance had resort been made to punitive action. Where there were indications of discrimination the Commission called the offending parties into conference and were able through this method to arrive at a "satisfactory disposition" of the cases.

Obviously, in matters where prejudices and social attitudes of various kinds are involved, it is better strategy that governmental agencies should, where possible, settle complaints concerning violation of the law by the method of conference rather than by a summons to court. If the offending employer can be persuaded into compliance, if he can be made to see the reason and the justice of the law in question, if he can have his fears or his doubts removed by those who have experience in the field, then he will be better disposed toward the law than he was before or than he would have been if more abrupt methods had been adopted. There is always of course the background knowledge that the state has the power to punish noncompliance, and there are no doubt other considerations that restrain men from maintaining resistance to constituted authority. There may be instances where the regulation is evaded or even defied—as happened not so infrequently in cases taken up by the FEPC —but so long as prejudice prevails in the community it may be wiser as well as more expedient to rely on the gentler method of consultation and persuasion. The various state commissions are at present operating along the lines of this policy.

To bring out the services rendered by public authorities administering antidiscrimination measures and to assess the limits and the possible extensions of such services we shall review, as briefly as possible, the history of the regulations that are or have been in effect since the initiation of the FEPC.

The history of the FEPC throws much light on the nature of the resistances that in this country oppose the right of groups of citizens to equal occupational opportunity with the rest. It was brought into being in 1941 not by congressional action but by executive order (no. 8802), because the adverse forces, including the Southern bloc, precluded the former method. Its initiation was in the main the result of pressures on government from groups suffering from discrimination, culminating in the project of a "March on Washington" promoted by Negro organizations. But such pressures would probably have been ineffective apart from the urgency of the wartime demand for labor and the rather favorable, if circumspect, disposition of the Administration. Nor would appropriations have been available had it not been for the emergency funds under the control of the Executive. Even so, the new FEPC held a somewhat precarious position, and was further weakened by the cancellation of the hearings it had scheduled in January, 1943, to examine the discriminatory practices of the refractory railroads and railroad brotherhoods. A second hearing took place in September of that year, after the Committee had been reorganized, but fourteen Southern railroads refused to obey its directives, and though they were cited to the President, no action came from the special committee appointed to look into the matter. Throughout its career the Committee encountered many obstacles to the fulfilment of its task and political considerations limited the cooperation it sought from various agencies of the government itself.

The FEPC went through several reorganizations. In July, 1942, it was transferred from the War Production Board to the War Manpower Commission and in May, 1943, it was reconstituted and attached to the Office of Emergency Management. At the same time its failing prestige was strengthened by the new executive order (no. 9346), which made it applicable to "war industries" (no longer "defense industries") and authorized it not only to conduct hearings and report findings of fact but also "to take appropriate steps to obtain elimination" of the discriminatory policies against which it was directed. The Committee extended its front by establishing regional offices throughout the country. It still had no coercive power in its own right but it could issue "directives" and enlist the services of the various departments and agencies of the Federal Government and of any other cooperating authority, state or local. The executive orders establishing the FEPC had extended, first to defense industries and then to war industries, the contractual obligation not to discriminate against any employee or applicant for employment "because of race, creed, color, or national origin." The policy of nondiscrimination was binding also within the whole range of governmental service, though there were no public hearings in cases where complaints were brought against an agency of the government. The Committee developed various rules concerning the evidence that would show whether this obligation was being violated by employers or under trade union provisions.

There was widespread disregard of the contractual obligation. This attitude was manifested, though not equally, in all parts of the country. There were plants engaged in war work urgently in need of labor which nevertheless refused to accept available Negro labor. There were instances where the contractual obligation was clearly violated but where the attempts of the FEPC to secure compliance were frustrated by the "hands off" policy of the War Manpower Commission or some other high-up authority. There were even instances where employers, hungry for labor, were ready to employ Negroes or were about to increase the ratio of Negroes in their plants but were in effect warned against such action by

some authority, for fear of causing trouble. There were instances where publicity, as in the case of the Washington
Capitol Transit Company, seemed to stimulate hostile reactions without helping the cause. There was the famous case
of the railroad industry, where the intervention of the FEPC
was blocked by the indefinite postponement of hearings
through the action of the chairman of the War Manpower
Commission, Mr. Paul V. McNutt, a case in which before
passing judgment on any person, such as the Chairman, it
would be necessary to know the primary source of the order
in question and the political considerations on which it
was premised. The same caution should be applied in other
instances where hearings were suspended or postponed by
executive action. In short, the mission of the FEPC encountered inevitably the general unreadiness of public opinion
for this type of regulation on a countrywide basis, apart from
the strong opposition of certain groups and interests. Many
employers engaged in war industry evaded or flouted the
antidiscrimination clause in their contracts. Various unions
supported this procedure. There was some peril in drastic
measures. The complete fulfilment of the mission entrusted
to the FEPC was out of the question.

Does this mean that the FEPC failed to perform a useful
function? There are political scientists and sociologists who
claim that law cannot move ahead of the mores, that it can
be effective only when public opinion is already so manifestly on its side that legal procedures merely give institutional form to custom. Obviously the protagonists of this view
must be thinking only of democratic countries, for nothing is
more obvious than that under dictatorship, and to a lesser
extent in old-time oligarchies, law or decree can make strange
invasions into the sanctity of opinion. The price paid for this
kind of success is another matter, and if we reckon that price
we may discount the views of dictatorially minded groups
which in the name of liberty are prepared to support any

degree of legal coercion. But our argument is not concerned with other situations than those of a democracy like our own. And here the school that would do nothing whatever until the mores fully sanction it is guilty of gross over-simplification. In a country such as ours public opinion is endlessly variable and always much divided. To wait until the mores return a triumphant affirmative may be to wait for ever, or at least until opportunity passes us by.

There are certain types of situation, where public opinion is divided, distracted, uncertain, or ambivalent, in which the passing of a law can be decisive. To this order belongs the situation we have described under the name of the indifferent equilibrium. Again, there are not infrequently situations in which the opposition of a minority can block action on the part of the more fair-minded majority. In these situations leaders and policy-makers are unwilling to offend the minority by putting forward policies of nondiscrimination. They may need the support of that minority on other issues. The minority, animated by prejudice and appealing to the immediate economic interests of the larger group, is likely to be more determined and more energetic than the majority. The leaders are reluctant gratuitously to add to their problems or to jeopardize their own future. This situation occurs, for example, in various trade unions, both in locals and on a larger scale. Take the case where Southern all-White locals are bitterly opposed to a nondiscrimination policy for the national union. In such circumstances the enactment of a law—statewide or federal according to the conditions—would not only settle the issue but would end internal contention on the subject.

The support of strong public opinion is indeed necessary, but no group or party is content to be the passive register of the voice of the people. Each seeks to make that voice more responsive to its particular cause. That is the principle of every democratic struggle. Government is always in the thick of the battle. It too can, does, and indeed must use the legitimate weapons at its command to strengthen the forces working on its side. Otherwise it convicts itself of a lack of purpose, other than the empty desire to keep in office. Hence the pragmatic test is whether the institutional controls it sets up further or retard the major ends to which it proclaims allegiance and on the appeal to which it won a mandate from the people.

By this test the FEPC was, within the limits of its means, a reasonably successful experiment. FEPC had a share in the combination of forces that extended the economic opportunities of groups subject to discrimination, particularly the Negroes. And it did not create, by and large, unfavorable repercussions such as might militate against further advances in this direction. It acted with discretion, but it loyally sought to fulfil the charge entrusted to it.

In the first place we can scarcely doubt that the remarkable change occurring in the employment policies of government departments and agencies themselves was stimulated by the establishment of the FEPC, with the strong announcement of administration policy that it conveyed. Some barriers to the employment of Negroes fell all along the line and in some of the newer agencies, notably the OPA, discrimination was in effect nearly eliminated.[5] Again, the hearings initiated by the FEPC, especially those in large cities like New York, Chicago, and Los Angeles, were given considerable publicity, and this fact had influence in inducing not only the plants thus exposed but also others that feared similar exposure to modify their policies. In some instances such exposure, as in the case of the International Association of Machinists at the Los Angeles hearings, had also an appreciable effect on the attitude of discriminatory trade unions.

The statistical record shows important increases in the

5 *The Wartime Employment of Negroes in the Federal Government*, mimeographed report issued by the FEPC, 1945.

employment of Negroes in plants involved in FEPC hearings and also, what is in the longer run more significant, a sizable amount of up-grading and of first admission of Negroes to skilled and semiskilled jobs.[6] The urgency of the demand for labor by reason of the increasing military draft on man power and the increasing scale of governmental contracts for war products, together with the mandatory antidiscrimination clause contained in these contracts, make it impossible to determine the extent to which the activities of the FEPC contributed to the improvement of the Negro's industrial position. But while we may admit that wartime urgencies were more potent than anything else in opening the gates of industry to Negroes there is still substantial evidence that the FEPC made good use of the opportunity thus provided. The resistance to the employment of the members of various groups, but particularly of colored workers, or to their promotion was still obdurate at many points. In many, though not in all, instances the result of the hearings was an agreement, at least partially implemented, to discontinue discriminatory practices. The following cases are cited as examples:

In October, 1943, the New York City USES reported that the laboratory of a noted telephone company had overlooked well-qualified Negro girls who had been referred and apparently was selecting trainees on a discriminatory basis. Investigation revealed that the charges of discrimination were justified, and USES service to the firm was suspended. In a subsequent conference at the Committee's office in New York, company officials stated that although the policy of their organization was to comply with Executive Order 9346, their supervisors had not been following it. Instructions were sent out to remedy the situation.

When the case was closed the firm employed only 57 nonwhites, primarily in service jobs, in its New York establishment. But by August, 1944, the number had risen to 186, and many of

[6] *First Report,* FEPC, pp. 65–78.

these workers held professional and clerical jobs, as well as skilled positions in shop and maintenance departments. One Negro member of the firm's technical staff attends meetings with other companies as a representative of the laboratory.[7]

There are now more than 500 Negroes working on Chicago's transit lines. Three companies and the unions of their employees worked with FEPC in achieving integration, which has taken place without incident, and colored personnel serve as trainmen and conductors on elevated trains, as bus drivers and as streetcar conductors and motormen. In the fall of 1943, when the cases were opened, Negroes were employed only as laborers or in service positions.

Negro and white organizations had been trying for several years to obtain skilled jobs for Negroes, and FEPC started negotiations soon after the opening of its Chicago office as a result of referrals by these organizations. Ill feeling had been growing in the Negro community, with tension high between white operators and colored passengers. There were even preparations for the boycotting and picketing of Chicago streetcars. After conferences, the largest of the three companies informed FEPC that it would accept applications from Negroes for platform jobs. The other two firms followed suit a short time later.[8]

We should clearly realize that such instances of successful intervention represent only one side of the story. The FEPC had hard sledding and encountered many obstacles. It was pioneer work; the first blazing of the trail is usually the hardest. There were miscalculations and defeats. There was also the fair prospect that more matured and more sustained activities along similar lines would have greater effect.

Besides the direct result of FEPC intervention we must enter in the reckoning the sustenance it has given to the forces working against discrimination and the greater compliance with the Executive Order that its guardianship no doubt has inspired. Moreover, in assessing the service of this and other governmental agencies engaged in combating dis-

7 *Ibid.,* p. 76. 8 *Ibid.,* p. 77.

crimination we must give weight to the moral effect on groups which have been the victims of social prejudice and which take greater heart and begin for the first time to feel that their citizenship is a reality and that the claim of democracy is not an idle formula.

We may note in passing that one evidence of the effectiveness of the FEPC was the bitter hostility to it of a section of the Congress, led by the Southern bloc, and the successful fight of this section, aided by the apathy of many other senators and congressmen, to prevent the enactment of a statutory equivalent, a fight characterized by a remarkable amount of parliamentary chicanery.[9]

Even in its brief life span the FEPC revealed some primary lessons for the strategist in group relations. We endeavor to set some of them down. First, political measures of this type can be effectively applied only where some preparation has already been made for their reception and where they do not rouse a widespread public resentment. There were instances where an order of the FEPC led to serious disturbances. One was the case of the Alabama Dry Dock and Shipbuilding Company, where a riot ensued when the Company sought to carry out an order to up-grade Negroes. It is not unlikely that the Company itself could have saved the situation had it taken the workers into its confidence instead of keeping its plan secret and abruptly putting it into effect.[10] But wherever the responsibility lay the cause

---

[9] See Will Maslow, "FEPC—A Case History in Parliamentary Maneuver," *University of Chicago Law Review* (June, 1946), vol. 13, pp. 407–445.

The reader should note that the proposed legislation for a "permanent FEPC" goes further in its provision than did the executive orders above referred to. Thus the bill advanced by Mrs. Norton (H.R. 2232, 79th Congress, first session) provides that the Commission to be set up can issue orders subject to judicial enforcement and review, and the right to work without being subject to discrimination is declared to be "an immunity of all citizens of the United States, which shall not be abridged by any State or by any instrumentality or creature of the United States or of any State." The bill also prohibits "unfair employment practices by labor unions affecting commerce."

[10] Cf. Northrup, *op. cit.*, p. 227.

of the trouble was sufficiently clear. No preparation whatever had been made for the reception of the new policy.

Another very important lesson is the need to secure the widest possible cooperation in the implementation of anti-discrimination measures. It can be reasonably charged against the FEPC that its operations were too insulated in this respect. Its task was an enormous one. That task could not be handled to the best advantage unless the Committee explored and marshalled the resources, both within the scheme of government and in the community, that could be utilized in the attainment of its objective. The executive order that brought it into being specially invited it to call to its aid the other agencies and departments of government. The agencies that did most of the contracting with war industries might, one would have thought, have been more fully enlisted in supervision of the contractual obligation against discrimination. It is true that these agencies were engaged in a perpetual hustle to increase production. It is true also that the FEPC was born during a great emergency and that the industrial situation was a hectic kaleidoscope. Moreover, the Committee itself went through various transformations in its brief history. It never had a staff adequate for its task. The Committee undertook singlehanded more than it could manage. One result was that its orders sometimes went forth without sufficient exploration of the situations to which they applied and sometimes without sufficient reckoning of the conditions under which these orders could be effectively and without undue resistance fulfilled.

At the date of this writing no thorough investigation of the work of the FEPC is yet available, and our comments, based on the published records, may need modification in the light of a more complete analysis. A careful detailed investigation of the successes and failures of the Committee and of the conditions under which it respectively succeeded or

failed in the fulfilment of its function would be illuminating.[11]

We conclude this survey by noting a limitation to efficiency
inherent in the procedure followed by the FEPC. It is perhaps
inevitable that a still fledgling body of this sort should devote
itself mainly to the hearing of specific complaints raised by
individuals. It prefers not to take the onus of initiating investigations. The field is very wide, the staff required for
thorough inquiry into conditions would have to be very
large and competent, and there is always the danger of creating friction and resentment if so inclusive an inquiry were
attempted. The Commissions set up in those states that have
passed antidiscrimination laws also rely so far mainly on
complaints addressed to them by parties who claim to be
sufferers from discrimination. But while in the early stages
this procedure is convenient and not unreasonable there are
serious disadvantages attached to it. In the first place, there
is no reason to assume that all who suffer discrimination are
in a position to make complaint to a political authority.
Many may be unaware of their title to do so, many may not
know how to do so. People used to subjection are afraid of
authority. The groups that have active organizations working on their side are more likely to have cases of discrimination brought to public notice. The weaker or less organized
groups—for example, the "Mexicans"—may take far less
advantage of their new right than the stronger groups. In
the second place, a complaint is usually the expression of a
balked expectancy. Now where a concern has pursued a
rigid policy of exclusiveness the individual who belongs to
the excluded group is not likely to seek admission. Against
such concerns few individual complaints are likely to be
made. Where instead a firm has shown more flexibility and

[11] The former chairman of the FEPC, Malcolm Ross, has published a
revealing and very reasonable account of it, *All Manner of Men* (New York,
1948). I am indebted to Mr. Ross for various comments and suggestions.

openmindedness many of the workers who feel the pinch of discrimination will hope for opportunity in its service. A similar phenomenon occurs in educational institutions. Those that have no hard-and-fast policy against the admission of the members of any group are more under pressure because of their limited acceptance of the applicants belonging to these groups than are the institutions that bar them almost altogether. It is a perfectly understandable situation, but the complaints to which it gives rise are skewed against the more tolerant organizations. The experience of the FEPC illustrated this principle, and since they relied mainly on individual complaints the result was that the attention of the Committee and its orders "to cease and desist" were directed to a considerable extent against the more liberal employers whereas exclusionist employers, especially if they operated on a relatively small scale, were able to pursue their discriminatory policies without a challenge.[12]

The obvious conclusion is that any commission entrusted with the task of maintaining political measures against discrimination must rely to a large extent on charges brought by its own investigators after careful surveys and not mainly on complaints initiated by affected individuals. Furthermore, complaints of the latter type, although they play an important role, require skilled scrutiny and considerable discernment before they are made grounds for positive action, especially when they apply to organizations that in general display a tolerant attitude. The FEPC did not adequately realize this need. Sometimes the Committee failed to make a sufficient investigation and thus did injury to its own cause. The major attack should be developed against organizations that most flagrantly practise discrimination and not against those that are more sympathetically disposed.

The most comprehensive measures so far passed against occupational discrimination are the recently enacted state

12 Cf. Weaver, *op. cit.*, p. 143.

laws the first of which came into force in New York State in
1945. Prior to this date a number of states had legislation
prohibiting economic discrimination in particular areas,
such as public work contracts, state civil service, and work
relief. The New York (Ives-Quinn) Act was squarely directed
against all discrimination in employment. Similar measures
were then passed in New Jersey and in Massachusetts.[13] Connecticut has more recently followed suit.

The antidiscrimination laws of these states have generally
the same pattern. We shall take as example the New York
law. It set up a Commission of five members with adequate
powers to inquire into and to prohibit discrimination in
employment "because of race, creed, color, or national
origin," whether such discrimination was made by employers,
trade unions, or employment agencies. The orders of the
Commission are subject to judicial enforcement and review.

The records to date show that cases of anti-Negro discrimination constitute more than half the total number of cases.
Next in volume come cases of anti-Jewish discrimination, and
there follows a scattering of cases concerned with various
ethnic and racial minorities, of which only the Italian cases
amount to any considerable number. As we have already
pointed out, the mode of recording cases, making complaints
on grounds of religion one of the primary categories, is misleading. This category would be almost blank except that all
Jewish cases are referred under it. The New Jersey Commission makes a very partial attempt to meet the problem by
seeking to distinguish cases of anti-Italian discrimination
when it is prompted by ethnic considerations from cases that
might be listed as anti-Catholic. But the line is rarely clear.
No doubt there are cases of discrimination where the religious factor is prominent, but it would be less confusing if
complaints were classified in the first instance according to
the ethnic or racial origin of those affected, without presump-

---

[13] For the text of these laws see Konvitz, *op. cit.*, pp. 167–192.

tion as to the grounds that motivate or determine discrimination.

The act has worked, and worked smoothly. All contrary anticipations have been falsified.

The act has been beneficial in reducing the range and extent of discrimination. The Commission has been largely concerned with the hearing of complaints and the readjustment of situations out of which the complaints have arisen. We have just seen that this method has considerable limitations though at the same time it is the least invidious method in the early stages. The Commission, however, has a staff of field investigators and already a sizable number of charges of discrimination are made on its own initiative. It is to be hoped, and expected, that the latter mode of operation will become more important as the spirit of the new law takes deeper root in the consciousness of the community. There is good reason to believe that the number of complaints advanced is no indication whatever of the actual extent of discrimination.

The Commission has begun work to this end. Part of its task under the act—and the New Jersey and Massachusetts acts have a similar provision—is to set up cooperative councils throughout the state. Some of these councils, composed of citizens serving without pay, are in being, and they may be expected to rally and sustain the sentiment against discrimination in the local communities. They are designated as advisory agencies and conciliation committees and are also expected to explore the nature and conditions of intergroup relations in their respective localities. Research groups mainly drawn from colleges and universities have been developed to carry on more comprehensive studies. Thus in the three states under consideration there is already in process a new mustering and orientation of community resources.

The Commission has begun to act in two other directions,

pursuant to its instructions under the act. One is the attack on discriminatory inquiries on the part of employment agencies or of employers in the process of recruiting labor or filling jobs of any kind. No questions can be asked of prospective employees and no advertisements or other statements can be issued by employers which directly or indirectly express an intent to discriminate on grounds of "race, creed, color or national origin." The Commission reports (March, 1947) that pre-employment discriminatory inquiries are now the rarity rather than the rule. There is, however, still the problem that there are various ways of evading this regulation, especially on the part of employment agencies.

The other activity is directed against trade union discrimination. Here the Commission has already registered important gains. According to its records (January, 1947) its work with national or international labor unions has had the following results:

(1) Two A. F. of L. unions and one independent union have eliminated discriminatory clauses from their constitutions;

(2) Two A. F. of L. unions and one independent union—all of them in the railroad industry—have agreed to recommend changes in the discriminatory clauses of their constitutions at their next conventions; [14]

(3) Three A. F. of L. unions and two independent unions—four of them railroad unions and one the International Association of Machinists—have taken action to waive union rules that conflicted with the antidiscrimination law.

Again, there is the problem of evasion. Many unions against which discriminatory practices were alleged have claimed that they have no constitutional provisions or by-laws favor-

[14] In May, 1947, the A. F. of L. Brotherhood of Railway and Steamship Clerks, meeting in Cincinnati, removed the qualification "White" from its requirements for membership. "New York State has told us," said the Grand President, Mr. George M. Harrison, "that we have to change our constitution or be enjoined from operating in that state."

ing discrimination. Nevertheless the results are highly significant. And those who regard the intrusion of law into this field as useless or detrimental should ponder the fact that some of the unions that have amended their constitutions or made promises to do so have hitherto been most obdurate adherents of discriminatory practices.

We conclude that the new laws against discrimination in employment have been salutary and successful. In particular, they have already served the cause in the following ways:

(a) The mere right to appeal against discrimination is an assurance to the groups that feel discriminated against, gives them some sense that they too are citizens, takes away some edge of the sense of frustration.

(b) The existence of such laws affects the type of questions asked applicants for employment and thus weakens one of the devices of discrimination. The New York Commission reports regularly show that employers after a hearing on a case of discrimination agree to cooperate by removing such questions.

(c) The laws lead a number of firms and trade unions that previously pursued an exclusive policy to change this policy. The increased range of employment thus opened up to the discriminated tends to set an example for the future. The employment of even one Negro in a plant where none were employed before is the thin end of the wedge. It is far easier to introduce others than to admit the first.

(d) The negotiations between the Commission and the members of firms involved in hearings have an educative effect. The element of coercion is properly kept in the background. The discussion is good-natured and must not infrequently help to bring out the principles that justify the law.

(e) The foremen and the hiring personnel have now a special responsibility to avoid unfair and discriminatory treatment of applicants and of workers alike. There is less scope for arbitrary action. The dismissal of arbitrary foremen, which sometimes occurs as the result of the complaint and the ensuing negotiation, must have a salutary effect.

3. THE LAW AND THE COURTS

One great function of the courts is to protect civil rights against infringements, encroachments, and violations. But the courts can fulfil this function only so far as the Constitution defines and prescribes civil rights, and then so far as the states and the Federal Government enact statutes supplementing and making specific the rights assured by the Constitution, and then so far as public opinion corroborates and endorses the guarantees of the Constitution and the enactments of the states. Only through the cooperation of all three, the Constitution, the laws, and public opinion, can the conditions be established under which the courts become the final and sufficient guardian of civil rights.

The impact of the antidiscrimination forces needs to be applied in all the three directions here indicated. Contrary to widespread belief, "in so far as the Constitution is concerned, the civil rights, privileges and immunities can be counted on one hand." [15] It is true that if the Constitution, and particularly the Thirteenth, Fourteenth, and Fifteenth Amendments, were given a sufficiently broad and liberal interpretation the vast edifice of discrimination would crumble beneath it. But the tendency of the Supreme Court has been, though modified in recent years, to give instead a narrow and legalistic interpretation. One can go further and say that as guardian of constitutionality the U. S. Supreme Court has in the past lent its authority to dubious and highly technical decisions with the effect of reducing to a minimum some of the liberties guaranteed by the Constitution.

Thus for many years the Southern states, through various

[15] Konvitz, *op. cit.*, p. vii.

devices including the famous "grandfather clauses," dis-
franchised Negroes contrary to the tenor of the Fifteenth
Amendment. In 1915 the Supreme Court held that the
"grandfather clauses" violated the Fifteenth Amendment
(*Guinn and Beal* v. *United States,* 238 U.S. 347). But other
devices set up effective barriers to Negro citizenship. The
educational qualifications, manifestly intended for this purpose, were given clearance by the Supreme Court. The poll
tax was not questioned. The Southern states could keep the
Negroes poor and uneducated and make the result a legally
acceptable reason for disbarring them from civil liberties.
The "white primary" received also the green signal from the
Court.

Constitutional guarantees are not explicit statements of
the manner in which the people may enjoy and exercise civil
liberties. They are only the foundations on which an effective
system of liberties may be built. The Constitution must be
interpreted and applied, and the interpretation will depend
on the climate of opinion, on the conditions and trends of
the times. Courts are not themselves primary agents of social
change. They register, often laggingly, the changes that move
in the community. This is well illustrated by the record of
the Supreme Court. For a long period it was more concerned
with stability than with reform, with property rights than
with human rights, with state rights than with the principles
of the Bill of Rights.

Perhaps the most fateful judgment ever passed by the
Supreme Court was that in the Dred Scott case of 1857, when
Chief Justice Taney and a majority of his colleagues were
not content to rule on a disputed constitutional issue concerning slavery but went on gratuitously to declare that Congress had no power to exclude slavery from the Territories
or to forbid citizens from carrying slaves, which were a species
of property, anywhere into the public domain. After the
passage of the Thirteenth and Fourteenth Amendments the

Court continued its obstructionist career by invalidating as unconstitutional the fundamental Civil Rights Act of 1875. This act was supplementary to other legislation intended to abolish the old distinction between the slave and the free man. It required that Negroes be given full social equality in the use of theaters, hotels, and public conveyances. "In the history of the people of the United States the *Civil Rights Cases* have played almost as tragic a role as has the Dred Scott case." [16] The decision of the Court opened the way for the whole machinery of segregation, which ever since has been a clamp on the cultural and economic development of the Southern states.

The Court went on to ratify the segregation principle it had thus inaugurated, further whittling away the Fourteenth Amendment. One important case was *Plessy* v. *Ferguson* (163 U.S. 537), in which the Court confirmed (1896) a racial segregation statute of Louisiana respecting common carriers. In his dissenting opinion Mr. Justice Harlan, already distinguished as the sole dissenter in the Civil Rights Cases, cogently showed that the Court had advanced entirely specious grounds for its decision—arguing as though the issue were whether law could control social prejudice, proclaiming the law could not do so, and then identifying segregation with "racial instinct" as beyond the power of law, a series of fallacious grounds for a judgment concerning a positive piece of prohibitory legislation.[17]

It is highly important that all concerned with antidiscrimination strategy should realize the fallacious character of certain arguments used by the Supreme Court in the opinions

16 Konvitz, *op. cit.*, p. 9.

17 For the Civil Rights Cases see Konvitz, *op. cit.*, Chap. 2. For a short survey of the relation of the Courts to race discrimination see Carey McWilliams, "Race Discrimination and the Law," *Science and Society* (Winter, 1945), vol. IX, no. 1, pp. 1–22, and Robert E. Cushman, "The Laws of the Land," *Survey Graphic* (January, 1947), pp. 14–18. For a thorough analysis of *Plessy* v. *Ferguson* see the March, 1946, issue of the *Minnesota Law Review*, devoted to a study of the subject by Judge Edward F. Waite.

they handed down in the Civil Rights Cases. These arguments are still prevalent today. "Legislation is powerless to eradicate racial instincts," declared the Court. In this brief dictum there is abundant confusion. Racial attitudes are made eternal as racial *instincts,* although these attitudes are often changing. Then the inference is drawn that law is powerless to control them. Why should this inference apply only to laws that reject discrimination and not to laws that enforce it? If the one kind is vain why not the other kind? Even if law had no power over prejudice why should it have none over discrimination, which is not an attitude but an action? Laws often check behavior to which the attitudes of people prompt them. Law does have a much more direct power over discrimination than over prejudice—should it leave the one alone because it cannot control the other? But if it makes discrimination a social *institution* it is indirectly indoctrinating people into prejudice. For one of the conditions to which the attitudes of men are responsive is the institutional structure. Men generally accommodate themselves to the institutional system in which they are brought up.[18] Within it their habits are formed and their attitudes developed. The *mores* are not a set of fixations independent of the social environment. Law cannot order men to abandon their prejudices, but it can strengthen or weaken the conditions under which prejudice develops. Law cannot—or should not, because of the dangerous reaction—bid Whites to change their opinions about Negroes but it can help, along with other agencies, to create conditions under which the opinions of Whites will freely and responsively change toward Negroes. Law cannot take the place of education but it can be a good ally. Once more we must understand that no one of the forces that work against discrimination can forego the aid of all the rest.

[18] Cf. Mark A. May, *A Social Psychology of War and Peace* (Yale University Press, 1943), Chap. IX.

We have shown how the courts can constitute a powerful agency for abridging civil liberties, but they can be an equally powerful instrumentality for advancing them. Fortunately they have, in recent times, been much more prominent in the latter role.[19] Following up the outlawing of the "grandfather clauses," the Supreme Court in 1927 held that the Texas statute of 1923, which first introduced the "White primary," was unconstitutional under the Fourteenth Amendment (*Nixon* v. *Herndon,* 273 U.S. 536), and in 1923 invalidated a later device for specifically barring Negroes from the primary (*Nixon* v. *Condon,* 286 U.S. 73). Another device to maintain the White primary was upheld by the Court in 1935 but the decision was in effect reversed in the Classic case (*United States* v. *Classic,* 313 U.S. 299, 1941). Since then the White primary has been a lost cause.

The courts have been active also in undermining the system of racial segregation they formerly ratified. To cite some recent instances, the Supreme Court ruled out social segregation on interstate buses (June, 1946). A Federal Court of Appeals in the District of Columbia declared against segregation of interstate Negro passengers (September, 1946). A Federal District Court of Southern California enjoined school authorities from establishing separate grammar schools for "Mexicans."

The courts remain in the thick of the battle. On the whole they have, in recent times, taken sides with the antidiscrimination forces. But the gains thus achieved are insecure. They can be stabilized only by the strong support of public opinion and of such specific laws against discrimination as public opinion promotes or sustains. The courts do not sit on dis-

[19] Osmond K. Fraenkel, *The Supreme Court and Civil Liberties* (pamphlet of the American Civil Liberties Union, 1945), gives a list of "leading cases" concerned with civil liberties. Of these cases 34 may be reckoned as having to do with interracial relations. In 30 of these 34 cases the decision was favorable to the maintenance or advance of civil liberties. The 4 unfavorable decisions in this list all belong to the period between 1875 and 1893.

tant Olympus, weighing with timeless mind the logic inherent in the Constitution. As we have seen, their judgments change with the times. But on various issues affecting discrimination there is often in the courts division, and sometimes vacillation. The very important decision in the Screws case (*Screws v. United States*, 325 U.S. 91) of 1945, which brought the Negro under federal protection when his rights have been violated by state officers of the law, was dissented from by a minority of three distinguished justices. A minority may turn at any time into a majority.

The stronger public opinion against discrimination grows, the more effective will the laws against it become. The more effective the laws, the more will the courts be of aid. The campaign must be directed toward all three objectives. Even the courts should not be regarded as beyond the reach of proper influence, such as, for example, is exerted by the American Civil Liberties Union, acting as *amicus curiae* and submitting briefs drawn up by the best legal talent.

In this section we have been concerned mainly with laws that promote or prescribe discrimination and the attitude of the courts toward such laws. Let us note, however, that there are various laws and ordinances that purport to protect the consumer, the worker, or the property owner, but are in effect, and sometimes also of design, instruments for the maintenance of discrimination. For example, the licensing laws of the plumbing industry have been used and developed for the purpose of keeping Negroes out of a craft that is exclusionist in policy.[20]

Finally, besides restrictive laws there are restrictive agreements of various kinds that, so long as they are legally valid, have the same effect within their range as restrictive laws. Since the beginning of the twentieth century discriminatory agreements of this kind have expanded in an extraordinary manner. They have been directed primarily against Negroes

[20] Northrup, *op. cit.*, p. 23.

and other non-White groups, including Latin Americans, but they are also employed against Jewish people and occasionally against religious minority groups. The restrictive covenant is a concerted arrangement between property owners of a particular residential area in which they pledge not to sell or rent to members of certain groups. "It has been estimated that as high as 80 per cent of the residential area of Chicago is covered already by these restrictions." [21]

So far as public policy is concerned there are a few principles that should already command general assent. These include the following:

(1) It should be a requirement of every housing project, public or private, that it does not diminish the reasonably accessible living space for groups against which there is any kind of social prejudice, and that it should not diminish the opportunity of such groups for the relief of congestion or for reasonable expansion;

(2) It should be a requirement of every large-scale city planning or housing development that it provide proportionate space for such groups;

(3) No new restrictive covenants should be anywhere permitted such as would have the effect of intensifying the segregation or increasing the congestion of such groups.

Beyond such general stipulations we must rely mainly on local action. A campaign of social education should be developed, wherever possible, to reveal the pernicious results of segregation and in particular of restrictive covenants as a basis of residential segregation. A clear line should be drawn between restrictive agreements designed to maintain objective residential standards in a neighborhood and those directed against fellow citizens on the ground that they are as such undesirable. Public opinion should be instructed

[21] Robert C. Weaver, "Northern Ways," *Survey Graphic,* January, 1947, p. 45. We cannot place much reliance on such estimates, but the essential consideration is that all the areas contiguous to the "black belts" are solidly covered by restrictive agreements.

regarding the evils of the latter type. Investigation abundantly shows that the following charges can be brought against them: [22]

(1) They create segregated areas, and segregated areas become social problem areas. Within them the "vicious circle" has free play. They become hives of disease, poverty, hopelessness, delinquency, crime, and social tension. The conditions bred in these areas infect the rest of the community. Not only the physical health but the social sanity of the community is threatened by them.

The prevalence of these conditions confirms the sense of caste in the non-segregated groups. The fact of residential segregation involves segregated schools, segregated recreations, segregated facilities of all kinds. Thus an alien and secretly, if not openly, hostile colony is planted within the larger community. The future of the community is mortgaged. It is committed to an increasingly more intolerable burden. Disruptive tensions take the place of the healing influences that accommodate group to group when they enjoy a system of live-and-let-live.

(2) Where the principle of segregation is rejected and the people have become habituated to this situation the presence in any residential area of a properly qualified owner or tenant, whether he be Negro or Oriental or Jew or anything else, has no adverse effect on property values. In England or in France, for example, the fact that a Negro lives in a high-class neighborhood, so long as he maintains the requisite standards, does not lower the residential desirability of the area. It is significant, by the way, that even in our own group-conscious society some of the most exclusive residential areas of the great cities do not object to the presence of a few Jewish members. Such members are usually persons of great wealth and the neighborhood remains as "select" as ever.

---

[22] See Robert C. Weaver, "Housing in a Democracy," *Annals*, American Academy of Political and Social Science (March, 1946), pp. 95-105.

Where there is no social fear there is no social peril. But
once the prejudice-begotten fear of a Jewish "invasion" or
of a Negro "invasion" takes hold of a neighborhood the
exodus and the deterioration begin. The social fear evokes
a new sequence of economic costs and social liabilities.

Little can be done about it until a sufficiently influential
portion of the local community comes to realize the evil
consequences of segregation and is at the same time emanci-
pated enough to accept the residential proximity of the
members of any ethnic or racial group—provided they meet
the conditions and standards of occupancy on which the
objectively definable amenities of the neighborhood depend.
Then the necessary legal controls can be adopted, in the
form of municipal and county regulations barring restrictive
covenants based on differences of race, ethnic origin, or religion—we must here add "religion," since it is often used
as a mask for ethnic discrimination.

In recent years some doubts have been cast on the constitutionality of restrictive covenants of this sort, and particularly on the validity of the enforcement of such covenants
through federal or state courts. The judgments of the Supreme Court that have hitherto been handed down recognize
racially restrictive covenants when effected by private action
(*Corrigan* v. *Buckley*, 271 U.S. 323) but not when organized
by a public authority (*Buchanan* v. *Warley*, 245 U.S. 60).
The issue is again before the Supreme Court. There is now
the new argument that the adherence of the United States
to the Charter of the United Nations—which repeatedly,
beginning with the first article, endorses the principle and
the objective of "fundamental freedoms for all without distinction as to race, sex, language, or religion"—renders the
principle thus ratified by treaty superior to municipal or
state law. Important new influences are at work to change
and, sooner or later, to reverse the attitude of the courts. It
should, however, be recognized that even if the courts cease

to uphold restrictive covenants, where the restriction is based not on standards of occupancy but on racial or ethnic exclusiveness, the pattern of residential discrimination would still persist. The denial of the recourse to law in order to enforce these covenants would be a signal gain, but chiefly because it would clear the way for direct attacks upon them.[23]

4. MARSHALLING THE POLITICAL FORCES

In the United States any compact group possessed of the vote has a lever of power out of proportion to its own numbers. This fact is due to the particular structure of the party system in the United States—a point we shall not pause to develop since it is recognized by all authorities on the subject. If the group can hold together as a minority bloc it will find ample occasion to make its influence felt. There may be good reasons why on most issues ethnic or racial groups should not constitute solid voting blocs but there can be no objection to their doing so with respect to this issue. It would be well if they realized their power and marshalled their forces in the struggle against discrimination.

There is a second reason why voting power is of peculiar importance for minority groups in this country. It is that so many officials are directly elected who in most other countries are appointed. The lower judiciary and numerous administrative officials are locally elected. Now there is a large amount of particularly vexatious discrimination that depends not on the law but on the attitudes of officials. The law may be liberal but the administration of the law may be oppres-

23 On the constitutional issue see D. O. McGovney, "Racial Residential Segregation by State Court Enforcement of Restrictive Agreements, Covenants, or Conditions in Deeds is Unconstitutional," *University of California Law Review* (March, 1945); Harold I. Kahen, "Validity of Anti-Negro Restrictive Covenants: a Reconsideration of the Problem," *University of California Law Review* (February, 1945); Sidney A. Jones, Jr., "The Legality of Anti-Negro Restrictive Covenants," *National Bar Journal* (March, 1946).

sive, as the Negro has often found.[24] The law may be enlightened but the behavior of the police may be brutal, as members of minority groups have good cause to know. If, however, the elected officials fear they will lose an important body of votes through such behavior they are likely to change their ways. District attorneys and police commissioners will see to it that their men in uniform give fair treatment to the underdog—if the underdog knows how to use his vote. It will be to the interest of the higher-ups to deflect tensions and avert disturbances, and to develop appropriate techniques to this end. Some fine instances are already on the record, in Washington, D.C., New York City, and other centers, showing how intelligent forethought can avert race riots and other clashes.[25]

So far as minority groups are organized to make proper use of their voting power they will be able to affect not only the attitudes of those in office but also election to office, and to influence the composition of school boards, of city councils, of courts. They will have greater equality before the law and more assured enjoyment of their civil rights. They will have greater bargaining power for the attainment of group status. And they will seek through more efficient forms of struggle to satisfy the needs that otherwise prompt nothing better than sporadic insurgence.

Let us see how these considerations apply to the largest of all specific minorities in the United States, the Negroes. For them the political situation has become distinctly more favorable. In the Southern states White primaries are passing out. The poll tax, in the eight states that retain it, has lessening

---

[24] Cf. Henry J. McGuinn, *The Courts and the Changing Status of Negroes in Maryland* (a collection of published articles accepted as Ph.D. dissertation at Columbia University, 1940); see also Myrdal, *op. cit.*, Chap. 24.

[25] Alfred McClung Lee, *Race Riots Aren't Necessary*, Public Affairs Pamphlet no. 107, New York, 1945; Joseph E. Wechler and Theo. Hall, *The Police and Minority Groups*, American Council on Race Relations, Chicago, 1944.

importance as a barrier in a period in which both wages and prices have risen. It is a small tax—one to three dollars per head—and the growth of political consciousness can gradually overcome its deterrent effect, even if it remains on the statute books. With the advance of education the literacy test will exclude smaller numbers, and although some Southern states have been tightening their restrictions—Alabama passed a law in 1946 requiring of would-be voters the ability to "read and explain" the Constitution—we may agree with Myrdal that "the entire work around 1900 to legalize political discrimination is being rapidly undone by various social trends." [26] More Negroes are acquiring the right to vote and more Negroes are exercising it.

With this change the whole structure of Southern politics is changing. There are now genuine political contests between the reactionary and the liberal forces. The agreement of rival candidates to accept the verdict of the primaries and close their ranks in the later elections is losing hold. The liberal candidates continue their opposition to the reactionary standpoint, should it win out in the primaries, and carry it to the polls. In various Southern states the Negroes are no longer resisted by a united front.

As a portent of the changing times we may take the political history of Georgia in recent years. That state had as Governor a bitterly narrow partisan of "White supremacy"— Eugene Talmadge. Talmadge in his campaign against any liberal influence took action to dismiss a number of educators as not "sound" on the racial question. To his surprise sharp opposition was aroused, with the students of the universities taking an active part. Talmadge lost ground and suffered defeat at the next election. His place as Governor was taken by Ellis Arnall, who within political limitations showed a more enlightened spirit and who has since published a book, *The Shore Dimly Seen*, depicting his vision of

26 *Op. cit.*, vol. I, p. 514.

a better South. When election time came in 1946 it was already manifest that the old order in Georgia had been challenged. In the spring of that year the head of the Augusta party machine, Roy Harris, was roundly defeated in an election in which he made the race issue paramount, and Negro voters participated more freely than on any previous occasion. In July came the first Georgia primary in which they were permitted to vote. Talmadge emerged the winner, but only because of a prejudicial electoral system according to which the majority of unit districts is the decisive factor—thus giving undue weight to small rural districts. Elected as Governor he died before he could assume office. This was in December, 1946, and thereupon Governor Arnall announced that the Lieutenant Governor elect, M. E. Thompson, was the rightful successor, in whose favor he would in due course resign. Immediately thereafter Talmadge's son, a faithful follower in his father's steps, came forward as a candidate for "election" before the state legislature, disputing the constitutionality of Arnall's action. On a "White supremacy" platform he was elected by the legislature in January, and proceeded forthwith to seize by main force the Executive Office and the Governor's mansion. The issue was taken to the courts and finally to the Georgia Supreme Court, which ruled five to two against Talmadge, Jr., and in favor of Thompson.

The political events thus briefly sketched reveal the ferment of social and political change that is occurring in the South. Here the enfranchisement of the Negro is a primary condition of progress. We conclude that of all the means at hand for the elimination of Negro subjection *the vote in the hands of the Negroes themselves is likely to be the most effective.* The increasing admission of Negroes to Southern polls and the strength of Negro blocs in Northern cities can together, if wisely utilized, assure the gradual advancement of Negroes toward a status of full civic equality. By this means the vicious circle of discrimination can in the course of time be completely disrupted. Already in certain Northern cities, such as New York, Chicago, Detroit, and Philadelphia, no political party can afford to antagonize the body of Negro voters. In numerous other cities, from Boston to Los Angeles, there is a sufficient Negro vote to have distinct influence where it is organized. Already in the states immediately south of the Mason and Dixon line the political significance of the Negro is receiving recognition.

But the efficacy of the means depends entirely on the strategy that presides over it. We should bear in mind also that the new voting power of the Negro may arouse more bitter opposition to his claims. There is first the task of educating the Negro voter. There seem to be curious differences in the attitudes of Negroes in one locality as compared with another. In Chicago, for example, they have shown a greater readiness to register and vote than is characteristic of the voting population as a whole.[27] In other cities, such as Detroit, they have been voting in smaller proportions than have Whites.[28] Since all Negroes have a most obvious common cause it is a reasonable assumption that skilful leadership could dispel the inertia that in various areas prevents Negroes from making effective use of their voting power.[29]

There is no likelihood that Negroes will form a third party, and there would be serious disadvantages in any attempt to do so. There are also important reasons why they should not identify themselves too closely with either of the major parties. They have to depend mainly on the bargaining power of a compact bloc that throws its weight to whichever side does most to advance their liberation. Success in this

[27] Harold F. Gosnell, *Negro Politicians* (University of Chicago Press, 1935).
[28] Edward H. Litchfield, "A Case Study of Negro Political Behavior in Detroit," *Public Opinion Quarterly* (June, 1941), pp. 267–274.
[29] Much useful information on the subject is contained in the monographs of Ralph Bunche prepared for the Myrdal study, *The Political Status of the Negro* and *A Brief and Tentative Analysis of Negro Leadership* (available in Schomburg Collection, New York Public Library).

enterprise can reasonably be anticipated. This strategy would rule out violent denunciation or revolutionary programs, for no major party could afford to espouse a cause so advocated. Intransigent and all-out demands, untempered to the trends of change and the susceptibilities of public opinion, although they may have moments of success or even of triumph, are likely in the longer run to be self-defeating. Whereas the vigilant discernment and resolute pursuit of each strategic occasion will bring successive gains cumulating into a transformation of the social and economic status of the whole Negro group. To carry out this strategy there is much need for the development of Negro political leadership.

For the Negro of the Deep South, a gradual process of enfranchisement, accompanied by appropriate advances in Negro education and in economic opportunity, would be far more feasible, and might be more desirable, than an all-at-once revolution of Southern ways. We must face the consequences of the fact that the South has denied to the Negro the conditions under which democracy can flourish. Democracy cannot consort with illiteracy and hopeless agricultural poverty. The vote without educational preparation and social provision is a menace to the democracy that grants it. It means corruption and boss rule. What can be sought without any qualification or time interval is the complete equality of the Negro and White before the law. This advance would also do less violence to the mores of the South. As Myrdal points out, there appears to be much more sympathy in the South for equal treatment before the law than for equal voting rights. "The lingering inequality in justice in the South is probably due more to low and lagging professional standards . . . than it is to opinion in favor of legal inequality." [30]

The effective use of Negro voting power is beset by various difficulties. Its organization is highly localized. It lacks ade-

[30] Myrdal, *op. cit.*, vol. I, p. 534. The passage is italicized in the original.

quate direction from any center. The National Association for the Advancement of Colored People has, according to Mr. Bunche, assumed the general role of watchdog over Negro rights. But what we have in view is a more concentrated and more positive superintendence of strategy. In the old days, when the Negro vote counted for little, the Negro people had at times a general leader who might also be, like Booker Washington, a prophet of the folk. Another kind of leadership may now be required. The local Negro leaders are immersed in locality problems, and there are local perquisites that sometimes bulk large in their ambitions. The time may be ripe for some wider strategy. Local insulations and the divisions between left wing and right wing groups become more embarrassing as opportunities for united action increase. Even in the South there are shrewd politicians who have become highly conscious of the importance of the Negro vote. A central strategy board could take advantage of favorable trends. Possibly a lesson might be taken from the Jewish book. The manifest and often bitter conflicts between the more radical and the more moderate sectors, between orthodox and "reform" groups, between Zionists and non-Zionists, have stimulated the organization of a coordinating body for common ends, the National Community Relations Advisory Council. By means of quiet and careful negotiations this body seeks, and has to its credit some success in finding, a united front for specific common programs.

The recent advancement in the voting status of the Southern Negro should itself be regarded as a function of the socioeconomic change that is stirring in the South. The breakup of old political machines, the increase of industrialization and with it the growing sense of the economic immaturity of the South, the consequent disruption of the old standpat "regularity" of opinion, the concomitant tendency unobtrusively to enlist Negro opinion on this side or on that, these are all aspects of the same slow ferment of change that is de-

throning the White prerogative of political rights, that is
undermining the poll tax, that is setting here and there an
example of "equal pay for equal work," vindicating here
and there the principle of justice against racial prejudice,
and generally endowing the Negro with some measure of a
curious kind of segregated citizenship. Moreover, the experience in the South, shared by Negro along with White, of the
concrete economic benefits of the protective legislation inaugurated by the "New Deal," has given the people as a
whole an appreciation of what government can do directly
for them. Wartime prosperity has worked in the same direction. New expectations have been forming and the old sub-
sistence standards of living, so much below the general level
of the nation, no longer are looked upon with the old complacency.

Finally, we should note in this connection that disprivileged groups may achieve notable gains through laws that
have no direct relation to the issue of discrimination. The
broad effect of social security legislation and other general
welfare measures has been to improve the relative status of
such groups. We do not include here such policies as that of
the Agricultural Adjustment Administration which, because
of its weighted bonuses, led to the displacement of many
Negro and White sharecroppers and many Negro farm
tenants, though possibly, in the longer run, it may prove not
disadvantageous that these low-subsistence cultivators had
to find other forms of employment.[31] We are referring instead
to federal policies assuring protection, unemployment benefits, minimum wages, and other forms of social security. In
the nature of the case the Federal Government cannot, like
some state governments, discriminate in the benefits assured
by the laws it passes. Constitutionally, it knows no distinction
of color or creed. The greater role of the Federal Government is therefore by implication favorable to Negro oppor-

[31] Cf. Myrdal, *op. cit.*, vol. I, Chap. 12.

tunity. While local agencies through which it operates tend to
take on some of the discriminatory attitudes of the localities
concerned they can at most, as in the administration of the
Federal Emergency Relief Administration, skew the intention of the law; they cannot block it altogether. Moreover,
if the federal administration is genuinely concerned that the
disprivileged groups obtain a fair share of legislative benefits
it can at important points override the bias of localities. Thus
the development of social security measures has helped to
raise the economic status of the great mass of low-subsistence
Negroes. The Farm Security Administration, one of the
latest of the "New Deal" devices, followed constructive policies that strengthened the position and improved the opportunities of agricultural workers and poor farmers. All measures assuring a minimum level of security mean a special gain
to the least sheltered groups. For example, since Negroes are
more subject to unemployment than Whites, measures of
unemployment relief, so far as they are fairly administered,
are of greater net benefit to them than to the rest of the
population. Perhaps even more important, these groups gain
thus a sense of participation in the common weal that has
great significance for their morale as citizens.

Chapter Eight

The Distorting Mirrors

---

1. WHY PREJUDICE IS PREJUDICIAL

OUR THEME is discrimination, not prejudice as such, but since on the educational front, more than on any other, the line of battle against discrimination advances over the defeat of prejudice we must devote our attention first to some considerations on the nature and operation of inter-group prejudice, and on the primary forms in which prejudice takes shape, adapting itself to the demands or conditions of personality. We shall deal with these topics as briefly as is consistent with our major purpose.

The way the members of a group think is the way they have learned to think. The way they think about other groups is a social product, responsive to social conditions. Only the very tough-minded, or those who are seriously maladjusted to their group, can resist or overcome in any significant manner the social stamp of their environment. Social indoctrination, direct and indirect, inculcates attitudes and beliefs. Habit confirms the lesson. This elementary conclusion is borne out both by psychological and by anthropological investigation. Every group, particularly when it is insulated from other groups, develops its characteristic and distinctive attitudes and beliefs.

It is not difficult to recognize how these attitudes, the thought ways and folkways, are transmitted to each rising generation. What is more difficult to investigate is the manner in which the social codes that are thus transmitted are initially developed and then undergo change and transmutation. Obviously the changing economic and power interests of the group are important factors. Obviously the changing relative position of the group over against other groups plays some role. But these conditions are only part of the story. There is no fixity in the mores. There is a subtle process in which the changing myths of the tribe interact with their changing techniques.[1] In the multigroup society there is also the impact on one another of the diverse codes of the various groups, making this type of society more changeful and more exposed to the cultural dominance of one over another and to the leadership and skill displayed on behalf of one or another set of values. It is this last consideration that makes the question of strategy so important in the modern community.

In this type of community the diverse groups, moved by the influences at work within each, construct highly simplified, and for the most part highly prejudicial, concepts of the other groups, not as persons, but as embodiments of a type character attributed to these groups as such. In every kind of society human beings have been prone to construct such mental pictures of the "out-group." Every tribe does it for the tribe beyond its borders. Every social class does it for the class above or below it in the social scale. But in the multigroup society the tendency takes on new dimensions and a new significance. For with its plethora of cultural differences and its clashes of economic interest, with its specialization and its stratification, it develops an antithesis for every thesis, for every group a counteractive group. The socialist carries around his mental image of the capitalist,

[1] See the author's *The Web of Government* (New York, 1947), Chap. I.

and vice versa, and so it is with the employee and the employer, the Protestant and the Roman Catholic, even (at election times) the Republican and the Democrat. These, however, are only a few broad examples of a way of thinking that has numerous other manifestations. This tendency to think in "stereotypes," as Walter Lippmann called them, is particularly uncontrolled when we come to racial and ethnic differences. In other antithetical relations the ground of difference is a matter of specific interests or of cultural viewpoints. Here, however, the difference is undefined and there is nothing to limit the play of prejudice in its image-making activity.[2]

One evidence is the derogatory names that in this country are applied to racial and ethnic groups. Such names in popular speech are attached to the Negro, the Chinese, the Jew, the Italian, the Pole, the Mexican, the Slav, and various others. The names in themselves are frequently meaningless, but they are loaded with contempt or misprision.[3] They become in effect summations and symbols of the prejudicial misconceptions that prevail in our society. A Negro poet, alluding to White attitudes toward his fellow Negroes, has finely expressed the point as follows:

> The mirrors in this country are convex
> And show our bodies distorted,
> Are concave, and show our minds hilarious.[4]

Clearly there is here an important line of educational attack. It is a task of enlightenment, to expose false generalizations, seeking to substitute for symbols based on ignorance and narrow interest other symbols that convey the truth.

[2] See the author's chapter, "Group Images and Group Realities," in R. M. MacIver, ed., Group Relations and Group Antagonisms, pp. 3–9.

[3] Note for the critic: we are aware this word is archaic, but it is a word we need.

[4] Owen Dodson, Powerful Long Ladder, New York, 1946. Quoted with permission of the publishers, Farrar, Straus, and Co.

Education can set itself to no more beneficial enterprise than to impress on the people, whether school children or adults, but above all addressing itself to the young, the lesson that these prejudicial concepts blur our vision of the human reality, put blinkers on our eyes so that we cannot deal with people as they are and cannot understand why they should be different from ourselves, as though we were the norm and sole standard for all humanity.

Education should set forward in all practical ways the objective that in our dealings with others, those outside our group, we see them as persons, not as samples of a race or stock, and treat them as persons, thus gaining for ourselves a new liberation, opening to us the world of men as it is, and making our relations with others more sincere, more genuine, and more intelligent. Much thought and devotion should be expended on the discovery of the most effective ways to impart this wisdom and—what is indeed most needed—on the selection and training of the teachers on whom this responsibility lies. There is good reason to think that the expenditure of the best educational skill on this problem would be well repaid, since the evidence of schools and summer camps in which the removal of inter-group prejudice has been a goal suggests that the young are amenable to this lesson, especially if they are given under favorable conditions an opportunity to practise it at the same time, through everyday contacts with members of the groups that carry the burden of prejudicial disesteem.

What makes this educational enterprise even more important, so much so that for the sake of the unity and strength of the nation it ought to be inaugurated in every school in the land, is the fact that the same years in which the lesson is inculcated are the years in which specific prejudice first takes hold of the personality. This conclusion is established by psychologists and pedagogical investigation. It is summarized by two psychologists as follows:

"(a) The young child undoubtedly starts his life without prejudice, and during pre-school years seems almost incapable of fixing hostility upon any group as a whole.

"(b) The great bulk of prejudice attitudes originate in the school years (elementary and junior high). Seventy-three per cent of the subjects date their first dislike of Jews in this range of years, 77 per cent their first dislike of Negroes." [5]

One caution, however, is needed at this point. The reader should not infer that very young children are free from the *tendency* to prejudice—all he can safely accept is that in the earliest years any such tendency is not directed against particular groups. The natural tendency to extol what is ours by depreciating what is theirs has not yet been "fixed" by social conditioning.

The school, if properly oriented, could no doubt become a powerful influence in counteracting the influences that work to canalize prejudice in the child, and thus might have some effect, through the child, on the grownup community. In the report cited above the authors suggest that school instruction could have more vitality than it usually does. Here is their conclusion:

"(a) Children apparently do learn *something* in school that decidedly affects their ethnic attitudes . . . but what it is they have learned they are in later years seldom able to tell. Vivid teaching seems to be rare. (b) The only specific teaching the subjects recall (in sufficient numbers to be reported) concerns 'scientific facts about race.' Where this lesson is reported the subjects fall predominantly in the less prejudiced half. *But only eight per cent of our subjects recall hav-*

---

[5] Gordon W. Allport and Bernard M. Kramer, "Some Roots of Prejudice," *Journal of Psychology* (1946), vol. 22, p. 22. The subjects to whom the percentages above given referred were 437 college undergraduates from Dartmouth, Harvard, and Radcliffe. The study has been reissued as a pamphlet by the Commission on Community Relations of the American Jewish Congress.

ing learned scientific facts about race. This useful lesson is apparently neglected in our school curricula." [6]

In passing we remark that students young or old are not likely to remember "scientific facts" about anything if they have been presented to them merely as detached facts. If they are to have meaning for the learner facts must be taught in a frame of reference. Facts about race become significant to the student only if the teacher can convey through these facts some larger truths about human beings. If he succeeds in doing so he will succeed also in checking the process in which, to quote from the same report, "prejudice is woven into the very fabric of personality." If that process is allowed to develop it ends in "the dull unaware stencilled quality of the prejudiced mind," which refuses to recognize facts or at best finds ways of "rationalizing" them.

The Allport-Kramer study indicates also—though here we must be careful not to draw general conclusions from a particular sample—that the children of more educated parents show a lower propensity to prejudice. For the subjects of the investigation the difference is given as follows: [7]

TABLE 2

PERCENTAGE DISTRIBUTION OF PREJUDICE SCORES
AS A FUNCTION OF PARENTAL EDUCATION

	Less Prejudiced	*More Prejudiced*
Both parents college graduates	60.3	39.7
One parent college graduate	53.0	47.0
Neither parent college graduate	41.2	58.8

We draw one broad conclusion various aspects of which will occupy us as we proceed. The potential role of education in the combating of inter-group prejudice is enormous, but the adequate development of that role is beset by many diffi-

6 *Ibid.*, p. 21. Italics as in original.
7 *Ibid.*, p. 31. For an intensive study of prejudice among college students see Eugene Hartley, *Problems in Prejudice* (King's Crown Press, New York, 1946).

culties. Some of these difficulties lie in community attitudes and in the controls they exercise on the educational system. Others lie within the system itself. Let us as a starting point set out some considerations regarding the kind of education that would be most effective in checking and redirecting the social processes in which the minds of the young are turned into distorting mirrors.

There are certain truths regarding inter-group relations that, could we find the way to inculcate them, would by their very nature dispel much of the prejudice that prevails. The fundamental task of social education is to make these truths live in the minds and hearts of men.

In the first place it is necessary to learn that we cannot understand the behavior of other men or of other groups unless we conceive the situation within which they act, the conditions to which they respond. We must know what that situation is, and then we must ask ourselves how we would act in the same situation. We must form the habit—if we wish to understand—of projecting ourselves imaginatively into the place of the other group.[8] We put this requirement forward not as an ethical postulate but as a condition of intelligent action. The failure to meet it is responsible for a vast amount of miscalculation, loss, and disappointment. We have constantly to relate our behavior to that of others. We must therefore be able to calculate, as far as we can, the response of others to our behavior. Yet in small affairs and in great we make endless errors for lack of doing so. In the

---

[8] The new role of the United States in the international scene is an additional reason why we should bend our educational efforts to inculate a lesson so important also for our domestic harmony. Already in our treatment of ex-enemy countries we can perceive that where we act with some attempt to understand the other people, as we seem to be doing in Japan, we are achieving far more success than where no such attempt is apparent. It is encouraging to find that some of our present-day writers show the same open-mindedness in their portrayal of other peoples, as is exemplified by Alexander Leighton in his book already referred to and by Edmond Taylor in *Richer by Asia* (Boston, 1947).

relations between nations, in making a treaty or in making
a peace, in dealings of every sort, statesmen miscalculate in
this account, often with disastrous results. They seldom ask
how they would respond to the treatment they mete out to
others and consequently their most elaborate plans go awry.
In the relations of employer and employee the same kind
of misunderstanding is very common. Our first lesson about
inter-group relations is therefore one that will make for
more intelligent and more successful dealings in every relationship.

When we learn the habit of asking how *we* would behave
were we *they* much that seemed alien and remote and meaningless and perverse in the doing and the thinking of other
people appears in an entirely new light. It brings other
groups and other peoples back into the circle of our common
humanity. Whether or no it increases our sympathy for them
it certainly increases our wisdom about them.

The second great truth is that in our closely knit society
—knit by interdependence if not by inter-understanding—
what we do to improve the lot of other groups raises the
entire standard of the community and thus redounds to our
own well-being. Furthermore, it reduces the wastage of conflicts and antagonisms that bring loss alike to the oppressor
and the oppressed. We have already cited the plight of the
Southern states and the backwardness of those Southwestern
states where the Mexican remains in a disprivileged condition. The principle operates on various levels. One aspect of
its operation is tellingly expressed in the following passage
from Bernard Shaw:

Now what does this Let Him Be Poor mean? It means let him
be weak. Let him be ignorant. Let him become a nucleus of
disease. Let him be a standing exhibition and example of ugli-
ness and dirt. Let him have rickety children. Let him be cheap
and let him drag his fellows down to his price by selling himself
to do their work. Let his habitation turn our cities into poison-

ous congeries of slums. Let his daughters infect our young men with the diseases of the streets and his sons revenge themselves by turning the nation's manhood into scrofula, cowardice, hypocrisy, political imbecility, and all the other fruits of oppression and malnutrition.[9]

It would be of signal service if social education could be so developed as to convey the lesson that the common good is the deep wellspring from which we all, individuals and groups, draw the cultural sustenance we need as well as our greater economic prosperity. It is part of the same lesson to show how the tensions and anxieties that arise in the prejudicial strife of groups and that work harm to the discriminator in the very act of discriminating are very largely based on false assumptions and on false fears. We deny a group full admission to the privileges of the community because we fear their "subversive tendencies," but these tendencies are created by our denial. Many historical examples are available. Thus before Roman Catholics were admitted to the franchise in England they were regarded as a divisive factor in the commonwealth, and dreadful evils were predicted should they be given the full rights of citizenship. Whereas the actual result of emancipation was to remove a ground of division within the realm and to widen the basis of unity. So it has been many times over. We have always to relearn the lesson that Julius Caesar so successfully practised. Ruthless conqueror though he sometimes was he had the insight to perceive that only by granting the Roman franchise to subject peoples could they be kept from causing strife and dissension within the Empire.

The world of prejudice, it would then appear, is a world of false fears leading to real sorrows. With false fears are linked false conclusions about the social reality, and education should be directed to their disproof. For example, false conclusions, contrary to the biological evidence, are rife re-

[9] Preface, *Major Barbara*.

garding the result of the intermarriage of ethnic or racial groups. The only genuine argument against intermarriage is based on social conditions, not on biological realities. In other words, the children of such marriages, as well as the partners, where the prejudice against them is strong, are exposed to serious social disadvantages. Here again the prejudice creates the evils that it fears. But so long as the prejudice is strong the evils will follow.

Finally, the truth we have been illustrating can and should be associated with the historical tradition of America, with the spiritual forces that lay back of its achievement of independence and its growth to greatness, with the processes that brought together many peoples and tongues into a "more perfect union," disregarding old distinctions of privilege and class, and with the explicit expression of the creed of Americanism in the Bill of Rights and in many undying utterances. The truth has many witnesses, the need for it is clear—it is the task of education to bring together the witness and the truth.

2. TWO TYPES OF PREJUDICE

Prejudice is protean, exhibiting itself in every kind of situation and expressing itself in the most diverse ways. It is not our province to examine or to classify its infinite variety, but we present a distinction between two types that seems to us to have an important bearing on educational policy. The distinction has been developed by Dr. L. J. Stone, one of our collaborators, and by Dr. Isidor Chein.[10]

The first, the most inclusive type, is the prejudice that is taken on through the regular processes of social responsive-

[10] For Dr. Chein's formulation see "Some Considerations in Combating Intergroup Prejudice," *Journal of Educational Sociology* (1946), vol. 19, pp. 412–419. Dr. Stone has been kind enough to prepare a special statement on the subject, which appears as Appendix 4.

ness, as the imperceptibly acquired result of indoctrination and habituation. It presumes the prior prevalence of prejudice in the social group, which the conforming individual accepts in the same way as he accepts the conventions, the labels, the gestures, and in general the folkways of his group. Some natures are more simply receptive than others, but all are in their degrees subject to the impressions made by the established scheme of things. Some are deviate and some, especially in the multigroup society, where there are always challenges to the myths of the tribe, outgrow certain prejudices and win their way to a greater tolerance or a better understanding. But in the primary process of socialization the thought modes of the group are perpetuated, and for the majority, unless in times of grave disturbance, these thought modes are "woven into the very fabric of personality."

There is another way in which, apart from direct indoctrination, the mere fact of growing up in a group exerts a powerful influence in favor of prejudice against other groups. It is natural for us all to magnify our own group, the nearer group to which we owe our origin and our nurture and the greater group that sustains and contains it and forms the orbit within which our interests are bounded. But to magnify our own group, which is also an immediate form of our native self-assertion, is to set it above other groups, is in all likelihood to disparage other groups. The emotional allegiance to one's own finds its compass point through the equally emotional aversion from other allegiances. The easiest way to magnify ourselves, the inevitable way of the untutored mind, is to belittle others.

On this theme Karl Llewellyn makes a significant point. "We misconceive," he says, "group prejudice when we think of it as primarily a prejudice *against* some one or more particular groups, as anti-Semitism, anti-Catholicism, anti-Anything-in-particular. It is instead at bottom a prejudice in favor of "My Own Group" as against all others, "pro-us" prejudice eternal, live, and waiting, ready to be focused and intensified against Any Other Group. . . . Our very ways of growing up produce this basis and drive for overwhelming group prejudices at every turn." [11] It would be interesting to follow this lead further and investigate, for example, whether even the relative degrees of prejudice entertained against different groups may not, in part at least, express the measure in which these other groups are conceived to be a threat or impediment to our own, either as being culturally alien or as being detrimental to our status or our economic interest. Incidentally, there is here a lesson that disprivileged groups, in their attacks on dominant prejudice, should carefully learn. It serves no purpose to tilt against the human nature they share with the dominant groups. If they realize how natural prejudice is to all humanity, how close it is to our virtues as well as to our vices, they will be less likely to attack at the wrong points and to pursue programs that antagonize without profit to their cause.

Besides the strong power of use and wont, there are also the sanctions of the code to deter individuals from aberrant behavior. To take the side of the "out-group"—to go in any respect counter to the prejudices of one's society—is to endanger one's own social status. The member of the group begins to feel like an outsider himself if he pleads the cause of the outsider. If, for example, in the camaraderie of the club he does not echo the sentiments that magnify "our" group at the expense of "their" group, even if he does not join heartily in the guffaw that follows the joke about "the Jew who . . ." or "the Wop who . . ." he becomes somewhat suspect, he is no longer so securely "one of us."

---

11 "Group Prejudice and Social Education," in R. M. MacIver, ed., *Civilization and Group Relationships,* p. 13. I know no more clear and pithy statement of the dilemma of socialization than is contained in Professor Llewellyn's contribution.

These considerations, which are in harmony with many findings of sociological and psychological research, lead to the conclusion that, however prejudice may first arise, a major determinant of its perpetuation is simply the tendency of the members of any group to take on the coloration of the established mores. We should therefore expect that, except in times of violent disturbance and change, the prejudice against particular groups entertained by the majority can to a very large extent be assigned to our first type.

Our second type is the prejudice that owes its chief impetus not to the social milieu but to the life history and personality problems of the individual. As the former type is an expression of conformism this type is an expression of failure to achieve a satisfactory conformism. The tensions and frustrations of the disoriented, of the misfits, of those who in their earliest years or in later life have suffered some traumatic experience, may find its outlet in hostility. The possible outlets are diverse but one of them is aggravated prejudice against those who are most exposed because of their inferior position in the community. The ego that is balked of constructive effectiveness in its own circle may compensate by destructive effectiveness against another. The ego that is fundamentally insecure within its own circle may over-assert its belongingness by denunciation of those who don't belong. The ego that fails in its aggressive drives within its own circle may take satisfaction through aggressiveness against the more vulnerable outsider.

Some cautions are necessary in the application of the distinction between our two types. In the first place there is no assumption that all inter-group prejudice must fall under one or the other of these types. They both presuppose the prior existence of prejudice. They both presuppose the conditions, psychological and social, that together generate the dominant prejudices of any group. What the distinction does is to throw a useful light on the relation between personality and prejudice, and thus helps to explain both how prejudice is sustained as a social phenomenon and how certain personality factors operate to create foci for the accentuation of prejudice. There are some indications, for example, that the more violent agitators and promoters of group hostility belong characteristically to the disoriented, the socially frustrated, and the psychologically insecure.[12]

Again, we should not regard our two types of prejudice as though they were manifested separately by two wholly different kinds of personality. They have some common ingredients, and prejudiced persons may exhibit any combination of the two types. For example, the first type is an expression, among other things, of the quest for social security while it is often the unsatisfied urge for social security that expresses itself in the second type. The difference then is a relative rather than an absolute one. What we find is that many persons, probably the majority, exhibit prejudice that is predominantly of type one while other persons, usually a minority, clearly exhibit prejudice of type two. Prejudice of the second type is likely to be more embittered and more aggressive. Furthermore, there are many variations of both types. Thus the first type may range from the chameleon-like acceptance of the mores by those who "take suggestion as a cat laps milk"—and can readily change when the mores change or at the bidding of authority—through the different degrees of incorporation of indoctrinated attitudes into the character structure, until we reach those so fixedly dedicated to the *status quo* that no influence or revolution can modify their stand.

We have drawn attention to these two types because a consideration of them has important implications for policy. If, as we have suggested, type one tends to be prevalent in normal times we have here a strong argument for the importance of *institutional* changes as an agency for the reduction of inter-group prejudice. There is in some quarters a tendency to deprecate institutional changes, especially legal changes, unless public opinion is "ripe" for them, and there are very good evidences in favor of this position so far as *moralistic* legislation is concerned. The history of American communities, especially of the larger cities, provides numerous warnings to this effect. But institutional controls against discrimination—rather than directly against prejudice—fall into a different category, if the source of discrimination is not so much an individually initiated as a socially conditioned response. A change of institutions, provided the institutions remain in force, means a change in social conditioning in a direction favorable to the new institutions. Under democratic conditions such a change requires not only a majority vote but also whatever degree of consensus is necessary to make the new institutions workable. Given this condition, the opposition to the institutions tends to wane. But this topic has already been dealt with in our review of the political front.

How does this typology of prejudice bear on educational programs? We saw that the very process of social initiation, of reception into the "we-group," generates the antithesis of the "we" and the "they," and tends to brand the "they" with the stigmata not only of exclusion but also of repulsion. We raise the question whether, given the right kind of training, the antithesis need be so absolute, so stark, so naive. Might not education, beginning with the young child, aim at the conditioning to embrace the "we" without implying the condemnation, the repulsion, or even, so far as we can rise to that level, the derogation of the "they"? There must be a "they" in antithesis to the "we"—that is a condition of group loyalty, of group unity. There must be some emotional warmth toward the "we" that is withheld from the "they." But the division of things into the beloved "own" and the hated "other" is primitive. It is the failure to see differences as they are, the failure to make *intelligent* distinctions.

We need not keep our training, even of young children, on the primitive level. We do not teach them primitive views about the sun or the stars. Is there any better reason for teaching them primitive morality than for teaching primitive science, especially when the primitive morality involves false evidence about other groups? Might it not be feasible—if we recognize the need for it—to indoctrinate in the loyalties of the "we" without also inculcating contempt and disparagement of the "they"? Children make the distinction for themselves in their sports when they fervently support the team they belong to without hating in any serious sense the team on the other side. They quickly learn the rules and conditions of the game. We do not propose or think it possible—or desirable—that children be turned into little angels. In their sports and in the rough and tumble of their relations with one another they find adequate outlets for their aggressive urges. There seems to be no logical ground, or convincing psychological evidence, for the position that they cannot win their socialization or in general fulfil the various urges of their nature without making the "they" into objects of fear, contempt, derision, or hate. Since the formation of social attitudes begins in the cradle this lesson cannot be conveyed at too early an age. But that involves not only the education of the child in the kindergarten and early school stage but also the education of the parent for the education of the child—a more difficult enterprise.

Anthropological studies show that the simpler peoples differ greatly in their attitudes toward the outsider. Some are aggressive and some are characteristically nonaggressive. We cannot presume that such differences are in some mysterious way genetic. In view of the high value set by children on conformity to the mores current in their own group we might reasonably expect that a different orientation of the learning process would have a powerful effect on their attitudes to other groups in the community.

We are here thinking mainly of type one prejudice. It is more universal and it is instilled through our present modes of education—unlike type two, which arises in the special conjunctures of personality and circumstances and which therefore needs on the whole therapeutic rather than preventive treatment. All men are under the impulsion to belong, but it is the young who learn the ways of belonging. Gardner Murphy writes: "Data suggest indeed that security, the need to be safe in the midst of the group rather than be a lone dissenter, is the central motivating factor, and that socially shared autisms in general derive basically from the need to be accepted by others." [13] If that be so, then it is unjustified to claim, so far as the majority of persons are concerned, that they have an inherent or "instinctive" need for antagonism against the "they-groups"—when that antagonism may be no more than a variable device to establish or confirm their fuller adhesion to the "we-group."

Some interesting confirmations of this conclusion are offered by the behavior of those who have migrated from one social environment to another. At the first they cling with the greater tenacity to their old mores, and if they form within the new environment a colony, settlement, or sub-community they tend to grow more conservative so that they adhere longer and more rigidly to the old ways than do the people from which they stemmed—a phenomenon exhibited, for example, by the French Canadians. The same tendency is manifested by colonies that retain a close link with the mother country and also by those groups from the mother country which, like the Anglo-Indians, live in the semi-detachment of a ruling class within a subject population. Many other manifestations of the tendency could be cited.

[13] *Personality* (New York, 1947), p. 380.

It is the counterpart of the tendency toward revolutionary or utopian unorthodoxy on the part of those to whom the established order refuses status or social integration. Hence they burn with the desire for a new order in which at length, or so they fancy, they will be able to satisfy their "homing instinct."

A sidelight on the universal need to belong and on the conditions under which a transference of allegiance takes place is afforded by Newcomb's study of Bennington students.[14] The girls who attend Bennington College come mainly from well-to-do homes where conservative mores prevail. Bennington, however, is a "progressive" college, and here the girls enter an environment in which different traditions prevail. Newcomb observed that many students who had absorbed the conservatism of their homes now took on the non-conservatism of the college. Some, however, rejected the new social outlook while some ignored it or even seemed to be really unaware of the change, maintaining a rigid allegiance to their former principles. It depended on personality type. Those with a greater sense of personal autonomy were likely to accept the new community. Those who were less autonomous or less adaptable retained the older conformism.

In a sense all these studies merely give modern instance and corroborative detail for the ancient maxim that "custom is the king of men." They show that this principle holds even where it seems to be most contravened. And they tend to show how social reactions, while of course varying with personality traits, are nevertheless expressive in diverse ways of the common need for social acceptance.

There is a clear lesson for policy-makers. It is that any changes they can inaugurate in favor of group equality, if effected either in the educational system or directly in the social structure, will not only immediately serve their end

14 See Theodore M. Newcomb, *Personality and Social Change* (New York, 1943).

but will also, provided they can be maintained for some length of time, have increasing potency as a new generation grows up, since they will permeate the major determinant of the social attitudes of all men, the scheme of the community to which they belong.

We observe in conclusion that even for our type two, although particular therapy is here indicated rather than the broader processes of education, some mitigating influences would be set in motion by the kind of program we have outlined. Type two may be regarded as no more than a deviation from type one, where social needs and social sentiments are diverted from their normal modes of satisfaction and expression to other channels, under the impulsion of personal frustration, the sense of insecurity or of inferiority, or some form of maladjustment of the individual to his group. The urge to conformism does not find adequate fulfilment and the lack of it and consequent tension is "compensated for" by aggravated hostility manifestations, by acute propensities to tyrannize, suppress, belittle, or humiliate. The relation of these propensities to neurotic tension and insecurity is affirmed by much socio-psychological, psychiatric, and anthropological evidence.

But the aggressions and hostilities of type two are directed against whole groups. As is the way with prejudice everywhere, those who exhibit these propensities respond to group "stereotypes." Their minds are distorting mirrors in which whole groups are seen as the incarnations of a set of unpleasant or menacing attributes. Frequently, under the goad of insecurity, they seek safety in a more rigid conformism, accompanied by intense dislike of groups that differ from the dominant pattern. Sometimes, instead, where the sense of rejection is too strong, they are likely to become equally intense in their repudiation of the established order and to join extremist movements dedicated to its demolition.

Thus the two types have in common the tendency to think

in undifferentiated group images, falsifying the social reality. In this primary respect the same educational approach is applicable to them both. Education should be directed so as to teach children the *habit* of making distinctions, in order that thereafter they may be less prone to lump people together in the slovenly rubrics of prejudice. All education is the learning of distinctions—why then should we be so backward in teaching children to make the distinctions that are most vital for the well-being of society? The infant begins by distinguishing the mother's breast; it distinguishes its mother from other persons, its mother and its father from the rest, its own family folk from the world outside. The young child distinguishes the larger family circle, those who belong from those who don't belong, his school from other schools, his play team from other teams, his associates of various kinds from nonassociates. The "ours" becomes enlarged and differentiated. *As he distinguishes he evaluates.*[15] But the differentiation is blocked at an essential point. The prejudice embodied in the mores blocks it at the frontiers of the "outgroups." At this point, as Llewellyn puts it, socializing becomes anti-socializing.

Here education can and should enter. Our survey of the two types of prejudice reinforces the conclusion that our social educating is still on the primitive level and needs to be redirected particularly in the following respects:

(1) We should not merely avoid, we should by our teaching reject, the tendency to dichotomize the social universe, dividing it into "ours" and "theirs"—"ours" being the good, the right, the proper, and "theirs" the antithesis of these qualities. We should in our teaching attack this tendency whether it has reference to the family, the near group, or the

15 For these processes see the works of Jean Piaget, especially *The Moral Judgment of the Child* (New York, 1932) and *The Language and Thought of the Child* (New York, 1926). One aspect of the subject is effectively developed in E. Lerner, *Constraint Areas and the Moral Judgment of Children* (Banta Press, Menasha, Wisc.).

nation. In our history books we should shun the implication that our cause was always wholly and altogether right and theirs wholly and altogether wrong. We should show our students that the social universe, like the physical universe, is complex and endlessly variant, and that different groups, peoples, and nations make different contributions to the sum of human achievement. We can teach them a deeper and more realistic regard for the achievement of our own group or our own people if we do not cheaply detract from the achievements of others. We can teach them that the group or the nation is distinguished not for some magic virtue of group or nation but solely by reason of the efforts, sacrifices, enterprises, and attainments of the men and women who compose it; nor does any one gain virtue or credit merely by belonging, for that property is common to the wise and the fool, the hero and the craven, the generous and the mean.

(2) We should teach them that they belong not to one community but to many, community beyond community, and that the greater embraces many groups, so that what is "ours" is also "theirs" and what is "theirs" is "ours." We should teach them particularly the multigroup nature of the nation community and of every great community—their city, their religion, their state. We should teach them the meaning of citizenship, which makes no distinction between group and group and which implies the equal rights and the equal opportunities of the members of them all. We should seek to give the students practice in thinking about the members of other ethnic or racial groups as citizens like themselves, as persons like themselves. We should seek to remove the sense of alienation from the members of these other groups, if possible by establishing and maintaining contacts with them in such wise that the students learn to know them as persons and not as wearing the badge of an alien tribe. We should not teach them that the others are *wholly* like ourselves, that differences are insignificant, but instead we should

teach them respect for difference and for the right to differ within the greater community.

(3) We should teach them that their personal likes and dislikes, their preferences and aversions, should not leap from the individual to the unknown group; that this is childish primitive thinking, and that hasty generalization is as pernicious in social conduct as in scientific investigation. What they hate and what they love, what they admire and what they detest, is another affair. But whatever their feelings and reactions they should be taught not to project these on whole groups because in some instance they have been so moved toward individuals. They should never assume that because, according to their kind, they dislike this Jew or this Gentile, this Baptist or this Roman Catholic, this Italian or this Mexican, the experience qualifies them to judge, or to generalize about, the multitudes who share the name or the faith or the origin of the particular offender.

Is it necessary to add that these many "shoulds" are not the elaboration of an ethical code professed by the writer and against which another code might set its own contradictory "shoulds"? *They are scientific "shoulds."* They are ways of stating that truth should be taught and falsehood convicted of its error. If this be the demand of *science* where the truth may have little relation to human behavior it is a still greater responsibility of *scientists* where the truth makes an important difference to social well-being.

Chapter Nine

The Educational Front

1. THE MOBILIZATION OF RESOURCES

THE EDUCATIONAL resources available or recruitable for the attack on inter-group discrimination are immense, but the difficulty of mobilizing them and of rendering them effective is great. Let us briefly review the major forces.

(1) First, there are the public schools, through which pass the vast majority of the children of the land. For the most part the schools are committed to the principle of group equality. It is hard to imagine the scale of the service the schools could render if they were fully equipped and ready to carry through their mission.

But there are many obstacles. Some lie in the educational system, some in the attitudes not infrequently found among the teachers or in their lack of training for the task, while another is the absence of any concerted and well-conceived overall program to unify, direct, and sustain the efforts of the teachers. In the first place the public schools are responsive to the socially dominant forces of the community. The policy that directs them is not prescribed by any central ministry of education. Not only has each state its own system but every city and town has its board exercising fundamental controls.

The boards are subject to the political forces that determine popular election. Hence they vary widely in competence and insight. But even the better ones are rarely qualified to construct the kind of program that would achieve the desired end, while the worse ones are often unwilling to advance it even if they could. The authority exercised by superintendents and deputy superintendents limits the policy-making of the school principals, and again the qualifications of the former for the educational promotion of inter-group equality are often inadequate.[1]

One particular fault on the administrative side is the maintenance of teacher segregation on racial or ethnic lines. Intergroup instruction is skewed at the outset so long as educational segregation exists and so long as minority groups are not properly represented on the teaching staff. Of seven "more or less representative" school systems in the United States, while all accepted the concept of inter-group democracy few followed it very far. "Administrators belonging to minority groups are very few indeed—a total of only seven Negro principals, two assistant principals, two Jewish principals, and one Jewish adult education director were found in all the systems together."[2] Discrimination in selection of candidates for college and university positions is also rife. It should be added that these serious flaws at the very heart of the educational system are not to be laid solely at the door of the administrators. There is, back of them, much resistance also from the dominant groups and sometimes a certain amount also from the teaching staff.

In computing the obstacles we should not forget the chronic weakness of the educational system in that the

[1] Cf. Theodore Brameld, *Study of School Administrative Practices and Policies Affecting Intercultural Relations*, Bureau for Intercultural Education, 1945.

[2] Theodore Brameld and Eleanor Fish, "School Administration and Intercultural Relations," *Annals of the American Academy of Political and Social Science* (March, 1946), p. 29.

scanty economic reward of the teacher not only affects his
status in the community but also diverts to alternative occupations many of those most qualified to follow the profession.
The difficulty is enhanced by the fact that in the poorer
areas, the areas largely inhabited by the foreign-born, the
areas in which the Negro or the Mexican forms a large part
of the population, educational standards are lower and the
chances of recruiting high teaching ability correspondingly
smaller. These conditions are reflected in such disparities as
the following: "Comparably for the nation as a whole, the
educational status of the foreign-born is, depending on residence, from one to two and a fourth years below that of the
native-born Whites. The Negroes, who of course are native-
born, are from three to four years behind." [3]

There is a second line of obstacles to be surmounted.
Whatever may be the limitations of the educational system it
is after all the teachers themselves who set the tone of the
instruction and by their attitudes and sympathies give or fail
to give wings to the lessons they seek to impart. The teaching
of the democratic equality of groups is not simply, perhaps
not even mainly, a matter of special courses or of a series of
lessons in courses in "civics" or "social studies." It is conveyed in the teacher's whole approach, in the spirit that
animates his teaching, in his attitude to the students, in the
incidental comments he makes on many things. The mere
routine performance of an assigned program is entirely ineffective. If the teacher is not himself alive to the issue no
recital of "facts" about races or ethnic groups will serve any
purpose. Many of his pupils come from homes where prejudice prevails. This makes the task of even the most convinced teacher a difficult one. But if the teacher has no
special competence or no special conviction—since he is

---

[3] E. de S. Brunner, "Groups and Educational Opportunity," in R. M. Mac-
Iver, ed., *Civilization and Group Relationships*. See in the same volume I. L.
Kandel, "Education and Group Advantage."

often a representative of a group which harbors prejudice—
the service he will render is negligible.

There remains for consideration an obstacle that meets
us everywhere when we survey the forces ranged against discrimination. These make a great array but they spread out
like detached commandos making independent and unrelated
forays on the enemy's lines. Some are trained and some are
untrained; some have good leadership and some have none;
there is no common strategy, no agreement on programs or
even on objectives. Hence there is much loss of energy, much
lack of direction. To discover the best procedures for attacking prejudice and discrimination requires careful study
and wise preparation. The proper training of the teachers,
the establishment of cooperative relations between the school
and the community, the making of an effective curriculum,
the selection of the best aids to the teacher in the way of textbooks and reports, these are matters that demand some sort
of headquarters staff or at least some central clearing house
to give advice and general guidance.

Some recognition of this need already exists. Some steps
have been taken to enlist the cooperation of school systems
in concerted effort toward a common goal. The National
Education Association has taken a lead in this direction.
Its Department of Supervision and Curriculum Development
has been taking an active part, in alliance with the Bureau
for Intercultural Education, and its Commission on the Defense of Democracy through Education has been making a
nationwide survey of the situation in the public schools, so
far as the teaching of democracy is concerned. This survey
should be very revealing. Another significant development
has been the project on Intergroup Education in Cooperating
Schools, under the auspices of the American Council on
Education with the support of the National Conference of
Christians and Jews. "School systems associated with this
project included Milwaukee, Cleveland, Pittsburgh, South

Bend, Denver, Hartford, Minneapolis, Newark, Oakland, Portland (Oregon), Providence, St. Louis, Wilmington, and Shorewood, Wisconsin." [4]

Through concerted action of this sort, based on studies of the situation in the schools and guided by carefully devised programs of genuine training and teaching, the educational system could be redeemed from its laggard neglect to give instruction in this important part of the business of living in America. There has been more than enough talk in the schools about the virtues of democracy; there have been more than enough orations in higher places about "education for democracy." But the lessons and the orations alike have shied away from the issue of how to bring democracy into the relations of men—partly because there have been no effective programs devised for this end and partly because of the fear of offending the interests and the prejudices of those who like to applaud the sentiment of democracy but dislike the attempt to practise it.

Besides the projects already mentioned some movements are on foot that are helping to create both a consciousness of the educational need and devices for meeting it. One of these is the scheme of "workshops in intercultural techniques" now being adopted at various centers for teacher training, such as Columbia and Harvard. Since a few training centers have a very important influence on educational thinking throughout the whole country, the development of such "workshops," in which inter-group understanding is directly and realistically fostered, should be highly serviceable.

Again, here and there within the multitudinous schools of the country, or in summer camps or elsewhere, experiments are being conducted in bringing the young to understand and to practise the way of life that freely and intelligently treats persons as persons and not as embodiments of a racial

[4] For further details see Mordecai Grossman, "The Schools Fight Prejudice," *Commentary* (April, 1946), vol. 1, p. 36.

or ethnic type. The most publicized of these experiments is the "Springfield Plan," which had the great merit of reorganizing both its educational activities and the relationships between the school and the community in such a manner as to make the equality of races and ethnic groups a living thing throughout the whole program of administration and instruction. Various other school systems throughout the country have been influenced by its example and have adopted some or all of its procedures.

(2) The second line of the educational front is made up of the numerous organizations that either include education among their activities or else make it their main concern. It is beyond our scope to review them one by one or to assess their respective activities.[5] These organizations comprise a number of distinct categories, as follows:

(a) *Organizations engaged in combating the various forms of racial or ethnic discrimination and not themselves associated with any particular racial or ethnic group or groups.* Some of the organizations listed in this class have titles that suggest a special concern with one or another form of discrimination, though their actual activities are not limited accordingly. Again, some of these organizations attack discrimination on a particular front. Thus, for example, the American Civil Liberties Union is prominent in promoting judicial procedures.

The list includes the American Civil Liberties Union, the American Council on Race Relations, the Bureau for Intercultural Education, the Council Against Intolerance in America, the Common Council for American Unity, the

[5] It would be of great service to the development of strategy if a forthright and detailed assessment were to be made. A beginning has been made in the report by Goodwin Watson already cited, but the research we have in mind would give a specific and particularized estimate of the activities and the contributions of all the more important organizations. A survey and broad appraisal of these activities is given in a report of the Committee on Techniques for Reducing Group Hostility, entitled *The Reduction of Intergroup Tensions,* by Robin M. Williams, Jr. (Social Science Research Council, 1947).

Union for Democratic Action, the Independent Voters League, the National Council for a Permanent FEPC, and numerous others.

(b) *Organizations particularly directed against some area of inter-group discrimination or particularly associated with one or more groups subject to discrimination.* The two groups that are well represented in this category are the Jewish and the Negro. In some instances the organization is wholly a creation of the group concerned, as with many of the organizations specifically combating anti-Semitism—it should, however, be noted that these organizations extend their interest to other areas of discrimination. In other instances the membership is general though the interest is more specific. It is significant that some large groups which suffer considerably from discrimination have taken no organized action of their own. This is the case with the Italian-Americans and with the Mexicans or more broadly the Latin Americans.

The list includes the American Jewish Committee, the American Jewish Congress, the Anti-Defamation League of B'nai Brith, and the coordinating body, the National Community Relations Advisory Council, all these being organs of the Jewish group; the National Conference of Christians and Jews; the National Negro Congress, specifically a Negro organ; and the National Urban League, the National Association for the Advancement of Colored People, and the Southern Regional Council.

(c) *Organizations associated with churches or more broadly with religious groups.* We include here the American Friends Service Committee, the Federal Council of Churches with its Department of Race Relations, and the Catholic Interracial Council; also the Y.M.C.A. and the Y.W.C.A., working both through their central councils and through local agencies.

(d) *Organizations belonging to the economic order.* Here

it is not easy to particularize, since there are a multitude of economic associations with endlessly variant attitudes and policies toward practices of inter-group discrimination. As we have already seen, some labor unions fight against discrimination and some fight for it, and there are tendencies in both directions to be found in employers' organizations. In general, the most steady aid comes from consumers' associations, cooperative associations, and CIO unions.

(e) *Organizations ancillary to the educational system.* Many educational organizations are interested in the cause, the leading agencies being the National Education Association, which has various departments specially devoted to this objective, and the American Council on Education. Effective work is also being done by organizations associated with schools of social work, and we may perhaps include here, so as not to expand our classification, such bodies as the Council of Social Agencies and the National Conference of Social Work. For the same reason we shall broaden our category to include training agencies such as the Boy Scouts and Girl Scouts. The full list would be considerable.

(f) *Organizations directly bound up with the political order.* We do not refer here to boards, commissions, agencies, or departments that are themselves a part of the governmental system, conducting administrative or executive functions, such as the state commissions against discrimination or the former FEPC. We have in mind the various advisory or auxiliary organizations set up or sponsored by local or state governments. There are, to begin with, many city or state committees appointed by mayors or governors the objective of which is to promote inter-group unity and to recommend measures calculated to reduce the barriers of discrimination between groups. Sometimes such bodies are merely a facade, serving the political interest which fears to alienate either the groups that discriminate or the groups that are discriminated against. Sometimes they work effectively for better inter-group relations and promote serious measures to this end, as has been done by the Mayor's Committees of New York and of Chicago. To this category belong also the local councils now being set up in states that have commissions operating under enactments against discrimination. Their function is presumed to be largely one of public education.

(g) *Research agencies proper.* There are of course research departments connected with many of the organizations already mentioned, but we reserve a special category for those research units that are free to initiate their own investigations, that are not subject to the direction of a more inclusive body, and that have no other commitment than that involved in the scientific pursuit of knowledge. Research work in inter-group relations is being pursued in a number of universities and colleges. We may instance the studies made under the direction of Kurt Lewin at the Massachusetts Institute of Technology (Research Center for Group Dynamics), under Paul F. Lazarsfeld at the Bureau of Applied Social Research of Columbia University, by Gordon W. Allport and his associates at Harvard University, and by Grace Coyle at Western Reserve, by Alfred M. Lee and others at Wayne University, and by Louis Wirth and others at the University of Chicago. Useful studies, especially of a local character, have also been made at various Schools of Social Work. Some of the great foundations, including the Rockefeller Foundation and the Carnegie Corporation, have sponsored, supported, and sometimes initiated, important investigations in this field, including the comprehensive Myrdal investigation made under the auspices of the Carnegie Corporation. A number of foundations place research in inter-group relations among their interests, including the Field and Harmon foundations, and one in particular, the Rosenwald Foundation, is primarily dedicated to this purpose.

Our list is quite selective and makes no pretension to give

techniques used to produce such effects. There is no mystery about them, they are known to every demagogue and rabble-rouser. They are easy to learn, though of course the "success" of the practitioner depends by no means solely on the techniques themselves but to a considerable extent on his own persuasive personality. But if we turn about to ask how the same techniques can be employed on the other side we make an untenable assumption. For these techniques are designed to play on already prejudiced attitudes in order to intensify them or at least to fan into activity established predispositions to prejudice. They may be of no avail when instead of seeking to stir the prejudices of the "in-group" against the "out-group" our object is to win the sympathies of the "in-group" for a cause that is out of line with their attitudes or predispositions.

Nor again can we learn any direct lesson from a study of propaganda operating under the condition of monopoly. The extraordinary power of propaganda where mass communication is monopolized is sufficiently illustrated by the history of Nazism and of Russian "Communism." But, whether the propaganda be directed to stimulate group antagonism or to suppress it, the condition of monopoly, with its concomitant of indisputable authority, with its hypnotic effect where no opposing voice can be heard, with its high premium on orthodoxy, and with its background of terrorism, precludes any satisfactory transference to the condition of democracy. Moreover, monopolistic propaganda can maintain itself only by identifying truth with official pronouncement, thereby making it impossible to search for truth or to convict prejudice in the only way in which prejudice must finally be convicted, by revealing its falsity.

The agencies of mass communication that take a stand against prejudice cannot then adopt, in any unqualified way at least, the methods employed by the other side. They have a more difficult task. This reflection brings us back to the point from which we started, that the mobilization of the educational forces engaged in the fight against prejudice is a process requiring the most careful investigation. The problem is still largely unexplored. In the sections that follow we shall deal with some of the leads that emerge from the evidences already before us.

2. COUNTERINDOCTRINATION

It is of high importance for the educational strategy-maker to realize that his business is not simply indoctrination, but primarily counterindoctrination. True, he can take advantage of favorable traditions and of congenial thought ways, but at the point of impact he is engaged in attacking established indoctrinations, not in sustaining them and not in promulgating novelties to which the prevailing attitudes are initially more or less neutral. In this sense he has to work against the grain of the mores. He must therefore avoid various approaches that would be permissible under other conditions—he must combine considerable discretion with his courage. Good intentions will give no wings to his message. Enthusiasm without perception of the resistance made by the folkways may be detrimental to the cause. Exhortation, at least before an audience unprepared for it, is usually vain, and reliance on it suggests either immaturity or naiveté. Denunciation is usually idle and often foolish. Gross satire or caricature is misunderstood, evokes countermockery, and has often a boomerang effect, especially where the viewpoint or attitude caricatured carries some social prestige or sanction. The hypothesis may be ventured that caricature is more powerful when directed against minority groups than when it is devoted to the cause of these same groups.[9]

9 Satire is a device that is more effective among the sophisticated than among the unsophisticated. Addressed to the latter, its point is often wrongly

We have in the preceding paragraph rather summarily dismissed certain obvious modes of appeal. We do not deny that there is occasionally a place for them, but the consensus of experience gives them a low rating.[10] There is another educational method which might seem to be both more effective and more scientific but which again experience, supported by psychological tests, shows to yield on the whole very disappointing results. This is the imparting of specific information calculated to refute prejudice, information about the groups who are its victims, information proving that the opinions of prejudiced people about these groups are contradicted by the evidence. Since this approach naturally—we might add, properly—appeals to the scholar we shall deal with it at greater length. Such information has certainly its proper usefulness, but we shall find that the truth that liberates us from prejudice does not consist of particular *facts*. The primary assault is on attitudes, not on opinions.

It appears to be a fair inference from observation and from research that information about the "out-group" is not of itself a potent determinant of our attitude toward it. The informed are hardly less prone to inter-group prejudice than the uninformed. There is frequently less prejudice against an "out-group" when few of its members live in the community than when many do—though presumably in the latter situa-

---

taken. Even the simplest satire, when designed to be educational, frequently misses fire. Thus a series of satirical cartoons against inter-group prejudice, the "Congressman Rancid" series, proved on test to be the subject of amazing misconceptions. (See report, *The Congressman Rancid Cartoons*, Bureau of Applied Social Research, Columbia University, 1946.) These cartoons, though still somewhat crude, were superior to another series entitled "Mr. Bigott," which portrayed a shrivelled, sickly-looking old-fashioned ogre who was fanatically proud of being a "one hundred-per-cent" American and displayed his profound contempt for all groups but his highly exclusive own. These cartoons were also subjected to tests, and the result showed that they rather completely failed to get their message across. See Paul F. Lazarsfeld, *The Personification of Prejudice as a Device in Educational Propaganda*, Bureau of Applied Social Research, 1946.

10 See Goodwin Watson, *op. cit.*, Chap. II.

tion the "in-group" has better opportunities to learn the facts. There is much less prejudice against the Negro in France or in England, where there are scarcely any, than in the Southern states where they abound. There was much less prejudice against the Japanese in California when they first arrived than later when they became a considerable group with important economic interests. Travellers to foreign lands are not remarkable for being less prejudiced than people who stay at home. More specific evidence comes from various researches, which suggest that there is a quite tenuous linkage between more information concerning an "out-group" and more favorable attitudes toward them.[11] All we can claim for instruction of a purely factual kind is that it tends to mitigate some of the more extreme expressions of prejudice and that, where there is any readiness to receive it, it provides some protection against the mob-rousing appeals to which ignorance is exposed. But where prejudiced attitudes exist any facts that run counter to it are likely to be discounted by the imputation of motives congenial to the prejudice. Indeed the imputation of motives, even among the educated, make attitudes proof against inconvenient facts. Thrift becomes selfishness and generosity ostentation; discretion becomes wiliness, caution cowardice, and courage aggressiveness. Information is a respectable ally of the forces that work against prejudice, but only when joined with these forces can information grow into understanding and understanding ripen into wisdom.

What knowledge of facts does is to enable us to apprehend differences more accurately, to discriminate more correctly, to avoid false or too sweeping generalizations concerning likenesses and differences. But the more accurate perception of differences is one thing and the evaluation of differences is another. Greater knowledge may not seriously change our

[11] Since the evidence is complicated and not free from seeming contradictions we examine it in Appendix 5.

evaluations, since the latter are so dependent on our prior indoctrinations and since our interests as well as our indoctrinations are constantly at work suggesting appropriate impu-
tations of motive such as will reconcile them with whatever
facts we may recognize or admit.

We conclude so far that neither exhortation (the evangelis-
tic appeal to principles and values that transcend prejudice)
nor the imparting of information (the logical appeal to facts
that contradict the misconceptions of prejudice) has any
considerable power to dissolve or seriously to undermine the
discrimination of group against group. Instead, however, of
taking on that account a defeatist attitude we should rather
explore the reasons why such methods carry so little weight
and make this explanation the basis of new and more potent,
if also more exacting and more slowly matured, attack upon
the problem.[12]

Let us examine a particular case. There is a consensus of
opinion that the counterindoctrination of delinquent youth
in institutions to which they are committed has little effect.
We are thinking particularly of one institution, a state school
for delinquent boys, that is exceptionally up-to-date in its
equipment and endeavors to apply the best-accredited pedagogical methods. Nevertheless the record shows that the great
majority of the boys remain impervious to its instruction.[13]
These boys are mostly members of youthful gangs or of
circles within which they become acculturated to delinquent
ways. They bring this culture with them and the inevitable

[12] There has recently arisen some controversy over the role of education,
especially in the schools, in promoting better relations between groups. The
defeatist attitude is suggested by a statement of Dean William F. Russell, of
Teachers College, Columbia University (quoted in an article in the *New
York Times*, November 24, 1946) that "there is considerable doubt as to how
far a school can serve human relations in areas outside of reading, writing,
and arithmetic." But Dean Russell had mainly in mind the methods of
exhortation and of the purveying of information, and it is well that the
limitations of these methods should be publicized.

[13] Fred Robin, *Crime School: a Study in Institutional Sociology* (to be published).

coercion and confinement of the institution makes them regard the staff as the agents of an alien and hostile culture, seeking to undermine the scheme of things to which they have been conditioned. Their response from the first is one of resistance. It is a struggle of wills, more particularly since the boys are subjected against their will to an external authority representing the alien culture. They devote their energies to eluding and stultifying the discipline thus imposed upon them and to re-affirming in their free relations with one another the old mores. The new rules, to which they must give a perfunctory obedience, are regarded as a temporary restraint to be thrown off, with all they stand for, when the great day of liberation comes. No process of education takes place under such conditions.

The lesson is clear. It is hard to know how to apply it to the training of delinquent boys, where the element of alien coercion is implicit in the situation, though even here promising experiments have been made.[14] But for the more normal give and take of education all that is needed for its application is a proper orientation on the part of the teacher. The lesson is that only where the sense of cultural barriers between group and group is dispelled can the prejudice that separates them be overcome. We do not mean that the sense of difference must disappear—not the difference but the barrier between differences is the peril. (So elementary a truth would not need to be stated except that there still lingers the ancient error that identifies concord with mere likeness.) The exclusiveness of the group must be broken by an educational process that integrates it within a more inclusive group. Prejudice is the expression of alienation and only the experience of the greater community can establish the bond of membership above the division of groups. The prejudiced person must learn to feel that the object of his prejudice

[14] E. M. Haydon, "Re-education and Delinquency," *Journal of Social Issues* (1945), vol. 1, pp. 23–32.

also "belongs." All communication—and education is simply one form of it—is the transcendence of separation. This principle has significance for the regular business of teaching, since if the class can be transformed into a team of which the teacher becomes himself a member there is awakened the feeling of participation in a common cause to quicken the whole process of learning and teaching.

The value of this principle is beginning to be recognized in the battle against prejudice. It is central in the programs of such investigators as Gordon Allport and the Kurt Lewin group.[15] It has a special role in the recently developed "workshops" in inter-group relations set up at various training centers. One type of such "workshops" brings teachers in training into cooperative contacts with members of the groups which are subject to discrimination. Another type brings together people of diverse positions and interests who are united in the objective of combating discrimination and prejudice. An example of this second type was the "workshop" convened in the summer of 1946 at New Britain, Connecticut. Under the direction of the Research Center on Group Dynamics, with the co-sponsorship of the Connecticut Advisory Committee on Inter-Group Relations and of the Commission on Community Interrelations of the American Jewish Congress, representatives of fifty communities met, teachers, administrators, businessmen, and others, and while they worked and planned for the common cause they developed among themselves the sense that they were not separately fighting for it but were, in their different communities, all members of the same team. When men pursue any cause, especially if it be an idealistic one, it is essential, in this modern world of many

15 Gordon W. Allport, "Psychology of Participation," *Psychological Review* (1945), vol. 53, pp. 117–132; Kurt Lewin and Paul Grabbe, "Conduct, Knowledge, and Acceptance of New Values," *Journal of Social Issues* (1945), vol. 1, pp. 53–64, and Ronald Lippitt and Marian Radke, "New Trends in the Investigation of Prejudice," *Annals*, American Academy of Political and Social Science (March, 1946), vol. 244, pp. 167–176.

interests, and of many divisions, that they first find sustenance in association with those to whom the same cause is dear. When the cause is that of inter-group understanding those who make it their interest must then carry the same principle further and seek to evoke in those to whom they appeal the consciousness of the greater many-grouped community that is frustrated by prejudice and discrimination. This task of education is no easy one, to be accomplished by resort to any ready-made techniques.[16]

To convey this understanding the teacher himself must be not only sympathetic but also alert and well-trained. Here again we find a serious limitation to the service of the schools. There is no reason to presume that the average teacher is liberated from the prejudices of the social group to which he belongs. The teachers designated to give this instruction should be carefully selected—which again implies wholehearted support on the part of principals, superintendents, and school authorities.

We have been pointing out that mere information, the purveying of "facts" about disprivileged groups, is quite insufficient for the dislodging of prejudice. Nevertheless it is very important that educators and leaders should be well equipped with relevant knowledge. Apart from other considerations those engaged in counterindoctrination must be prepared to rebut defamation. Prejudice is always cocksure of its "facts," the cocksureness of ignorance. If the speaker or teacher cannot properly refute such misrepresentations he loses control of the argument. He needs training on this account—at the very least he should be familiar with easily available literature in which the more common misconceptions of prejudice are corrected.[17]

[16] See Palmer Howard and Ronald Lippitt, "Training Community Leadership Toward More Effective Group Living," *Adult Education Bulletin*, August, 1946; also A. Zander, *Centerville Studies Itself*, University of Michigan (Adult Education Program), Ann Arbor, 1941.

[17] Convenient brief compendia of information, suitable for popular reading,

If, for example, the adversary is anti-Semitic and asserts in the style of Hitler that the Jews run an international financial conspiracy with headquarters in Wall Street the lecturer should know that only 18 per cent of the membership of the New York Stock Exchange is Jewish (*Fortune* survey) and that all of the eight leading banks in the business of private international finance—a no longer flourishing business—are non-Jewish. Or if the anti-Semite claims that in the United States the Jews control the press and overrun the professions the lecturer should know that less than one per cent of the press owner-publishers are Jewish (*Editor and Publisher,* December 17, 1938) and that, according to the *Fortune* survey, "the Jewish advantage in the professions . . . is rather shadow than substance."

Or again, if the adversary denies the claim of Negroes to economic opportunity or economic advancement on the ground that they are "unreliable," "dirty," "disease-carriers," and so forth, the lecturer or the teacher should have at his command the evidences of such reports as those issued by the New York State War Council or the Army and Navy reports already cited. Whether the objectives raised by the adversary are his genuine beliefs or merely some of the numerous smooth pretexts under which obstructive prejudice masks itself the most effective reply to his false generalizations is the ready appeal to actual experience.

On the other hand, many of the arguments made on behalf of prejudice are not of the kind that specific facts can refute. These are usually based on specious misconceptions of the

include Ruth Benedict and Gene Weltfish, *The Races of Mankind,* Public Affairs Committee Pamphlet No. 85, New York, 1943—directed against racial prejudice—and *To Bigotry No Sanction,* a brochure of the Philadelphia Anti-Defamation Council, revised and reissued by the American Jewish Committee, 1944—directed against anti-Semitism. A more inclusive popular work of this kind is needed. It should be sponsored by some educational authority and should carefully avoid the intrusion of social philosophies not directly relevant to its theme. Margaret Halsey's *Color Blind* is a well-written popular presentation of the case against race prejudice.

larger relationships of human beings. Most racial arguments
are of this kind. Or the prejudiced person will take another
line and maintain that the Negro ought to be thankful for all
that White civilization has done for him instead of complain-
ing because it doesn't do more. The Negro, he says, owes a
lot more to White civilization than he ever gave to it.[18] This
is a sample of the fallacy of collective responsibility and collective obligation. The conception of a racial debt is mytho-
logical. Moreover, every human being and every human
group owe a debt—if we accept the basis of the argument—
that is quite incalculable. All they have and all they enjoy,
all the civilization they possess, is the cumulative contribution of all the past, beside which any service they may render
is microscopic. There is no reckoning this way, and in any
event the particular contribution of any group to this sum
of achievement has nothing whatever to do with the question
of fair dealing between group and group. Ethical obligation
is not measured by such criteria.

It is inherent in the process of education that it leads
people along the road from rationalization to reason, for,
after all, rationalization postulates the validity of the reasoning process it abuses. Rationalization is an appeal to evidence,
a presumptive submission of the case to the logic of evidence.
The speciousness of the appeal is apparent in that, when the
evidence is refuted, the rationalizer is most likely to resort
instead to some other rationalization and, if driven far
enough, may finally take refuge in a dogmatic hide-out, such
as the tenet that there is a "God-made" difference between
White and Negro. Nevertheless, for the effect on others if
not on the protagonist of prejudice himself, it is highly desirable that the speaker or teacher be not caught unawares
by the twisted arguments turned against him. Even the ancient catch-question, "Would you like your sister to marry a

---

[18] Myrdal, *op. cit.*, vol. II, p. 1233, quotes a "letter to the editor" in the
Richmond *News Leader,* in which the writer makes much of this argument.

Negro?", may cause trouble unless a fitting answer is immediately forthcoming. There are various ways to put the questioner in his place. One answer might be: "No, not so long as there are so many prejudiced people like yourself to make the situation intolerable." Or, more simply, "Do you disapprove of dealing fairly with people unless you would like your sister to marry them?"

We have in the foregoing discussion been diverted from considerations of strategy to those of tactics. Let us sum up the main argument. The educator cannot put his main trust in the logical power of facts that rebut prejudice. Facts alone cannot rebut prejudice. Owing to the operation of the "vicious circle" there are always *some* facts that support the position of prejudice. At the same time, since prejudice by its very nature distorts the truth, the educator should be well-grounded in the requisite knowledge, not only because it should be part of the instruction he offers but also because otherwise he is unprepared to meet the false charges and the rationalizations of the prejudiced. Nevertheless his fight is not against scientific misconceptions but against emotionally charged attitudes. Prejudice becomes "woven into the very fabric of personality." He must seek to counteract that process in the young, and where it is already well advanced he must face the long and difficult task of enlisting on his side and strengthening those elements of the prejudiced personality that can be made responsive to his appeal.

3. NOT BY WORD ALONE

A serious difficulty meets us when we ask for tests of the efficacy of educational programs, whether they take the form of sustained indoctrination in the schools or of organized social activities or of sporadic appeals through the agencies of mass communication. We saw that little attempt has been

made to assess the value of school courses and of the more ambitious "plans" developed by some educational systems. But
we are no better off if we want to learn how far press or radio
campaigns are of service to the cause. To take the radio, for
example, we find a study by two members of the research
department of the Columbia Broadcasting System, the purpose of which is "to demonstrate that educational programs
have been relatively unsuccessful." [19] Now what these authors
do is to use an ingenious device called the "Program Ana-
lyzer" to test the responses of a sample of listeners. By this
test educational programs show up none too well—and it is
useful to know that fact. But even if the showing were a
good one it would not necessarily be an indication of success
from the educational point of view. It would show that the
listeners liked the program—not that their education was advanced by it. They might like it for certain adventitious
features of popularity—how far it influenced them, and for
how long, is a different matter. The criterion of responsiveness is better than none at all, but it is quite inadequate. We
lack the kind of test that measures the success of the advertising of toothpaste or of the wartime appeal to buy Victory
bonds. Incidentally, the authors of the article in question
suggest that the reason for comparative non-success is that
"producers of such programs have not completely adapted the
educational content to the peculiarities of radio as a medium."

Certainly we have very little *conclusive* evidence at our
disposal concerning the effectiveness of educational appeals.
We know from tests that some devices should not be employed, such as the repetition of rumors in order to refute
them, or the use of cartoons that grossly caricature the ways
of prejudice, or the proclamation of the special merits of
minority peoples. We can without great difficulty apply tests

to define whatever change of attitude is the immediate response of students or listeners. But, apart from the difficulties of analysis and interpretation considered in Appendix 5, there is the more serious problem that we cannot reckon the longer-run results. The student is exposed to many other influences, in his home and in his social contacts of various kinds. It is unlikely that we can trace the more permanent influence of the indoctrination he receives. Possibly, it is entirely dissipated in later years. Possibly, here and there it is like seed sown in receptive soil, which in time comes to full growth in the value-system of personality. As for the more sporadic broadcasting of appeals against inter-group prejudice, their value is still less amenable to direct assessment.

These considerations should lead us to take with caution the claims sometimes made by sponsors of educational programs. There has been a tendency to extol the merits of certain experiments in this field, *though practically no checkup has been made of their efficacy*. Such experiments may be very valuable but they need to be subjected to constant critical re-examination. Without constant skilled appraisal the pursuit of programs for the betterment of inter-group relations, no matter how finely sponsored, no matter how heavily financed, no matter how loudly applauded, may be not only futile and wasteful but even detrimental to the cause they support.

At the same time we should avoid the opposite tendency, so congenial to a certain type of scholar who demands infallible proof in a context that offers no prospect of its attainment, and when it is not forthcoming dismisses the experiment altogether. This attitude fails to recognize the conditions and limitations of all social strategy. In the first place there can never be any *proof* in advance of action that action will succeed. The business man when he makes a decision can never be *certain* that it will achieve its objective.

The wisest general can never have absolute assurance that his plan of campaign will work. It is the very essence of strategy to go by the best indications available and never to flinch from making decisions because there is always a possibility that they will go wrong. If the scholar does not accept the same limitation then the guidance he is qualified to give in matters of social strategy will be lacking. He must be content to follow the lead given by his experience, his knowledge of social situations, his analysis of probabilities, and he must not let his very proper longing for complete verification have a paralyzing effect on his social wisdom. In the second place, when the decision is taken and the experiment made, he must again be content to make his verdict discretional. Having assessed the results by the best methods at his disposal he must then set aside his measuring rule and use his judgment.

We have some knowledge, and we can attain more, on the basis of which this judgment can be exercised. We know that some modes of appeal are better calculated than others to produce results. We are learning a good deal concerning the social psychology of discrimination and aggression. We are learning where gains have been made and how these can be advanced. We know some of the weak parts of the enemy front. We are discovering what potential resources can be evoked and enlisted on our side. We know something of the conditions under which inter-group tensions are increased or diminished. We know the speciousness and hollowness of many arguments put forward in defense of discrimination and segregation. By mustering and focusing this knowledge we can with reasonable confidence develop the art of strategy, recognizing that every practical art succeeds when, based on the appropriate knowledge, it has the fortitude and the imagination to take the steps necessary for its application to the problems it must face.

The primary reason why we cannot measure the long-run

efficacy of educational programs and policies—and it is one that holds for every other mode of attack on prejudice and discrimination—is that their power is relative to the degree in which they support and are supported by other forces working within the community. Education is dynamic only in its dynamic interaction with the trends of social change. Social education is itself a process of molding the thought ways of the group, and especially of the young, so as to bring them into harmony with the presumptive demands and needs of society. To serve this end the scheme of education must not be limited to the purveying of information. For social education is practical education, instruction in the art of living. To teach an art is to teach the practice of that art. Hence education against prejudice implies the provision of conditions under which the student learns to abjure prejudice. In other words, social education acts not by word alone: it seeks also to provide occasions and situations, contacts and adequate opportunities, for acting out the principles it promotes.

That is the merit of such educational schemes as bring the student into cooperative relationship with members of groups against which the bias of his society is turned. Through continuing relationships of this kind he can hardly fail to learn, if properly instructed, the difference between real human beings and the false image of them constructed by prejudice. To educate against prejudice is to promote new relationships in which the element of prejudice is banished. It is not enough to establish contacts where none existed before. Some kinds of contact, as we have already suggested, increase, instead of diminishing, prejudice. The overseas tourist is not conspicuous for his better understanding of the peoples he visits. The slave owner had plenty of contacts with his slaves but he generally remained profoundly ignorant of them as human beings. In our present multi-group society men come into frequent relations with groups against which they bear prejudice, but the prejudice is not thereby lessened. If we enter into social relationships within a pre-established frame of prejudice and under the drive of interests that are sustained by prejudice no progress in understanding is to be expected. The educational mission is at the same time to set up a truer frame of reference and to introduce and develop a corresponding system of relations.

Education should plan for the same kind of free intergroup relations that emerge without any planning where conditions are favorable. We saw that a not infrequent result of the working side by side of Whites and Negroes in the same plant, where the initial prejudice is not too virulent, is an accommodation in which the Whites accept the Negroes into the partnership of labor. During the last war, when Whites and Negroes shared continuously the same perils and responsibilities the Whites are reported as having come to learn their common humanity with the Negroes. A Southern officer on a submarine chaser that went through a perilous expedition is quoted as saying, of the Negroes on board, "half way through the trip I forgot they were black." [20] A War Department study of White officers and platoon sergeants who served in companies with Negro platoons showed that while 64 per cent reported having originally felt unfavorable toward serving in a "mixed" company (having both Negro and White platoons) 77 per cent stated that after service in such units their attitudes had become more favorable.[21] Other army studies showed that the rank and file were also more ready to participate in "integrated" programs after they had some experience of them. That White workers tend to move, through experience, in the same direction is confirmed by an OWI survey, which contains the following state-

[20] Eric Purden, "The Story of the PC 1264," *The Nation*, August 25, 1945.
[21] "Opinions about Negro Infantry Platoons in White Companies of Seven Divisions," Information and Education Division Report No. B-157, Hq., A.S.F., July, 1945.

ment: "Those who reported having worked with Negroes were more inclined than those who had never done so to advocate equal pay for equal work." [22]

What happens in these situations is that a process of spontaneous inter-group education takes place. The common task, the common problem, the common cause, the common danger, or whatever it be, requires that the members of the one group deal realistically with the members of the other. They come to know one another as they actually are, to test out one another, as human beings face to face, and this knowledge eats through the distorted images, the "stereotypes," with which they started. They may remain critical one of another, they learn the shortcomings of one another as well as their good qualities, but the White man sees the Negro as he actually behaves, no longer through the blur of prejudice. He sees him as a person, and if we could teach men to look on other men, the members of other groups than theirs, as persons, the primary goal of inter-group education would be achieved.

The same process of spontaneous education frequently occurs where people of different groups live side by side, on shipboard, in camps, in settlements, in housing developments. Segregation, here as elsewhere, is the ally of prejudice. Let us consider, for example, those housing experiments in which Negroes are allowed to participate along with Whites. It is a common charge that if Negroes are admitted within a general housing program Whites will refuse to enter and in any event property values will be deteriorated in consequence. Occasionally public housing proposals, in areas where antidiscrimination regulations would not permit the exclusion of Negroes, are limited in scope or even abandoned altogether because such charges are believed to be true. Nevertheless there is a growing amount of evidence

[22] "White Attitudes toward Negroes," Report No. 30, Extensive Surveys Division, Bureau of Intelligence, OWI, in conjunction with NORC, July, 1942.

that the charges misrepresent the facts. Given a well-planned and sufficiently large-scale housing project, chances are that the investment in it will not be adversely affected by the presence of Negroes and that the Negroes accepted under it will not seriously lower the social status of the area.

The contrary view has been supported by two main considerations. One is that the areas in which Whites and Negroes are usually mingled are run-down and dilapidated. But in such areas it is precisely the deteriorating conditions, such as the invasion of business or industry into a residential district, that account for the "mixed" character of the residents, since these areas no longer maintain the restrictions that bar the Negro from other areas. The second consideration is that, owing to the congestion of the Negro sections, the admission of Negroes into another area is likely to be followed by a continuous expansion of its Negro inhabitants so that it becomes in effect a Negro district, with all the effects on its amenities that flow from a decline in residential status. Hence it is perfectly natural that White residents should become panicky when there is a prospect of the entrance of Negroes into their neighborhood. What the Whites fear is the consequence of their own discrimination, a consequence no less formidable on that account.

However, in various larger-scale housing experiments the proportions of the two groups are stabilized—the percentage of the Negro population may range from 5 to 70—and under these conditions mixed housing has, according to the available reports, been remarkably successful. There has in most instances been no exodus of White residents. There has been a strong tendency for Whites and Negroes to come to look on one another as neighbors, after the first apprehensions of the Whites were allayed. The children of the two races join in the same games and tend to forget, if they ever knew, any barrier between them. These housing experiments need more careful study than they have yet received. They have been in effect experiments in inter-group education.

Not all the experiments have been successful. Much attention has been directed to the "race riots" that prevented, for about two months, the occupation by Negroes of the Sojourner Truth development in Detroit. This housing project was designed to provide quarters for Negroes engaged in war work. It was not strictly a "mixed housing" project but it gave Negroes access to an area beyond the limits of previous segregation. There was vacillation on the part of the political authorities, and the lack of resolution gave an opportunity to opposing elements to stir up serious trouble. Though we cannot go into particulars here there is much evidence that the problem, an old one in the city of Detroit, was badly mishandled. It is true that Detroit presented a particularly difficult situation. Mr. Frank S. Horne of the National Housing Agency speaks of this city as "housing problem area number one." The city maintained a pattern of rigid and sealed residential segregation in the face of a vast influx of White and Negro workers of every sort. Intelligent leadership, political and social, was requisite to meet an urgent need—and it was not forthcoming.

Wartime conditions brought with them a considerable number of public "mixed housing" projects. These fell into various categories. Of 468 projects 171 were "controlled" in the sense that the management assigned buildings or sections exclusively to Negroes or to Whites, 142 were "partially controlled," and 80 were "uncontrolled," the remainder being left unclassified in the statistics.[23] The reports for the different categories are on the whole encouraging. Some projects of "open occupancy," in Seattle, New York City, Los Angeles, and Chicago, have been highly successful. Of the Seattle war housing project, for example, it was reported

[23] Statistics provided by Mr. Frank S. Horne.

that "all men live side by side, without conflict or disturbance, proving that racial harmony is possible." [24] There
was, however, some contrary testimony. One project (Bremer-
ton) in the state of Washington reported that the situation
was unpleasant until Negro tenants were separated from
Whites in the dormitories. But the more general verdict was
that the program had worked out successfully, even where
there was initial restiveness or friction. It is evident that a
clear-cut policy, announced from the first, is essential. It is
also evident that a great deal depends on the management.
One of the first responsibilities a wise management will
accept is that of the careful selection of the initial representatives of minority groups. The lessons to be derived
from these crucial experiments in democratic education are
numerous, and they should be carefully explored. [25]

[24] *Housing the People,* 6th Annual Report of the Housing Authority of
the City of Seattle, 1945.

[25] A study now being made by my colleague, Professor Robert K. Merton,
on behalf of the Lavanburg Foundation gives admirable point to the statement above. It is an intensive study of residential morale in two communities,
one of which has a population half White and half Negro while the other
is a combination of Jewish and non-Jewish residents. We cite with permission
the following passage from the report, unpublished at the date of writing:
"From three-quarters to nine-tenths of a cross-section of the American
public has expressed itself as favoring residential segregation of Negroes.
The great majority of Whites expressing this view in the North have not,
of course, lived in the same neighborhoods with Negroes. In the absence of
direct experience, they could only give voice to a deep-seated prejudice.
That a considerable proportion of these would have different opinions is
indicated by the Lavanburg Foundation study of Hilltown, an inter-racial
housing community in Pittsburgh. Before moving into this project, only
4% of the whites expected race relations to turn out well, whereas 21%
were convinced that it would involve nothing but conflict. Most of the
remainder had their doubts. After a few years, fully 21% found that race
relations had turned out better than they had anticipated. Only 6% felt
that it was worse than their expectations. More importantly, 3 of every 4
who had expected serious racial conflict found that their fears were un-
founded. Direct experience had shown what general admonitions for tolerance would probably not have shown: that inter-racial fears and hostilities
were exaggerated and distorted beyond all resemblance to the reality."

Chapter Ten

Some Conclusions

---

1. THE INVESTIGATIONS WE NEED

OUR INTENTION, when inaugurating the present work, was to levy tribute on the work of scholars in this field, seeking to derive from their investigations such leads or evidences as had a practical bearing on the social control of discrimination. As the work advanced, we were led to broaden the basis of evidence, partly because historical and contemporary experiences of the processes of discrimination supplement the testimony of specific researches but partly because the available researches proved less helpful than we had anticipated. Before, then, we seek to sum our direct conclusions we shall offer some comments respecting the kinds of scientific research we need as aids to social strategy.

The initial questions we set to ourselves and our collaborators (Appendix 1) proved largely unanswerable from the available data. There is no reason why research should not supply adequate answers to these questions. The reason it fails to do so at present is that so little of it has been focused on matters of strategy. Thus, one of our colleagues, Dr. Hartley, remarks: "To date, research workers in social psychology have not been oriented toward the problems of social control in any direct way." Psychologists have been much more concerned with the inner structure of the prejudiced person than with the social impacts that determine it or the social impacts that might, especially in early years, recondition it. Sociologists have been more concerned with the modes of discrimination than with modes of control over it.

One reason why social researchers tend to shy away from the practical problem is that they do not care to commit themselves to findings that are not susceptible of complete demonstration, or that are not invincibly verified by the evidences they present. It is hardly necessary to point out that these desiderata can never be satisfied with respect to any conclusions whatever regarding strategy. If strategy had to depend on such verification it would never develop—never even begin. The judgment that decides between practicable alternatives is in this particular different from the judgment that decides between true and false. Nevertheless every intelligent choice of alternatives is determined by the weight of evidence. It is of vast importance in all practical affairs to calculate probabilities, and the calculation of probabilities is just as scientific a procedure as the verification of data and assuredly requires no less competence. If the social engineer has to take some other kind of scientist as his model he should choose rather, say, the meteorologist than the laboratory chemist. The cases are not really parallel but at least the social researcher should recognize that the meteorologist is performing a thoroughly scientific function—and a very useful one at that—in predicting the weather, even although he must deal in probabilities. And because he is willing to deal in probabilities he learns to make his predictions progressively more accurate.

We hold that much of the potential social benefit of the already vast amount of investigatory energy now directed to inter-group relationships is lost because this activity has so little bearing on the question of strategy. As we have pointed out, there have recently been some real advances in this respect, but very much remains to be done. While we have much knowledge that challenges the policy-maker we have very little that can guide him.

What is needed for practical purposes is not so much a new series of detached studies concerning the nature, conditions, and effects of inter-group prejudice and discrimination, but far more a direct and coordinated exploration of the methods by which these phenomena may be combated and controlled. New research projects should be designed primarily to meet this need so that any practical findings they may offer will not be afterthoughts but the fulfilment of the primary objective.

This conclusion is fully corroborated by those social scientists who have devoted themselves to the subject. Donald Young, for example, sums the matter up as follows:

What the social engineers need from research in addition to data about the nature and causes of Negro-White discrimination is information about the conditions of cooperation and the relative merit of techniques by which group hostilities may be reduced. So far most research has been on problems of racial maladjustment. It is much more exciting to study riots than it is to try to find out why no outbreaks have occurred in a community where they might reasonably have been anticipated. It is also more interesting and easier to write about barriers to Negro progress than it is to study conditions which have facilitated it. From the engineering point of view, this is analogous to learning all about defective timbers and flawed girders while ignoring the qualities of sound materials. Of course maladjustments must be studied, and much more effectively than they have been, but just as much and possibly more can be learned from the more common and less dramatic examples of inter-racial accommodation.[1]

One series of such investigations would be concerned with thorough analysis of the utility of the action programs conducted by organizations of various kinds. These investigations would fall under two types. One type would examine specific unified programs that have been put into operation, such as, say, the Springfield Plan. The purpose would be to

[1] "Techniques of Race Relations," *Proceedings,* American Philosophical Society (April, 1947), vol. 91, pp. 150–161.

assess its service as a teaching device, to sift the available evidence accordingly, to undertake experiments and tests where these are deemed desirable, to distinguish short-run from long-run effects, to consider the manner in which the plan cooperates with the forces and conditions in the community that work in the same direction, to examine the impediments, in the teaching system itself, in family life, in the mores of the various groups, to the fuller attainment of the objective, and so forth.

The second type would take up the action programs of specific agencies, whether group-oriented agencies, community organizations, political organizations, foundations, and so forth, in order to weigh the use of methods and techniques, the coherence of the program, the selection and distribution of resources in pursuance of objectives, the conditions determining the choice of projects, the follow-up of past projects, and so forth.

Studies of this kind would give much-needed guidance where little now exists and would certainly aid in redirecting activities so as to minimize waste, duplication, false starts, hit-or-miss efforts, untenable ideas about the value of certain organizational procedures, while at the same time they would give a new impetus and backing to the more advantageous lines of social action. Among foundations we might instance the Rosenwald as providing opportunity for such a study; among group-oriented organizations the American Jewish Committee and the American Jewish Congress; among civic endeavors the Mayor's Committee on Unity in New York or the similar committee in Chicago or the Cleveland or Detroit programs.

A related and equally promising mode of study would be to have researchers act as "participant observers" of action programs as these are being carried through. Their function would be that of checking the reactions of those to whom the program is addressed, keeping them under continuous observation so as to estimate the evanescence or permanence of the impacts of the program, examining the relation between the successive stages of the program and the responses it elicits, all with the constructive purpose of making recommendations for its improvement.

In some areas there is a fine opportunity for the combination of project activity with investigation into its success, but in none more so than in the educational area. Take particularly school programs designed to reduce prejudice against minority groups. Let us suppose plans have been made by a research group to investigate the utility of these programs. It would be highly serviceable to invite, on a voluntary basis, the participation of teachers of psychology and of the social sciences in the schools throughout the area. No doubt a considerable majority of such teachers would be ready to cooperate. They would be furnished with various tests for school use and with other materials useful for the purpose of the investigation. They would be expected to report regularly to a staff of trained investigators. With their aid different techniques could be tried out with different groups and comparative studies made of student reactions. A program of this magnitude would involve the support of the school authorities, and probably it could be undertaken only under the auspices of a large foundation. But it promises results well worthy of the effort and of the expenditure. For it would give not only intimate guidance on methods of inculcation but also a new stimulus to the teachers themselves. All the more alert and capable teachers would gain new interest and deeper experience. Not only the methods of teaching but in many instances the attitude as well as the skill of the teachers would be advanced.

The same principle could be applied to the exploration of various problems that can be effectively studied only over a large range. For example, we know that parental attitudes are of significance for the attitudes of the children. But some children react one way, and some another. How do the various types we might thus distinguish respond to this or that mode of school indoctrination? What are the characteristic responses of children of different age groups, status groups, and so forth, to the teaching of social tolerance? It is easy to see that such inquiries might be developed in various ways and on various scales of magnitude. But our object here is not to propose specific programs of research but only to suggest an orientation that, while offering no easy or short road, nevertheless would turn to more promising endeavors the accumulating interest in one of the most challenging of social problems.

2. THE BROAD LINES OF STRATEGY

In this section we set down some major recommendations that have emerged in the course of our work. Some of them obviously require much fuller development than we have been able to give them in the course of this preliminary survey.

(1) *The primary attack on discrimination should rally to the cause of* national *welfare and* national *unity. It should not uphold the banner of particular groups.*

The national aspects of inter-group discrimination have not received adequate attention. The distinctively inter-group culture that has developed in the United States and that is reflected in its national tradition and in its political structure is threatened by the growth of inter-group tensions and by the prevalence of inter-group discrimination. The consequences to national unity, to the strength and the integrity of American nationhood, are ignored or disregarded. Discriminatory practices are sustained by narrow interests and are accepted by a larger public that remains unconscious of their more profound import. Prejudicial and defamatory conceptions of large groups of their fellow citizens are entertained by the more influential circles of practically every community. In their clubs comfortable gentlemen refer with frivolous unconcern to groups of other ethnic origins as though they were lesser breeds. Everywhere groups accept irrational and highly distorted images of other groups. Intellectuals are as susceptible to this social contagion as are the unlettered—sometimes even more susceptible. "Vicious circles" of many kinds abound in which smouldering resentment lies at the other end of a diameter from smug superiority. The frustrated groups, unable to share in and contribute to the community life, develop their quotas of racketeers, black market operators, gangsters, and so forth, and though these form only a small minority of such groups they suffice to confirm the prejudice of which they are themselves a product. The more sensitive members of the disparaged groups become frustrated, socially inbred, and not infrequently psychopathic. The intellectuals among them not only are subject to the same tendencies, but also are tempted to become the leaders of subversive movements. All disparaged groups tend to become disaffected—and there is some evidence that the degree of disaffection is proportional to the intensity of discrimination—and when the range of discrimination is so great as it is in the United States the resulting loss to the solidarity of the national life, to its healthful vigor and strength of purpose, must be considerable.

Not only does discrimination generate disunity and a masked caste system wholly alien to the faiths and loyalties in the strength of which America has become a distinctive nation, not only does it stimulate and sharpen the exclusiveness of all the narrow interests that in pursuit of immediate prestige or economic gain override considerations of the common welfare and of their own long-run advantage, it has a further consequence of particular moment at a time when the United States is thrust into a position of world leadership. It diminishes our influence in world affairs and tends to discredit the more far-reaching programs of our statesmen.

It follows that those who seek to educate our people should

lay primary stress, not on the disadvantages and frustrations suffered by the disparaged groups or by any one of them in particular but on the common loss, injury, and discredit that the country as a whole, majorities as well as minorities, sustains from the cleavages, rifts, and tensions that ensue from the prejudicial and undemocratic treatment meted out to large portions of the citizen body. *This lesson should be the background of the teaching of citizenship, for the young and for adults alike.* The untoward effects of all kinds, cultural, intellectual, and economic, that proceed from our attitudes and practices of discrimination should be brought home to the consciousness of the people. This knowledge should provide the perspective for the application of the more specific considerations discussed in our study.

To make this knowledge dynamic it must be presented so that any moderately intelligent person can see its significance and understand its bearing on his own behavior. Instead of regarding the abstention from discriminatory practices as at most an external obligation, something that may be abstractly owing to an unesteemed fellow man, it should be seen as something every man owes to himself and to his own group and in a very practical sense to his country. If this side of the case were clearly and tellingly exposed it might count heavily against the gratification of egotistic aggressiveness, the comfortable sense of belonging to a superior group, and the occasional calculation of a possible economic advantage, so far as these are the motivations that determine the discriminatory behavior of the average man. There are types of prejudice that are more deeply rooted in community conditions and community mores, particularly the color prejudice in the United States, and in some areas the anti-Semitic prejudice. Such prejudice would be challenged by indoctrination that no longer segregated it from the more inclusive prejudice to which it belongs but showed it as a more extreme form of the same thing, confirmed by old traditions and by the established acceptance of the relationships conformable to

it. Thus challenged it would become less resistant to the
forces that can be marshalled against it.

(2) *There is no one direction of attack on discrimination
that should be given pre-eminence or overall priority. All
the fronts are strategically important, and the attack on several at once is more effective than the attack on one alone.*

There are those who say the only cure for discrimination
is the economic one, and some advocates of this view pin their
faith solely on economic transformation or economic revolution. There are those who, from a quite different approach,
deprecate any action on the politico-legal front. Such claims
needlessly divide the forces making against discrimination.
They ignore the lesson of the "vicious circle." We should not
minimize any agency of attack. We should not regard any of
the fronts, say the educational or the political, as either subsidiary to the others or as dominant over the others. There
need be no question as to *where* to attack, but only over the
how. There are, it is true, particular merits associated with
one or another front, and we have sought to do justice to
these in the text. But the total situation that sustains inter-
group discrimination is constructed of complexly interwoven
forces, and when we weaken any one of them we weaken the
whole.

(3) *Wherever the direct attack is feasible, that is, the attack on discrimination itself, it is more promising than the
indirect attack, that is the attack on prejudice as such. It is
more effective to challenge conditions than to challenge attitudes or feelings.*

It is better strategy to raise the economic level of the disprivileged, to remove the barriers to economic opportunity
or to occupational status, to assure the right to vote, to break
down the wall of segregation, to drive wedges into the discriminatory system at its weaker points, and so forth, than to
refute directly the prejudices or myths that justify these
handicaps. It is more expedient to strike at tangible than
at intangible impediments. Above all, it is most rewarding

to promote changes that, once inaugurated, are hard to revoke, to establish institutional forms that, once accepted, tend to create habits and conditions favorable to their maintenance. This is likely to happen when specific laws against discrimination are passed and carried into operation, or again when a higher standard of living is attained for a group that has been exposed to prejudice.

In putting forward this conclusion we are not at all contradicting our previous principle, that the attack, to be successful, must be developed on every front and not on any one front alone. We are not in the least minimizing, for example, the vital importance of the educational campaign. We are talking here about more promising *methods*, not about more promising fronts. No front can be more important than the educational. But when we deal with the service of education we lay stress on such aspects as the provision of avenues for easy and natural acquaintanceship of the members of one group with those of another. In other words, we think of education as doing two things: on the one hand as providing a basic understanding of the situation so that those who are responsive to the lesson will be more ready to take positive action against discrimination, and on the other hand as setting up appropriate conditions, such as opportunities for congenial inter-group contacts, so that anti-prejudicial habits and reactions may be stimulated. We have just shown that education has the grand function of exposing the national perils of discrimination, and of inducing those who are thus awakened to these perils to organize and seek remedies against them. In fulfilling this function education is making precisely the flank attack on prejudice and the direct attack on discrimination that we regard as the most promising method—not the method that should *alone* be adopted but the method in furtherance of which the strongest forces should be deployed.

(4) *Discrimination and its evils are likely to be exacerbated by any changes that increase tensions or promote crises*

*in a society, no matter what their source, whether economic,
political, ideological, or any other. On the other hand discrimination is likely to be diminished by any changes that
make for the general well-being of a society or that provide
more constructive outlets for the aggressive tendencies of its
groups.*

A few brief illustrations must here suffice. We noted that
discrimination tended to be worsened by a depression. In
any aggravated disturbance feelings become narrowed and
embittered, as in the crises that accompany wars and still
more during those that afflict defeated peoples. On the other
hand, the processes that bring about general prosperity—
as distinct from the exclusive advantage of any class or group
—tend to reduce the discrimination of group against group.
Thus the recent economic gains of Southern Negroes, modest
though they have been, accompanying some general economic
advancement in the South, have worked to mitigate the
severity of segregation and of the attitudes that accompany
it. It is not implied here, however, that under all conditions
economic improvement will have favorable reactions, since
the conditions determining discrimination vary from case to
case.

Better conditions, better opportunities, better equipment
for living, at least permit the diversion of aggressive tendencies from the lower range of suppressive hostilities waged
between group and group and provide means that good
strategy can employ to encourage such diversion. Thus in
congested and poverty-stricken areas there sometimes arise,
among youths and adolescents, bitter inter-group feuds. Were
adequate playing grounds, gymnasiums, and so forth, available the urges that express themselves in these feuds might be
given healthier outlets in team rivalries and in the competition of sport.

(5) *It is the primary business of strategy to explore and
attack the weaker points in the position of the discriminatory
forces, the lines of least resistance.*

As one reviews the multiform activities of organizations working in this field one gets the impression that hit-or-miss programs have been the rule. There are notable exceptions, and generally there is an increasing recognition of the need for preliminary planning. In many cases, however, this function is still taken too lightly. The careful assessment of opportunities and obstacles, together with such accounting as may be possible of the results of earlier programs and of the experience of other organizations, is the most exacting and the most rewarding of the activities that such organizations can undertake.

In the text we give illustrations of two types of weakness in the enemy ranks. One is best seen on the economic front. Here the back lines are held much more strongly than the forward lines. There is, for example, powerful resistance to the entry of Negroes to positions of responsibility and authority in industry, but at the same time the intermediate functions that lead up to these positions are more exposed to infiltration and seizure, and each advance makes the next one easier. The other is evidenced on the ideological front. The myths, traditions, prejudices of various kinds that bolster up discriminatory practices are inconsistent with and contradictory to other principles upheld by the discriminators. Advantage can be taken of this ambivalence. *Here the most effective way may not be to accuse the discriminators of inconsistency, of the betrayal of certain creeds they profess, but rather the direct appeal to these creeds themselves.* For here the enemy cannot strike back, and he is strategically at a great disadvantage. When men, for example, proclaim the principle of "fair play," when they are committed, in defense of their own economic system, to the doctrine of "a free field and no favor," then we can powerfully use that plea by demanding that they apply it to the Negro when he seeks the opportunity to prove his economic worth.

(6) *It is of primary importance to evoke appropriate leadership. The opposing forces are organized. There are*

great potential forces that can be rallied and organized to fight discrimination.

What leadership can accomplish is indicated by the role it has already played in the establishment of the wartime FEPC and in the passage of antidiscrimination laws in a few states. It is indicated also in the initiation of far-reaching educational programs and in the recent advances made in some Southern states.

The kind of leadership we require varies according to the basis of discrimination. Where discrimination is dominantly social, as in the case of anti-Semitism, there is great need that men and women of high social prestige should take a clear stand and set a clear example. Where discrimination is strongly correlated with economic subjection men of standing in the business world can be very influential. Since discrimination raises primary moral issues and since it is often defended on pseudomoral grounds an unequivocal crusade by religious leaders is of the greatest importance. This leadership has on the whole been hitherto rather fitful and unimpressive, although there have been notable exceptions. Again, where the situation that has been designated the "indifferent equilibrium" is found, resolute action by business executives and by trade union leaders will be decisive.

(7) *Strategy should always be adapted to the prevailing mores.*

This principle has many applications, of which only a few are dealt with in this work.

It does *not* mean that no action should be taken until the mores of the community are ready and ripe for it. There is always division and some conflict within the creeds and thought ways of a modern community. The mores are always imperceptibly changing. Good strategy will seek to discern and to take advantage of the trends of change. Good strategy will at the same time endeavor so to frame its policies that they will not, then or later, arouse latent antagonisms or increase actual ones so as to endanger the

objectives it seeks. For this reason radical demands, where
the mores are strongly resistant to them, are often dangerous,
especially if they are put forward by the minority groups
themselves. They may serve sometimes to rouse the public
to a consciousness of the problem but if pushed too hard
they may provoke a revulsion that will militate against
progressive measures.

The public is not good at making distinctions. Good
strategy must always remember this. For example, *the public
easily confuses news prominence with importance.* Hence it
is injudicious to give prominence to false rumors, even for
the sake of showing their falseness. For the same reason legal
measures should not be taken, except in extremity or in the
face of a manifest and grave danger, against rabble-rousers.
The attention they thus receive gives them larger proportions
in the eyes of the public. The less notice taken of them, in
the press and through other agencies of communication, the
better.

(8) *Minority or subject groups themselves have an essential part to play in the conquest of the discrimination to
which they are exposed.*

The fact that certain groups are the victims of more severe
and more persistent discrimination than others is not due
to chance or caprice. Nor is it usually to be explained by a
sheer clash of interests, though sometimes economic conflict is involved. We have seen how the "vicious circle"
operates to maintain discrimination. This means, among
other things, that the discriminators find a justification for
their behavior in the plight, the attitudes, or the behavior
of those they discriminate against, even where these conditions are themselves the consequences of discrimination. In
this situation both sides react in a way perfectly "natural"
to human beings, and *both sides* have to learn, for the sake
of a better society, to control such reactions. The natural
resentments of disprivileged groups may take forms perilous
to their own advantage, whereas these feelings can be directed

instead into disciplined well-planned assaults not on the discriminating groups but on the common enemy, discrimination. The sense of frustration often drives men to rash compensatory behavior, to the consequences of which they themselves are blind. Wild denunciations, sporadic violence, incitements to subversive or antipatriotic behavior increase the resistance of the other side. We should not forget that the discriminators have no monopoly of prejudice; that malady may be just as rife among those who suffer from the prejudice of others.

The Jewish situation offers a good illustration of the general problem. Both because of their exclusive cultural tradition and because of the persecution they have suffered the Jewish people have been in an exceptional way set apart from other peoples. But detachment within a community is a strong stimulus to discrimination. To help defeat discrimination they must, in spite of obstacles, find ways of identifying themselves with the community as a whole. There are fine examples of how this can be done without resort to a colorless assimilation. They must avoid any imputation that they detach their interests from those of the community. They must particularly restrain the revulsion that expresses itself in doctrines that advocate the overthrow of the whole institutional scheme of things. They must somehow place the symbols of their own group under the sign of the great community.

3. CONCLUSIONS CONCERNING THE VARIOUS FRONTS

A. *The Economic Front*

The economic front offers particularly good chances for a breach of the "vicious circle" of discrimination. *Social* status is strongly guarded by tradition and ideology. Economic interest presents no such unified or deeply entrenched opposition. Economic interest is not solid against the economic

claims of the disprivileged. If their advance is against the
competitive interest of some it is in conformity with the bargaining interest of others. Moreover, it is easy to show that
the longer-run interest of all is seriously reduced by the
denial of economic opportunity. Besides these general considerations and others put forward in the text there are some
specific features of the economic front that indicate the direction of strategy.

(1) *The forward positions of the forces of economic discrimination are the least strongly held. It is eminently the
area in which continuous advance is feasible through the
lines of least resistance.*

We have given perhaps sufficient illustrations of this principle. There would be tremendous resistance if members of
a disadvantaged group, such as the Negroes, were to claim
admission to high executive positions in finance or industry,
where none of them had hitherto risen beyond the ranks of
semiskilled labor. But the way from semiskilled labor to
skilled labor, from skilled jobs to the responsibility of foremanship, from foremanship to lower executive functions,
and so forth, is a gradient that is nowhere too steep to be
climbed by successive well-directed advances. Each advance
provides an habituation on the part of the dominant group
and an experience on the part of the advancing forces that
together make the next advance no more or little more difficult than was the one before.

(2) *Changing economic and technological conditions offer
opportunities that should be seized at the earliest possible
moment.*

Economic conditions, largely as the result of advancing
technology, are always in a state of transition. New industries rise and grow. New methods of economic organization
are devised. New materials are developed and partially sup-
plant old ones. New forms of motive power are harnessed for
industrial purposes. Consequently new skills, new techniques,
new occupations of various kinds, new businesses and new

forms of business are always appearing. Unless concerted
action is taken at an early stage the old patterns of discrimination will fasten themselves on these new enterprises. What
has happened respectively in the business of airplane production and in the business of air transportation furnishes a
good object lesson. In the automobile industry, again, we
have an example of how a policy adopted in good time can
set new standards.

In various ways economic change can be turned to advantage in the fight against economic discrimination. For
example, the changing structure of industry, responsive to
technological change, has greatly increased the range of industrial trade unionism as opposed to craft unionism. Now it
is the older craft unions that have been particularly exclusive, whereas the newer industrial unions have on the whole
accepted a position opposed to discriminatory membership.
This gives an opportunity for an attack on exclusiveness in
the craft unions as well. For many members of craft unions,
such as the machinists, operate within plants and corporate
structures that include a predominance of industrial union-
ists and they can be put under pressure to accept nondiscriminatory policies applicable to the plant or the industry as a
whole. Apart from this development altogether the growth
of unionization makes it harder to segregate any group of
workers from participation in the wage scales and other
advantages the workers derive from trade union bargaining.

(3) *Modern trends have brought it about that government
itself, if taken in all its range, is the greatest of all employers
of labor. Considerations of political expediency, not to speak
of the professed principles of democracy, make government
as employer particularly susceptible to campaigns for the
equalization of economic opportunity.*
We have seen in the contrast between the governmental
employment of Negroes during the First and the Second
World Wars respectively what a difference it makes when

energetic and organized demands for fair employment practices are made on government. The change in civil service
regulations is another result of well-directed effort. Much
more can be achieved along the same lines. Where in the
country at large a group is in effect barred from certain occupational avenues or where its entry into them is severely
limited governmental action thus brought about can set a
precedent that will aid toward a wider opening throughout
the country of the gates of opportunity.

The policy we have just been advocating serves to illustrate again the danger of one-sided emphasis on any particular line of attack. We have pointed out the great advantages
of action on the economic front, but that action is far more
effective if it is supported by concerted effort on the other
fronts. If the economic sector offers remarkable promise it
does so only when educational campaigns proclaiming the
dangers of discrimination are brought to bear, only when
voluntary organizations of various kinds raise powerful protest, only when political action supplements and reinforces
economic trends. If during the Second World War there
were opened up "more than one-and-a-half million jobs to
workers once excluded from these jobs on grounds of race or
creed," [2] this advance was due to the combined impact of
many forces.

B. *The Political Front*

Before summarizing our conclusions under this head we
take occasion to refer to the report entitled *To Secure These
Rights,* issued in the fall of 1947 by the President's Committee on Civil Rights. The report itself is a sign of the
times, and tends to confirm our estimate of the significant
trend that has set in among the American people toward the
removal of the disabilities from which so considerable a body
of our citizens have been suffering. The reception of the

---

[2] Felix S. Cohen, "The People vs. Discrimination," *Commentary* (March,
1946), vol. 1, no. 5.

report is further evidence in the same direction—the "good press" it generally received, the fact that the 26,000 copies of the report were exhausted within two or three days of publication, the reprinting of it in full by the newspaper *PM*, and the immediate announcement of a popular edition by a commercial publisher. This reception was given to a program of action for the political control of discrimination that goes drastically further than any ever presented before in this country by an officially sponsored text. It recommends not only a series of measures to strengthen the civil rights enforcement agencies of government, including a permanent Committee on Civil Rights and a congressional Joint Standing Committee for the same end, but also numerous specific enactments to defeat certain forms or practices of discrimination, to abolish poll taxes, to remove present exceptions to the right of naturalization, to abolish discrimination in the armed services, to establish a federal Fair Employment Practice Act, to repeal obstructive laws such as the alien land acts, and so forth.

Some of these proposals may be realized in the immediate future, others are problematical, some are not within the present range of practical politics. The Committee, for example, roundly recommends "the elimination of segregation, based on race, color, creed, or national origin, from American life." It recommends that all the states of the union pass laws to end discrimination in employment and in admission to educational institutions. In other words, it is a statement of objectives that should be pursued, to be attained as soon and as far as possible. Our own proposals in this concluding section and throughout the work are of a rather different character. We are concerned with the strategy that can win the objectives of nondiscrimination, with the policies and modes of attack that can lead us to the goals and standards envisioned by the Committee.

We include here two major types of action, one expressing itself in legislative, judicial, and executive procedures on

the part of government and the other consisting in the
exercise by subordinated groups of political rights, beginning
with the right to vote, and in activities designed to assure
these rights and to give them extended scope and efficacy.

We pointed out the essential importance of political action,
so understood, and the unwisdom of minimizing its role.
At the same time we showed the undesirability and the peril
of certain forms of coercive political control over prejudicial
propaganda or over the discretionary judgment of qualified
authorities in the selection or rejection of *individual* candidates for professional training, educational recognition, promotion, honors, and so forth. Our negative conclusions may
be summed up as follows:

(1) *No expression of opinion should be outlawed merely
on the ground that it is defamatory of or prejudicial to any
social group, whether ethnic, racial or other. Still less should
any censorship be set up to check such expression of opinion.*

(2) *The machinery of the law should not be invoked to
prosecute rabble-rousers or the advocates of group antagonism except where definite incitements to overt injurious
actions against groups are made or where, in times of crisis,
such activities create clear and present danger to the immediate vital interests of the state.*

(3) *While government may reasonably take action to
check discriminatory policies in public educational organizations, in nondenominational organizations receiving special
grants, immunities, or privileges from the state, in organizations that control the training for, entry to, or right to practise, professional or other vocations, such action should not
take the form of determining whether particular candidates
are or are not qualified to meet the standards set up by these
organizations but should rather be directed to determining
whether the weight of the evidence is or is not adequate to
show the presence of discriminatory policies. Any political
regulations made on such grounds should not be of a local*

character but should have at least a statewide application.

We turn next to the great positive contributions that political action, in the inclusive sense already indicated, has clearly shown its capacity to make.

I. *Legislative and Executive Action*

We have pointed out that much legislation that is not in the first instance directed against inter-group discrimination may nevertheless be helpful in reducing it. Any measures of social legislation that improve the economic condition of the more depressed groups will tend to have this effect. During the recent war federal policies strengthened a movement in the Southern states that transferred a considerable percentage of Negroes from agricultural and domestic service employments to industrial employments—a change advantageous to their economic opportunity and their social status.[3]

Concerning measures particularly directed against discrimination the following conclusions are well established:

(1) *The experience of the FEPC and of four State Commissions against Discrimination shows that laws prohibiting discrimination in employment can work, smoothly and effectively, in all states where there is enough popular support to secure the enactment of such laws.*

It is not contended that such laws achieve the abolition of inter-group occupational discrimination. But they do reduce it and can be increasingly potent as they become fully operative and promote new habits and expectations.

(2) *Given concerted effort the chances are strong that similar laws can be passed in a large number of states and in the District of Columbia. Thus the way would be prepared for federal legislation and for an appropriate supplement to the Bill of Rights.*

(3) *It is a weakness in the operation of existing legisla-*

[3] Seymour L. Wolfbein, "War and Post-War Trends in Employment of Negroes," *Monthly Labor Review*, January, 1945.

tion that its implementation depends so largely on individual complaints brought before the commissions. This weakness should be remedied by carefully planned programs for positive action developed under these commissions.

(4) *Antidiscrimination forces should organize campaigns for the curbing of restrictive covenants, seeking to secure municipal and statewide regulation to this effect, with the further goal of having such covenants outlawed altogether, so far as discrimination against race or ethnic group is involved. Every new housing development, public or private, and every city-planning project should be required to take into consideration the impact of the program on the present living space and future opportunities of those groups that are suffering from residential congestion.*

Besides the policies advocated above there is, of course, the primary objective to turn law from being an agency for the maintenance of inter-group discrimination into an agency for the advancement of inter-group equality. In various respects, particularly though not exclusively in the Southern states, law ratifies and perpetuates discrimination. Through segregation statutes, poll tax requirements, and numerous special impositions law forges chains against the democracy it professes to serve.

II. *Judicial Action*

In this category we include two very different processes. The courts are engaged not only in the administration of justice but also, on the upper level, in the authoritative interpretation of the Constitution. Both of these functions may be, and have been, so conducted as to give aid and comfort to the advocates of discrimination. Both may be, have been, and should be so conducted as to serve the cause of evenhanded justice and democratic equality. There are obviously therefore strong reasons why strategy should be brought to bear on the judicial arm of government.

In the administration of justice the groups that suffer from discrimination have found, too often, that the scales have been weighted against them. The prejudice that prevails in the community has seeped up to the judicial level, especially in the lower courts. In the South the prejudice of juries against the Negro has been notorious and the judge has not seldom been of like mind with the jurymen. There have been happy signs of change, but there is still vast need for progress. Moreover, the biased attitude of the courts gives shelter to the brutality of sheriffs and police officers who trample down the most elementary rights of those to whom the community has already denied a decent chance.

The kind of strategy called for here is obvious enough. It is a combination of education and political pressure to ensure:

(1) *that injustice in the name of justice is exposed and remedy demanded;*

(2) *that biased officials and judges are exposed and defeated at the polls;*

(3) *that, particularly in the Southern states, Negroes are permitted freely to exercise their constitutional right to serve on juries; and that in the Southwestern states the same right is freely accorded to "Mexicans";*

(4) *that, where high-court decisions give a narrow or restrictive interpretation of the range of civil rights, campaigns are inaugurated for federal statutes to fill the gap in constitutional coverage;*

(5) *that when cases involving civil rights, especially as they relate to discrimination, are before the courts the liberal viewpoint is presented in as effective a form as possible, subject to the conditions of proper legal procedure.*

III. *Voting and Other Modes of Democratic Action*

We are here concerned with the exercise of political rights by the citizens of a democracy. Much more could be said on this subject than is suggested in the text. It is one of the most important areas for the development of strategy against discrimination. Many of our previous conclusions have inevitably introduced the method of political pressure. Here we deal with more specific kinds of political action.

In the last resort appeals and manifestoes and protests and even "marches on Washington" owe their effectiveness to the political consequences they portend. It is mainly because citizens can vote that politicians give heed to such demonstrations.

(1) *There is only one good reason why minority groups of an ethnic or racial character should be politically organized, and that is to combat discrimination and assure to themselves equal opportunities within the community.*

(2) *Groups suffering from discrimination have been slow to develop their potential voting power for this purpose. Such considerable groups as the Italian-Americans or the "Mexicans" have no effective organization. The Negroes have local organizations but have scarcely learned how these can make common cause for common ends. It should be a primary objective to organize, educate, and marshal these groups for the fight against discrimination.*

(3) *When we speak of the political organization of groups we do not mean that singly or in any combination they should constitute political parties. They should instead formulate programs with the object of getting them adopted by major political parties and should constantly be ready to throw their weight in favor of whichever party is more favorable to their cause.*

Before we leave the political front we should observe that government can fulfil one function of broader scope than those with which we have been dealing. We have throughout insisted that discrimination must be attacked on many fronts. But can we turn the many fronts into a united front?

There are many organizations but they all act not only independently but usually without much recognition of what the
others are doing. Can such recognition be brought about,
preparing the way for larger cooperation? There would be
many advantages; there would be less undirected effort, less
duplication; there would be new stimulation, better timing
of activities, an enhanced sense of the importance of the
common cause and a new concentration of the activities devoted to it. Probably the most effective agency for bringing
together the numerous and diverse organizations working in
the field would be the government, the government not as
lawmaker but as guardian of the unity of the nation. Our
government has already convoked in a similar way the organizations engaged in promoting certain aspects of national
well-being, such as public health or child welfare, calling
them all under its auspices to a forum for the discussion of
their common interests and their mutual needs.

No one can deny that the issue before us is one of great
national concern. It is equally certain that, however far-
reaching the direct function of government may be, it needs
to cooperate with the other agencies that by different methods
and especially through the education of public opinion are
working toward the same end. *Why then should not the
government provide a central bureau of information and
service, and convoke from time to time, perhaps through a
central Civil Rights Committee, conferences on inter-group
discrimination, enlisting in united effort all organizations that
are ready to make common cause against a common peril?*

C. *The Educational Front*

Education is a far-ranging activity. It may be thought of as
including every mode of persuasion and exhortation no less
than direct instruction. It may cover propagandism in all
its forms. In this broad sense most of the conclusions we have
already stated contain educational prescriptions. Now we

shall deal with educational action in a more definite sense, with special reference to school and other educational organizations, whether directed to the young or to their elders.

Here the primary function of education is to reveal the nature and the consequences of discrimination. To fulfil this function education must explore the background of discrimination and particularly its relation to *prejudice*. On this topic we limit ourselves to a few general conclusions.

(1) *Prejudice is natural to human beings but it becomes concentrated, sanctioned, and developed in the traditions and usages of the social group. The social acquisition of prejudice begins at an early age, and therefore it is important that the counteracting of prejudice should begin with the very young, when they are most impressionable and have not yet become structured in the attitudes of prejudice.*

(2) *The impact of social prejudice is continuous, and therefore the process of counterindoctrination cannot be effective if it is limited to any age period.*

(3) *The process of counterindoctrination demands great skill as well as great persistence in educational effort. Education should be concerned not so much to show the contributions and the qualities of particular groups as to impart a sense of the greater common heritage, the transcending common interest, so that the concept of what is "ours" becomes inclusive, not divisive.*

(4) *"Better education," in the sense of fuller and more accurate information about dispriveleged groups, accomplishes relatively little. To be effective, education against discrimination must be dynamic, that is, it must show the vital relation between the facts it teaches and the greater values and permanent interests of all groups alike.*

(5) *Besides the type of prejudice that depends mainly on social conditioning there is another type that takes its particular character from the frustrations or maladjustments suffered by individuals in their early life history. This second type, to*

*which the more extreme "agitators" and "rabble-rousers"
tend to belong, yields at best to more specialized treatment,
whereas for the first type the problem is essentially one of
effective counterindoctrination.*

We turn next to the services that are or can be rendered
by three major agencies, so far as they are enlisted in the
struggle against discrimination. There are (1) the schools,
including colleges and universities, (2) voluntary organizations engaged in some kind of educational activity, and (3)
the agencies of mass communication, particularly the press,
radio, and moving picture. First, the schools. We shall sum-
marize later concerning the appropriate content of education
in this area. Here follow preliminary propositions of the
"physician heal thyself" type.

(1) *There is still a considerable amount of discrimination
in the recruiting of teachers. So long as this continues the
schools are handicapped in the fulfilment of their educational
function. It is contrary to enlightened educational policy that
members of minority groups should be disadvantaged, apart
from their qualifications, as candidates for teaching positions.*

(2) *In certain areas the school systems are themselves wholly
dedicated to discrimination, carrying it to the limit of segregation. While in some of these areas no immediate reform
can be looked for there are others in which a concerted campaign might suffice to bring this practice to an end. This is
the situation with respect to the segregation of Mexicans
and other groups in the schools of California.*[4]

(3) *The schools and school systems that do undertake education against discrimination generally lack (although there
are outstanding exceptions) well-prepared programs. There
are too few qualified teachers, there is no adequate training
for a difficult task, better aids to teaching could be provided,
there is little overall guidance, and frequently no realistic*

[4] See, for example, Mary Hornaday, "Segregation in the Schools of California," *The New Leader,* May 10, 1947.

contacts are made with community conditions. Various surveys show the need for a much wider cooperation between school systems to remedy these deficiencies.

We come next to the organizations working on behalf of better inter-group relations. These are so varied and so numerous that little can be said about them within the scope of our investigation. Taken together, they constitute a great educative power. But while some of them are well adapted to the functions they undertake there are not a few others that follow hit-or-miss methods with little or no checkup on the results of their activities. Some of them do not realize that the cause they seek to advance requires of them much more than goodwill and missionary zeal. Very many of them would benefit by submitting their programs and policies to searching appraisal. In doing so they should consider also their relation to other organizations in the same field, so as to change mere duplication of effort into efficient cooperation.

Finally there are the agencies of mass communication. It is true of all the media through which education is conveyed that they can be employed to provoke intolerance and to heighten tension no less than to spread enlightenment and inter-group understanding. And unfortunately the techniques for the stimulation of passion and intolerance are simple enough, whereas there are no equally sufficient techniques for the dissipation of prejudice. The media of mass communication have generally two great advantages, first that they reach vast numbers of people and second that there is in one way or another, according to the medium, a constantly repeated exposure to their influence.

There remains the question of educational approach or educational strategy. We have devoted considerable space to this question and shall single out here only a few salient considerations.

(1) *Education against inter-group discrimination is necessary instruction for the business of living in our modern*

multigroup society. As such, it should not be directed simply or even mainly to the dislodgment of prejudice, but more positively to the advantages of tolerance, mutual understanding, fair play, and equal opportunity.

Education should not point merely to the evils of discrimination. It should dwell on the meaning and the conditions of democratic participation. If it exhibits cases of prejudice it should still more offer examples of the broader vision and present cases of large-minded finely tolerant personalities. It can find eminent instances of such in the history of the United States. If education brings out the consequences of discrimination it should be even more concerned to show the positive benefits that flow from community life where it is not rifted or cleft by inter-group barriers. We can find, in the United States, communities where there is relatively little discrimination as against others where discrimination rules. There are cases of successful accommodation in "mixed" housing projects. The gains that accrue to all from the spirit of accommodation should be shown, not merely the losses that are entailed by the absence of that spirit. It is a mistake to stress the differential, even if it is for the sake of bringing out the contributions of this group or of that group; it is essential to give meaning and vitality to the concept of the commonwealth.

(2) *The most plausible way to justify discrimination is to point to the undesirable habits, manners, and attitudes of the groups in question, to their inertness, lack of initiative, "immorality," and so forth, or again to their aggressive ways or subversive ideas. Education can effectively meet these pleas, so far as they have any ground in the facts, by explaining the principle of the "vicious circle."*

We can show by this method that the association between discrimination and unlikable or unpleasant qualities imputed to the groups subject to it does not at all justify but on the contrary condemns discriminatory practices. The lesson must, however, be thoroughly conveyed, since it disturbs the congenial complacence that goes with a sense of superiority.

(3) *Education should always combine action programs with whatever instruction it offers. It must not confine itself to facts and principles about group relationships; it must help to form habits appropriate to these facts and principles —habits of doing as well as habits of thinking.*

In this endeavor the schools must be in living touch with the community. They must train the student to enter into such relationships with members of other groups as will remove the sense of alienation or distance and will dislodge the distorted type-images that prevent him from meeting the members of these groups as persons in their own right. We need everywhere in modern society to develop personal contacts across the lines of specialization, and above all across the lines of ethnic and racial division. To be fully significant, these contacts should bring people together in cooperative activity toward common goals. They should not be merely sporadic or occasional. It is particularly desirable that they be initiated in childhood, so as to check from the earliest years the false constraints and prejudicial "stereotypes" that scar and threaten to cleave asunder the multigroup community in which our lot is cast.

Race and Ethnic Group

THE TERMS "race" and "ethnic group" are employed in a confusing variety of ways and sometimes are given a meaning that has no scientific warrant.

Race. The term "race" should never be used to signify *species* or permanent genetic divisions of the genus *Homo.* We know of no such species. "Our human groups, though biogenetically valid, are not fixed constellations in the universe of nature." [1] For taxonomic purposes we can distinguish three (or four) "races" of mankind, but here we use the term "race" in a freer sense. We mean by races clusters of peoples with some geographical identification, each cluster exhibiting typically a characteristic combination of minor physical differences genetically transmissible. But there is a vast amount of variation, and, moreover, the characteristic differences tend to be modified in the members of these races when their habitat is changed. The physical differences in question refer to color of skin, color and texture of hair, cranial formation (long-headed and broad-headed types), color of eyes, and so forth. We get different results according to the criteria we select as primary. On the other hand, there are certain more important genetic differences between human individuals, such as the differences between blood types, that occur within all peoples and have no association whatever with the racial distinctions we draw. We get our inclusive race groups by giving emphasis to skin color, so that in the usual classification we have the white, yellow, and black races.

Furthermore, there is no scientific confirmation of the socially

---

[1] W. M. Krogman, "The Concept of Race," in Ralph Linton, ed., *The Science of Man* (Columbia University Press, 1945), pp. 59–60.

derived theories that one or other of these races, so defined, is intrinsically superior genetically. There are marked differences of intellectual advancement, of artistic achievement, and of other historically exhibited qualities between human groups, whether taken as races or as ethnic groups. But these differences are so clearly related to environmental differences and to historical conditions operative through many generations that it is impossible to attribute them to different genetic potentialities. Given favorable environment and social opportunity the members of races or of ethnic or other groups that have low historical rating show such responsiveness as to discountenance the doctrine of innate racial superiority.[2] Heredity is of course a potent factor. There are great differences in the genetic potentialities of different individuals. But heredity, which works in exceedingly complex ways, offers no explanation of the differential achievements of different races or even of different peoples.

Ethnic group. By ethnic group we mean a body of people, a folk or folk-element associated with a particular territory in which its ancestors developed certain cultural characteristics of their own, usually including a distinctive language. Through prolonged exposure to the same physical and cultural environment, combined with inbreeding, the ethnic group may acquire distinctive, though highly variable, physical modifications. In its home territory the ethnic group often becomes a nation, that is, a community so coherent in sentiment that it possesses or at least strives to possess political autonomy. But the ethnic group as such is not a nation. For one thing, the original group, while remaining in its home territory, may be incorporated into a larger nation, as has happened to the Welsh and the Scotch. For another, portions of the original folk may become ethnic groups by migration to other lands where they retain for a time, within the new state, some of the characteristics of their forebears. Thus the Italians, the Czechs, the Poles, and so forth, may still constitute ethnic groups within the larger citizenship of the United States. Again, we should call the Jewish people, or the section of it resident within any state, an ethnic group, but certainly not either a nation or a race. There is no "Semitic" race, and the folk we call Jews spring from a Mediterranean area where many

---

[2] The researches of Boas, Klineberg, Dahlberg, Ashley-Montagu, and others bear out this point. See, for a short summary, Otto Klineberg, "Racial Psychology," in Linton, *op. cit.*

peoples mingled and mingled again but where out of the min-
glings there arose a distinctive group made coherent and compact
by religious faith and social usages.[3] Because of their separatist
religion, and because, after losing their home territory, they
became migrants into many lands where they clung tenaciously
to their religious culture and were often segregated and often
persecuted, the various Jewish groups have been strongly "en-
dogamous" and thus tend to have distinctive facial characteristics
and other visible signs of difference from the peoples among
whom they have dwelt. This fact has encouraged the false notion
that they constitute, in any sense, a race. They are an ethnic
group differing from most others by the fact that to a large extent
they adhere to a religion peculiarly their own.

Incidentally, there is no English noun corresponding to the
adjective "ethnic," just as there is no English adjective corresponding to the noun "folk." It would be more convenient if we
could use "ethnos" and "ethnic," "folk" and "folkic."

The identity of the ethnic group with the culture group is not
genetic but historical, a product of community life. Wherever
people form communities or demarcated groups within a larger
community they develop cultural differences. Wherever groups
live under different conditions or are exposed to different treatment within a community they develop cultural differences.
There is, for example, a Ghetto culture, but it belongs to the
Jewish Ghetto, not to the Jewish people as such. Where different
ethnic groups come together in the same environment the identity of the ethnic with the culture group ceases to hold. Cultural
differences develop within the same environment, for neither
environment alone nor native potentialities alone bring a cultural pattern into being—but they no longer follow ethnic lines
—unless social restraints prevent the different groups from shar-
ing in a common culture and imparting to it new elements from
their various heritages.

It is important for the understanding of the ethnic group that
we do not define it as a culture group. Neither the racial group
nor the ethnic group has as such, when it shares the conditions

[3] C. S. Coon, "Have the Jews a Racial Identity?", in J. Graeber and S. H.
Britt, *Jews in a Gentile World* (New York, 1942). One advantage of placing
the Jews as an ethnic group is that they no longer are regarded as in an
anomalous position, identified neither by "race" or by "national origin" but
given a pseudo identification as a religious group.

of a common citizenship in a common social environment, a separate culture. Some groups retain distinctive elements of their earlier culture, as does the Jewish group, but they also acquire many characteristics of the common or national culture, and many of their members become wholly absorbed into the prevailing culture. Some groups—and this is as true of the Negroes as of, say, the Italian-Americans—cease after a time to have any differential or at least any nonindigenous culture at all. In the United States they become as essentially American as any other portion of its citizens. Under these conditions conflicts and antagonisms based on ethnic or racial differences have no longer any intelligent ground or intrinsic meaning. They are nothing more than the factitious and wasteful strife of dominant groups and subordinate groups, majority groups and minority groups. The association of this strife with differences of economic interest as well as with differences of ideology is solely the result of relative position or standing. Such conflicts are as prejudicial and as futile—though fraught with very serious consequences none the less—as the squabbles of Swift's "big-endians" and "little-endians."

Social Science and Social Action

DOES KNOWING give guidance to doing? No one doubts that knowing how to do enables us to do. That is the realm of the applied arts, the techniques. But when the knowing is not the knowing how to do, when it is the knowing how things are, as is the case with the knowing of the scholar, and particularly of the social scientist? The student may know much about government—does it teach him to govern? He may know much about economics— does it teach him to construct wise economic policies? Can he, should he, draw conclusions regarding the practicability of social or economic measures? Does his knowledge instruct him concerning methods that offer the greatest chances of success in the fulfilment of social objectives?

Social scientists not infrequently refuse to draw such conclusions. Let us admit that there are two kinds of risk involved. In the first place the conclusion is always inferential. It is never categorical knowledge. Its formula is not "A is b, c, d" ("Water is H_2O") but always "If you want A do b, c, d," where A is an objective and b, c, d are processes. The technologist makes assertions of this type but he is dealing with repetitive processes, where the conditions can be held constant. The engineer can stipulate precisely the processes requisite to construct a bridge of given size and capacity, designed to serve a given purpose. The social engineer cannot emulate his exactitude. The engineer knows exactly the stresses and strains to which his structure can be subjected and the effects upon it of heat and cold and wear and tear. The social engineer cannot assess with any such assurance the reactions of human beings to the measures he may advocate. Should he therefore, as social scientist, refuse to advocate any? But that would be the denial of the validity of the knowledge he possesses. If he has understandingly investigated the relevant conditions he is better informed concerning the chances of success or failure of the different measures that may be applied to them. He knows better what resistances they will encounter and what forces can be marshalled on behalf of them. Take, for example, our own theme of prejudicial discrimination. If we have studied the variant susceptibilities of different personality types and of different groups we are in a better position to know how far and where certain modes of appeal against prejudice are likely to be more effective than others. If we have studied the genesis and the propagation of "stereotypes" or group images we are to that extent better prepared than others to give advice regarding methods of social education to correct the distortions and falsifications of reality that they contain. There is a large amount of such usable knowledge. If the social scientist does not use it, having first acquired it, is he not denying his social responsibility without thereby vindicating his title of social scientist?

The second risk springs from the fact that the objective to which the knowing is applicable is itself the product of a value judgment. In this respect this knowing differs, at least ostensibly, from the knowing of, say, the engineer. Possibly the difference is more apparent than real, but that is a question we cannot here discuss. Anyhow, the argument is that the scientist must maintain at all costs his objectivity. He must eschew value judgments. He must, to save his scientific integrity, not even participate, as scientific worker, in programs that are based on valuations of any kind. He has no place, as scientist, in the strife of creeds. If he utilizes his knowledge for the promotion of particular social values, being himself as human as anyone else, he is likely to let his bias as human being affect his scientific discernment and thus to undermine his primary obligation as a seeker after knowledge pure and undefiled.

It is not within our province in this study to disentangle all the implications of this argument. A shorter answer must suffice. In the first place the danger of bias besets the social scientist in every kind of investigation and his problem is to guard himself against it, in short to maintain his scientific-mindedness, and not to shun areas of knowledge where he may be susceptible to bias. In the second place applied science is in all fields the concomitant of pure science, and to it we owe all the civilization that man has built—why should it not be so in the social field? In this respect the social scientist is in precisely the same position as the chemist, the biochemist, the biologist, the physicist, and all the rest.

Our answer so far has been defensive. Let us now take the offensive. The social scientist who seeks to avoid bias by complacently refusing to investigate issues that are infected by it is not thereby saving his scientific soul. He is like the saint who would guard himself against temptation by abjuring the world where temptations abound—and then is beset by new and more insidious temptations in his retreat. His boasted objectivity is apt to develop into indifference or into a not too secret satisfaction with the *status quo*. We could cite not a few instances of social scientists who have gone down this road—take, for example, Sumner or Pareto. The refusal to study questions that arouse human emotions may itself become a bias. In taking this position the social scientist shuts himself off from a large area of social reality—and from the area that is of greatest interest and of greatest concern to his fellow men. His disinterestedness is likely to be or to become the expression of an interest, and he cannot protect himself against *that* bias because he proudly proclaims it to mean the absence of all bias.

There remains, indeed, an ethical question that any scientist may be called upon to face, whether he be physicist or social scientist. His science opens the door to some kind of "know-how." It will serve ends he disapproves as neutrally as ends he cherishes. Should he then devote his inherently neutral skill, when there is a demand for it, to serve only ends of which he himself approves or should he regard himself as a servant of the community or of the state and be willing to devote it to any ends that win popular approval or political sanction? Should a physicist who is also a pacifist be willing to apply his knowledge to the invention of the atomic bomb—unless of course he believes that thus he will be helping to make war impossible? Should a social psychologist apply his knowledge to the elaboration of propaganda techniques in favor of a cause that does not command his sympathy? Even more broadly, should the scientist be available as an expert somewhat in the manner in which a lawyer can be briefed by any

side to a dispute? There is no scientific answer to this question
—only an ethical one.

We raise it briefly here because the social sciences are more
closely involved in the issues of social policy than any other
branches of knowledge and because there is considerable doubt
among social scientists concerning their relation to policy-making
and even a certain amount of confusion concerning the significance of their research activities where they have a bearing on
the controversial questions of the political or economic arena. It
is hard for the social scientist to steer his true course between the
Scylla of indifference to or abstention from scientifically derived
conclusions that nevertheless sustain one side, one policy, against
another and the Charybdis of partisan advocacy of whatever
program. Research workers should realize that their large pre-
occupation with such subjects as housing, public opinion, crime
and delinquency, unemployment, tariffs, and so forth, is itself
directed by the social importance of these areas of investigation
and that if they refuse to draw inferences regarding preferable
policies they are like investigators of public health conditions
who refrain from recommending what should or should not be
done about them. It may be answered that there is little if any
controversy respecting the desirability of public health. The goal
itself is hardly in question. But neither is the goal of economic
welfare. The question is how that goal is affected by one kind or
another of tariff legislation or by one method or another of
dealing with unemployment. No group can offer so much guidance on these questions as the body of social scientists. But one
consequence of the attitudes to which we have been referring is
that this group, while it has been elaborating research techniques
for the discovery of factual evidences, has been slow to develop
the scientific methods and processes requisite for the application
of such evidences to the area of policy-making.

His very proper awareness of the danger of bias, of the primary
obligation of scientific objectivity, cannot absolve the social
scientist from this scientific task. On the contrary, if he refrains
from making practical applications he is the more apt to divorce
his particular ethics from his scientific faith and to make judgments as a layman, as a human being, without the regard for
evidence he insists upon as a scientist.

In his study of the Negro in the United States Gunnar Myrdal
offers the social scientist what might seem to be a compromise

solution. In one passage he states the aim of practical research as "to show precisely what should be the practical and political opinions and plans for action from the point of view of the various valuations if their holders had also the more correct and comprehensive factual knowledge which science provides." Dr. Myrdal is thinking especially of the "American creed" as held by those who nevertheless approve the social and economic subjection of the Negro, and of the rationalizations by means of which they seek to reconcile their behavior in this respect with their larger profession of faith. The judicious exposure of the rationalizations that buttress it is no doubt an important technique for the dislodging of prejudice. At the same time we must avoid the assumption that the cause is won when such rationalizations are exposed in the light of social science. There are always other rationalizations in which interested prejudice will tenaciously seek refuge, and even if they could all be exposed, and the lesson brought home to the rationalizers we must not assume that the larger creed would then be triumphant. It may well be that, where the prejudicial behavior is deeply rooted in the mores and jealously guarded by group interests, the uneasiness prompted by the exposure will lead to a new justification and a more intransigent reassertion of prejudice. There is abundance of historical evidence that authoritative creeds, accepted by peoples with entire conviction of their truth—religion offers many notable examples—can be so "interpreted" that they are adduced to sanction behavior flagrantly at variance with the explicit injunctions they contain. Devout slaveholders used their Bibles to prove that slavery was instituted by God, and today, in the Southern states, there are not a few who find a similar justification for the segregation of the Negro.

These remarks give point to a further comment on the compromise solution in accordance with which the social scientist "without prejudice," to use the word in another sense, confines himself to showing the contradictions between behavior and accepted creed. We are very far from denying that this type of investigation is useful and salutary, but we raise at once the question: Why should the investigator restrict in this wise his approach to important social problems? Why need he, for example, study the nature and social consequences of inter-group discrimination exclusively in the light of certain presumptively dominant creeds of the discriminating groups? Dr. Myrdal has shown how effective the latter method can be made, but he is too good an investigator to rely on it alone. Why, in short, should not the social scientist directly examine the consequences of discrimination? The consequences of whatever kind. He will discover, it may be, that these consequences are detrimental to social well-being, as he understands it. If others assess them differently they are no less free to do so. But if in the judgment of the investigator the consequences are undesirable it becomes for him a task wholly consonant with the principles of science to examine in turn the available methods for mitigating or removing their source. His exposition of the undesirable consequences may help to rally public opinion in support of the application of these methods. In all this, provided the investigation is honest and impartial, there is nothing that conflicts with the integrity of the scientist.

The exploration of the strategy and tactics of control over untoward social conditions, in the manner indicated above, is still in a rudimentary stage, especially in this country. In reaction from the naive dogmatisms of their environment and early training and also from the complacent generalizations of their predecessors American social scientists have tended to make their researches so "objective" that they have for the most part avoided this task or repudiated it, building up a kind of social philosophy appropriate to their abstention. They have thus escaped certain risks. They have escaped the contentions of participation in public policy, where their conclusions could be only probable or conditional. They have escaped the challenges of established interests. But they have done so at a price. They have failed to turn on social problems the light they alone could throw. They have not developed the skills that belong to this activity of their science. They have narrowed the range of their investigations.

The limitations of research in this respect have been stimulated by, and have in turn promoted, the belief held frequently by social scientists that they have and can have little or no influence on social conditions. This attitude has found typical expression in the work of Sumner and his followers. It is characteristic generally of those who emphasize the irrationalism of human behavior. The recent history of the world reveals the remarkable power of social movements, whether we think of them as rational or as irrational, under the drive of strong leadership with clear objectives. The success of these movements testifies to the responsiveness of men to persuasive appeals. These appeals link old values with new behavior, and *in this sense* the responsiveness is itself rational. The linkage may be false, but the adaptation of behavior to the presumed demands of value systems is an inherently rational proceeding. It is pre-eminently the task of the social scientist to show whether the claimed linkage is valid or invalid. The mores are not the static and irresistible force suggested by Sumner. They are full of inconsistencies and strains, unliberated tendencies in many directions, responsive adjustments to new situations well conceived or ill conceived.

The social scientist cannot move the world, but he may be able to learn the secrets of how the world is moved and so furnish aid and special directives to the forces on one or another side of the eternal struggle to move it this way or that.

In our own days the struggle is so momentous and the problems of a society beset by unprecedented changefulness are so urgent that social scientists are becoming more conscious of their potential role. The indifferentism of the previously dominant attitude has been shaken by the events that have shaken the whole world. Their absorption into wartime missions has given many social scientists a new orientation. A notable example has been given them by the physical scientists who, when with much misgiving they delivered the atomic bomb to the world, felt obligated to form an association to advocate methods for the security of mankind against its terror. Economists have been learning that a thousand pressing problems of the day, problems of prices and wages, of corporations and cartels, of the economic functions of government, of international exchange and international trade, involve them more and more deeply in practical affairs. Psychologists have given a lead by forming a Society for the Psychological Study of Social Issues, which has already done excellent work. Anthropologists are applying to the challenges of modern civilization the lessons they derive from the study of the simpler peoples. Sociologists, anthropologists, social psychologists, and political scientists are all contributing to the understanding of inter-group relationships. There is still a place for the ivory tower, but no social scientist can profitably ascend thereto who has not gained practical knowledge—and some wisdom—in the social arena.

To maintain his scientific integrity while participating in the resolution of social problems the social scientist must always be on guard against temptations arising both from his particular temperament and from his calling. He must regard himself not as an "expert" who is free to explore the social means to any end, but instead as a citizen who is guided by his own sense of the needs of society when he undertakes to explore the strategy of social control. Furthermore, when he embarks on this undertaking, he should be scrupulously watchful lest his own values lead him to distort, obscure, or overplay any factual evidences pertinent to the situation or to draw any scientifically unvalidated inferences to connect his facts and his values. No matter how good the cause there will be some evidences on the contrary side. However deplorable we may find racial discrimination to be there are *some* evidences in its favor. The propagandist suppresses or minimizes the unfavorable evidences; the social scientist must give them the same consideration that he gives to the evidences that support his cause. So far as he succeeds in doing so his science will become the ally of his citizenship.

List of Questions Relevant to the Inquiry

THE FOLLOWING is the list of specific questions, as revised for later use, the answers to which we hoped wholly or partially to uncover in the course of the investigation. As we proceeded it became clear that many of them could receive, in the light of available information, only very imperfect or tentative answers.

A. INSTITUTIONAL ASPECTS OF DISCRIMINATION

I. *Political*

(a) FEPC

In what fields of employment, in what regions, and in what respects did the FEPC succeed in controlling or diminishing the tendency to discrimination in employment?

In what respects did it fail? Has it had any unfavorable consequences?

Where did it meet most resistance and in what forms? Where least?

What evidences are there as to whether this device could be successfully extended?

How far did its degree of success depend on wartime conditions of employment? Can any conclusions be drawn as to its efficacy in times of diminishing employment?

(b) STATE LAWS AGAINST DISCRIMINATION IN EMPLOYMENT

What have State Commissions against Discrimination achieved so far? What further promise have they?

What conclusions can be drawn from the relative

frequency of complaints by members of different groups?

How far do Local Councils give promise of being effective and in what respects?

In what ways could the operation of these Commissions be improved or effectively extended?

(c) STATUTES OF CIVIL RIGHTS

How far and in what ways have state statutes guaranteeing equality of civil rights been operative, inoperative?

How far has enforcement been attempted? In what areas? With what success?

What effect, apart from attempts at enforcement, has the mere existence of such statutes?

(d) RIGHT TO VOTE

In what ways has this right been exercised by groups subject to discrimination and with what success with respect to the diminution or control of discriminatory tendencies?

How can this right become more significant to disprivileged groups so that they can enjoy it more securely or use it more effectively?

(e) PUBLIC HOUSING

How can public housing developments be made more serviceable to groups suffering from residential discrimination or congestion?

II. *Nonpolitical*

(a) BUSINESS

What evidences are there that discriminatory procedures stem (a) from the attitudes of employers (b) from the attitudes of workers?

Does the morale of the workers suffer where an employee who excites their prejudice is introduced or re-instated? Under what conditions does a satisfactory adjustment take place?

Where management is desirous of avoiding discrimination and there is opposition from some group of workers, what policies or methods have proved most successful in securing worker cooperation and under what conditions?

What forms of business activity show most evidence of discriminatory tendencies?

What policies of business leaders have been directed to the abolition of discrimination? Which have been most successful, and under what conditions?

(b) TRADE UNIONS

What conditions mainly determine union policy with respect to discrimination, especially racial discrimination?

What grounds, other than economic, are put forward to defend policies of discrimination? How far are such representations in accordance with the facts?

In what occupational areas have groups subject to discrimination, particularly Negroes, made most gains, fewest gains?

(c) PROFESSIONS

What are the main reasons for the varying degrees of discrimination practised against groups with respect to admission to professional training? Why for example is the extent of discrimination so apparently high in medical schools?

What accounts for the differences in policy with respect to admission shown by various colleges and universities?

How do private institutions—colleges, technical colleges, universities—compare in this respect with public or state institutions?

(d) CHURCHES

In view of the universalist claims of most religions (brotherhood of man, equality, etc.) what are churches doing specifically to discourage discrimination, and with what success?

What is the experience of churches that reject racial segregation or other forms of discrimination in areas where prejudice prevails?.

B. SOCIO-PSYCHOLOGICAL ASPECTS

Main topics on which evidences, supported by experiment, observation, and analysis, are sought are the following:

(1) The relative susceptibility of different personality types to particular appeals in favor of discriminatory or prejudicial treatment of other groups.

(2) The efficacy of different methods of combating rationalizations of discriminatory practices on the part of those who adhere to creeds, political philosophies, social traditions conflicting with such practices.

(3) The relative responsiveness of inter-group prejudice to the fluctuations of economic prosperity.

(4) The relative efficacy of different types of leadership in the combating of inter-group prejudice.

(5) The relative efficacy of different methods of educational attack on prejudicial social "stereotypes."

(6) The relative efficacy of different school programs designed to counteract inter-group prejudice, assumptions of group superiority and inferiority, and so forth.

(7) The feasibility of diverting aggressive tendencies from discriminatory to nondiscriminatory channels.

Memorandum on Types
of Prejudice

THE DISTINCTION between two types of prejudice, as embodied in the text, is derived chiefly from a report prepared for the author by Professor L. Joseph Stone of Vassar College. At our suggestion Professor Stone submitted the following analysis. In a preliminary statement he points out that while there is supporting evidence for the distinction he regards it as an hypothesis that has not yet been subjected to rigorous test.

The hypothesis. The hypothesis proposed is that there are two qualitatively different types of prejudice. It is not suggested that these are likely to appear often in complete purity, but that they involve different dynamics and hence should be distinguished. "Type 1" is simply a reflection of prevailing social attitudes by the individual. He has learned to regard members of certain other social groups as inferior or threatening and in general as very different from himself. The prejudice that he displays—which may lead him to various kinds of discriminatory acts or other overt hostility—is something that he has learned in simple and casual ways. They are part of the automatic structure of the life space offered by the culture upon which we all depend in organizing our simplest perceptions and our most complex attitudes. We find ready-made a classification of people in convenient groups and the feeling tones that we attach to each group are equally ready-made and inherent in the system of groupings that is passed on to us. It is part of the equipment that the culture builds into us along with our attitudes and expectations of spinach or ice cream, the value of home-run hitters, or the degree of respect due the garbage collector and the minister.

"Type 2" prejudice, on the other hand, while it may begin with the ready-made classification already described, becomes a necessary part of the personal economy of its possessor because it meets a need created by the dynamics of tension within his personality. For any number of reasons, determined by the individual life history, there is a store or backlog of hostility in some individuals. Such abnormal reservoirs of hostility are expressed in neurotic forms where hostility is directed inwardly. In others it takes a more nearly psychotic form and may be expressed in criminality or in violent hostility—often openly aggressive—toward individuals or groups. For an unknown proportion of the population, then, the ready-made target for hostility is very "valuable" and may be a necessity in maintaining a particular equilibrium, just as a neurosis or psychosis is a state of equilibrium.

Derivations from hypothesis. It should be repeated for emphasis that these types are not pure. It is granted that they become endlessly mixed and intertwined. Nevertheless, it may be valuable to follow out the implications of their existence even in qualified form. First it is clear that, except in the relatively rare instances where the entire population of a town or region is extremely violently prejudiced, the individuals who correspond to "Type 2" must be more strongly prejudiced but this prejudice—it follows from the hypothesis—is not merely stronger but must be more firmly held and more resistant to change because of the personal needs that it fulfils. It follows too that it must be numerically less common (although there are pessimistic psychoanalysts who might question this!).

Such an analysis, obvious as it is, is especially needed now that so many studies have been undertaken (and so many excellent ones completed within the last year or so) which purport to offer a portrait-of-the-prejudiced. As a rule, a portrait has been drawn of the *most prejudiced.* However, if our hypothesis is correct it will be seen that such a portrait is misleading and that a second portrait of the "casually prejudiced" is just as much needed.

Implications for strategy. It may be that this hypothesis can help to account for some discrepancies that have been noted in research on group hostilities and also point the way toward procedures to be followed in combating such hostilities. For example, in situations where Negroes have been introduced to housing facilities or job situations, it has often been remarked that the anticipated tension has failed to appear even where earlier polls have indicated the likelihood of its appearance. Our assumption would be that relatively few of the people involved in such a situation represented the second "character conditioned" type of prejudice. Certainly the casual acceptance of such a situation is incompatible with what we would expect from the pictures drawn in several excellent researches of the prejudiced individual. Moreover, this hypothesis may help to explain the psychological mechanism underlying the intensification of prejudice during periods of depression, when as Lazarsfeld has shown, for example, the unemployed individual may approach a neurotic lack of feeling of security, and flaws of personality structure may develop, dynamically necessitating "Type 2" prejudice in individuals who formerly had no such need. It will be noted that this is saying more than merely that in times of economic stress group hostilities are greatest.

In terms of the strategy of control it will be evident that our greatest efforts must be directed toward the weakest (and yet most numerous) strongholds of prejudice. By hypothesis, "Type 1" prejudice will fall fairly readily before strong and determined leadership or before any decisive indication that it is "not the thing to do"; in short, before any effective restructuring of the automatic classifications and attitudes of the culture. It might even be argued that the more deftly this can be accomplished as a matter of course and the less it entails verbal crystallization the more effective it will be. Educationally, or more accurately developmentally, it will tend to disappear in the measure that children are encouraged to see others as individuals; witness mingling rather than segregation; are encouraged to find individual rather than group labels and names to attach to those in "out-groups"; and tend to become aware of the fact that they themselves belong to many different groups and not to just one. All of these influences and experiences could readily be elaborated into an entire program of intercultural education and would be most effective against "Type 1" prejudice.

"Type 2" prejudice is not thus amenable to pressures and it might be better to wall it off or leave it, if possible, to stew in its own juices rather than attempt to influence or modify it. Dr. Elsa Frenkel-Brunswik has pointed out in a personal communication that the extremely prejudiced person very much resembles the psychotic in the airtight fashion in which he resists penetration of his system of ideas. She has indicated too that her data show a break toward the extreme prejudiced end of the continuum, perhaps suggesting the reality of the type distinction here offered on an *a priori* basis.

Appendix Five

Information and Attitudes

PRESUMABLY ONLY those readers who are specially interested in social research will care to study the exhibit that follows: it is a review of a large range of investigations the main objective of which was to test, and if possible to "measure" how far opinions about other groups and attitudes concerning group relations were affected by courses of instruction and other forms of communication. But the exhibit is well worth attention, because it reveals some weaknesses in prevalent modes of research not only in this area but in a much larger field of social investigation. If one asks what the survey here presented teaches us concerning the influence of instruction, especially instruction in college courses, on the attitudes of those exposed to it, one is hard put to answer. The findings are bewilderingly diverse. Sometimes there is reported a diminution of prejudice, or at least of adverse opinion; sometimes there is no diminution. Sometimes the conclusion is that prejudice is diminished in this respect but not in that; sometimes the relation is reversed. Sometimes one category of students is reported to be more responsive; sometimes another category.

What are we to make of all this? What, in sum, do we learn from all this assiduous researching? Let us acknowledge in the first place that much of this work is pioneering and that the lack of conclusiveness is or should be a spur to the development of more refined methods. The chief defect of many of these studies—there are some fine exceptions—is that they conceive

288

too simply the problem of investigation. Instruction about groups and group relations is not a clearly defined datum, the influence or effect of which we can proceed at once to examine. Instruction depends on the instructor—and also on the instructed. It may be merely informative or it may introduce value concepts. In either case the instructor himself displays an attitude. His personality, his experience, his outlook, his teaching ability, affects his instruction. His relation to his students is also a variable, and therefore the influence of his instruction. The students themselves are different in the different cases. There are many distinctions between one group of students and another. The influences that play upon them outside the circle of instruction may be very different for different groups. Instruction does not operate in a vacuum. Moreover, the method of testing for results is highly variable, no less than the situation in which the testing occurs. Attitudes are not separable unit factors to be isolated and identified by ready-made formulas.

In short, researchers are apt to ask too simple questions, partly because with simple questions that assume certain uniformities they can "quantify" the answers and so attain a specious accuracy. They treat a particular "factor," say instruction concerning other groups, as though it were a determinate dose of a specific drug acting on a type of organism and consequently possessing a measurable potency. But instruction is not a standardized commodity nor does it operate on a standardized "subject" called a class of students. The question is not, what is the effect of a course of instruction on a class of students? The question at issue is, under what conditions does what kind of instruction to what kind of auditors have what effect? It is multiple, not simple, and it cannot be simplified without confusion.

The evidence suggests that appropriate instruction under certain conditions does have an influence on attitudes toward "outside" groups. Research can do genuine service by giving us more satisfactory knowledge of the situations within which instruction is a significant means of combating discriminatory tendencies.

We now present the survey in question, for which we are indebted to Professor Robert Bierstedt of the Department of Sociology of Wellesley College. We wish at the same time to call to the attention of the reader another survey made by Dr. Arnold Rose and published by the American Council on Race Relations (Chicago, 1947) under the title: *Studies in Reduction of Prejudice.*

A bibliography is appended, arranged in alphabetical order, for the identification of the studies cited in the survey below.

The most numerous group of studies deals with the influence of such academic courses of instruction as psychology, sociology, social science, civics, immigration, race problems, contemporary problems, education, and so on; to such an extent indeed that one psychologist, McNemar, has complained about the "campus-bound inertia of researchers." Billings found an increase in liberalism as a result of weekly seminars and field trips, but three years later the same students had become more conservative again on race questions. Ford found a positive relationship between classroom instruction and favorable attitudes toward the Negro, but his "experience scores" changed only slightly. Schlorff and Whisler found reliable shifts in the favorable direction. Barkley, testing the influence of the first year in a Southern women's college, found reliable changes in attitudes toward war, law, and the Constitution, but none in attitudes toward evolution, God, the church, and the Negro. Campbell and Stover tested the influence of 18 weeks of teaching which emphasized respect for Germans and Chinese and found no reliable differences between the experimental and the control group. When one of their groups studied the Negro the students became reliably more favorable than the control group when measured by the Bogardus scale but not when measured by the Hinckley scale. Droba reports no reliable gains in tolerance toward the Negro on the part of 30 college students after a course on the Negro, but this study is criticized by Horowitz on the ground that the before and after forms of the test were not comparable and no control group was used. Gilbert found that a high school science course produced no statistically significant differences in the ability of some 2,000 pupils in Los Angeles high schools to ignore their prejudices on certain nonspecified controversial issues. Eschen similarly found that a course on contemporary problems in an Iowa high school changed attitudes toward the Constitution, patriotism, and the Germans but not toward censorship, the Chinese, communism, criminals, and war. Doob exhibited significant changes in 22 attitudes during a course in social psychology given to 176 college students, but decided, upon interviewing the students, that "reasons offered for real changes varied, but most of them seem to involve external events." These external events are not indicated except for the remark that Hitler's march into Austria was one of them. M. Smith discovered shifts toward greater tolerance after courses on immigration and race problems, and in another study discovered that attitude toward the Negro was less subject to change than other attitudes after an elementary sociology course. Young, in one of the earliest of these studies, found practically no change in the ranking of inborn ability of various ethnic groups after a course in race problems; his students, however, could have become more liberal toward all these groups without changing the relative ranking. Myers reports a change in the less liberal direction after a course on anti-Negro prejudice, but is inclined to attribute the unfavorable change to an increase in honesty rather than to an increase in prejudice.

Although not directly relevant to experimentally induced changes of attitudes, the question of the influence of broad fields of study (college majors, professional training, etc.) rather than specific courses is not without interest in spite of evidence which is again inconsistent. Barkley, for example, in the study mentioned above, found no difference in the effects of the commercial curriculum and the liberal arts curriculum. Allport and Kramer include among their tentative assertions on the psychology of prejudice the statement that students of the natural sciences tended to be less prejudiced than students in other fields. Boldt and Stroud, finding favorable changes which they attribute to college training rather than to age and maturity, say that the course of study exercised some influence in that social science majors were most liberal, physical science majors next, and humanities majors least liberal. Murphy and Likert, on the other hand, say that "If courses in the social sciences affect attitudes toward the Negro, they appear to do so but little more than do the courses in English literature and natural science." Murphy and Likert also found that business and engineering students were relatively illiberal in attitudes toward the Negro and that teaching and journalism students were relatively liberal. Pre-medical students were also relatively liberal and pre-law students were not far behind. The factor of selection obviously operates in this area, however, and it is consequently difficult to disentangle causes and effects.

With respect to educational level, as distinguished from particular courses and areas of study, Bugelski and Lester, Boldt and Stroud, Chase, Garrison and Burch, Haag, Jones, and Bolton

all find tolerance increasing with age or with additional educational experience. Bolton found the more advanced students
more liberal toward the economic, political, and social rights of
the Negro but not toward social intercourse with Negroes. Green
concluded that prejudices are already fixed at the age of seven
and that no age differences (up to 16) appear except in the
ingenuity of defending opinions. Minard found a consistent drop
in race tolerance in terms of personal practice from the 7th
to 12th grades. Korczak and Paznanska, as reported by Dunham,
found that among young children goodwill predominates over
aversion toward their companions but that the goodwill diminishes with increasing age. Moore and Porterfield failed to find
that the upper college classes are more tolerant; Murphy and
Likert say that sheer amount of college work had no effect on
their attitude scores; and Sims and Patrick found increase, decrease, and no change respectively in three different groups.
Chein and Laks, studying 200 highly educated persons in a
precinct in New York City, found that persons who gave more
unfavorable responses to out-groups (Negroes, Jews, Catholics,
or Protestants) had higher average education than the precinct
as a whole. Cantril investigated the intensity of attitudes and
concluded that extremes of attitude are more intensely held and
that education, along with wealth and age, is associated with
more intensity. Samelson, reporting a survey of 2,523 Whites conducted in 1944 by the National Opinion Research Center, says
that education is associated with information on Negro conditions but not with a desire to improve those conditions. She
concludes that, since Southern college graduates are better informed on all questions pertaining to the Negro than are Northern high school graduates, education does not alter fundamental
attitudes found in communities of residence. Brooks, reversing
the variables, found that attitudes of students are more favorable
to the well-educated than to the poorly-educated members of
other ethnic groups. On the general subject of changes of
attitude as related both to the incidence of racial attitudes in
children and to advancing educational levels attention is invited
to additional items in surveys by Horowitz and Rose.

A number of investigators have attempted to relate different
kinds of experience to attitude changes. Cole, for example, has
reported that tolerance for Mexicans and Japanese among Colorado high school pupils is inversely related to the number of

contacts with these groups; she found intolerance for Negroes, however, although there was no contact. Harlan reports that less frequent contact and greater intimacy of contact are related to more favorable attitudes toward Jews. F. T. Smith found a significant improvement in the attitudes of Teachers College students after visits with eminent Negroes in Harlem, but attitudes toward marriage and kinship by marriage resisted a change. M. Smith studied members of fraternities and sororities and found a very slight positive relationship between homogeneity in attitudes and length of resident membership in these groups. Unfortunately for present purposes, however, no ethnic or out-group attitudes were included in his study. Sims and Patrick found no significant changes in attitude from year to year among Northern students in a Northern university (Ohio State) and none among Southern students in a Southern university (Alabama), but Northern students in the Southern school exhibited a year by year decrease in favorable attitude toward the Negro. Tuttle and Murphy and Likert mention reading habits as determinants of attitudes, and the last two authors especially emphasize a factor they call "bookishness" as influential in encouraging, among other things, tolerance for out-groups. Williams reports an interracial Y.W.C.A. project effective in shifting the attitudes of the White group in a pro-Negro direction without a correlative shift in the Negro group. A visit of a Chinese girl to Cincinnati sixth grade classes is reported by Zeligs to have had a favorable result. LaPiere found that a large number of proprietors of inns and hotels said they would not accept Chinese guests after they had in fact accommodated them. Murphy, Murphy, and Newcomb conclude that familiarity as such seems to have no necessary relationship to tolerance. Rose, on the other hand, in a recent study of mixed and unmixed troops in the European Theater of Operations, found that opposition to the use of Negro troops in mixed companies declined markedly after experience with them. It may be of real significance that at first only a third of the White officers (commissioned and non-commissioned) in these companies favored the introduction of Negro platoons, but after two months 77 per cent favored the accomplished fact and none expressed themselves as less favorable. In a survey of enlisted personnel 62 per cent of those in unmixed divisions said they would dislike it very much if a Negro platoon became a part of their company while only 7 per cent of the White soldiers already in mixed companies expressed the same degree of dislike. It should perhaps be remembered, however, that in these two surveys no Negro officers or noncoms were involved.

Studies which indicate a positive correlation between relevant information and attitudes are those of Biddle, Closson, Reckless and Bringen, and Watson. Nettler also finds a low positive relationship between favorable attitudes toward the Japanese in America and amount of information about them, but warns that less tolerance is not necessarily correlated with little or no information. Murphy and Likert discount altogether the low positive correlation they find between information on the Negro and favorable attitudes, saying that factual information is "notoriously incompetent to dispel attitudes based on deep personal sympathy or antagonisms, or attitudes which are rooted in self-interest." Bolton found reliable differences in knowledge of the Negro among Southern female college students after a course on Negro education but no corresponding differences in attitude toward the social rights of Negroes. Zeligs and Hendrickson, as cited by Rose, studied 200 sixth grade children and discovered a correlation between information about ethnic groups and favorable attitudes toward them, as measured by a form of the Bogardus social distance scale, but attitudes toward the Negro proved to be an exception to this correlation. In another early study cited by Rose a group of California high school students acquired considerable information about the Japanese during a visit to Japan, but there was no significant change in attitude toward the Japanese. Horowitz exhibited a positive correlation between information and general tolerance for several racial groups, but the same tolerance appeared when he tested for three fictional groups, "Danireans, Pireneans, and Wallonians," about which his subjects could have had no information. He concludes that "Despite evidence of a positive relationship between knowledge about a group and tolerance for it, there is ample evidence of much tolerance and intolerance unrelated to the possession of relevant information." In a recent study, although one not on an ethnic issue, Newcomb found that both information and attitude toward the Spanish Civil War seem to be influenced by what he calls an "attitude climate" (Bennington College vs. Catholic University). Murphy, Murphy, and Newcomb, after a survey of the literature on this subject up to 1937, conclude that "Altogether, our rather meager present evidence suggests that those who know most about other races and peoples tend to have favorable attitudes about them, particularly in the case of more distant peoples and probably less so in the case of those more frequently met, such as Negroes in this country. And the conclusion also seems justified that 'liberal' attitudes tend to be found among those most adequately informed on relevant issues. Both of these conclusions must be regarded as highly tentative, however; our present understanding of the whole problem is colored by the particular type of information which is related to attitudes, and by the peculiarly selected nature of most of the groups which have been studied." A similar degree of uncertainty seems to obtain in 1947.

Turning to the effect of propaganda and other miscellaneous stimuli upon change of attitude, Annis and Meier, Bird, Chen, Remmers, and Stagner all show the positive effect of lectures, speeches, radio addresses, or printed material. Bayton says that propaganda is more influential in the formation of racial stereotypes than face-to-face contacts, and, in a later article, attributes prejudice to coercive, authoritarian, and capricious methods of parental control. Hartmann found emotional appeals much more effective than rational ones in a political campaign, as did Stagner in a classroom situation, while Knower found little difference between the two types. Biddle found that instruction in propaganda techniques reduces susceptibility to propaganda, but Collier found that even those who are aware of the nature of propaganda are influenced by it. Hay and Millson discovered little modification in attitude following a debate, and Millson found little difference among "academic," "exhibitionistic," and "conversational" modes of debate. Willis, however, found that dramatization was more effective than "straight talk," and a combined form least effective. The influence of motion pictures, considered as propaganda, has been studied by Thurstone, Peterson and Thurstone, Ramseyer, and Rosenthal, all of whom agree that attitudes change in the direction intended by the propaganda. Peterson and Thurstone studied attitudes toward nationality and race, crime, the punishment of criminals, capital punishment, and prohibition. They report that the most striking change occurred in attitude toward the Negro after showing 434 sixth to twelfth grade students the film entitled "Birth of a Nation," which was considered potent anti-Negro propaganda. They also report that pictures have relatively permanent effects on the social attitudes of children and that a number of pictures on the same theme have a cumulative effect. Ramseyer investigated attitudes toward the WPA and soil erosion, and Rosenthal subjected undergraduate students in general psychology to radical motion picture propaganda to observe the effect upon socioeconomic attitudes. In both of these latter studies, however, a minority of subjects changed their attitudes in a direction opposite to that intended, showing that propaganda sometimes has an adverse or counter effect. A recent study by Wiese and Cole on the effect of a commercial motion picture on attitudes toward the Nazis is inconclusive. For additional material attention is again invited to a special section on the differential effectiveness of propaganada techniques in the memorandum by Rose.

In an attempt to weigh the influence of certain prestige factors, Marple found that majority opinion was more influential than expert opinion in changing attitudes, but Burtt and Falkenburg found no difference between the two types. Lorge and Saadi and Farnsworth found that statements on various political issues received greater verbal acceptance among subjects tested when linked to a "liked" or "prestige" name than when linked to a previously disfavored or disliked name. Kulp similarly exhibited the effect of prestige factors on the acceptance of statements on liberalism, but when these same statements were attributed to conservative authors the subjects still changed their attitudes in the liberal direction.

That teachers might influence attitude changes apart from information and instructional material provided a useful clue to Kroll, who found that the conservatism of students increased under conservative teachers and decreased greatly under radical teachers. Longstreet found that a year's course on American history resulted in reliable changes of attitude only in the class of the teacher aware of the experiment, and Manske, comparing liberal teachers with those prejudiced against the Negro, found 8 of 22 classes showing slight changes opposed to the teachers' attitudes and only 2 in the direction of the teachers' attitudes.

BIBLIOGRAPHY FOR APPENDIX 5

Allport, G. W., and Kramer, B. M., "Some Roots of Prejudice." *Journal of Psychology*, 1946, 22:9–39.

Annis, A. D., and Meier, N. C., "The Induction of Opinion Through Suggestion by Means of 'Planted Content.'" *Journal of Social Psychology*, 1934, 5:65–81.

Barkley, K. L., "Relative Influence of Commercial and Liberal Arts Curricula upon Changes in Students' Attitudes." *Journal of Social Psychology*, 1942, 15:129–144.

Bayton, J. A., "The Racial Stereotypes of Negro College Students." *Journal of Abnormal and Social Psychology*, 1941, 36:97–102.

Bayton, J. A., "Personality and Prejudice." *Journal of Psychology*, 1946, 22:59–65.

Biddle, W. W., "The Relationship between Knowledge and a Measure of Autistic Thinking on Certain International Problems." *Journal of Social Psychology*, 1931, 2:493–496.

Biddle, W. W., "Propaganda and Education." *Teachers College Contributions to Education*, 1932, No. 531.

Billings, E. L., "The Influence of a Social Studies Experiment on Student Attitudes." *School and Society*, 1942, 56:557–560.

Bird, C., "The Influence of the Press upon the Accuracy of Report." *Journal of Abnormal and Social Psychology*, 1927, 22:123–129.

Boldt, W. J., and Stroud, J. B., "Changes in the Attitudes of College Students." *Journal of Educational Psychology*, 1934, 25:611–619.

Bolton, E. B., "Effect of Knowledge upon Attitudes toward the Negro." *Journal of Social Psychology*, 1935, 6:68–90.

Bolton, E. B., "Measuring Specific Attitudes Towards the Social Rights of the Negro." *Journal of Abnormal and Social Psychology*, 1937, 31:384–397.

Brooks, L. M., "Racial Distance as Affected by Education." *Sociology and Social Research*, 1936, 21:128–133.

Bugelski, R., and Lester, O. P., "Changes in Attitudes in a Group of College Students during their College Courses before and after Graduation." *Journal of Social Psychology*, 1940, 12:319–322.

Burtt, H. E., and Falkenburg, D. R., Jr., "The Influence of Majority and Expert Opinion on Religious Attitudes." *Journal of Social Psychology*, 1941, 14:269–278.

Campbell, D. W., and Stover, G. F., "Teaching International-Mindedness in the Social Studies." *Journal of Educational Sociology*, 1933, 7:244–248.

Cantril, H., "The Intensity of an Attitude." *Journal of Abnormal and Social Psychology*, 1946, 41:129–135.

Chase, W. P., "Attitudes of North Carolina College Students (Women) toward the Negro." *Journal of Social Psychology*, 1940, 12:367–378.

Chein, I., and Laks, L., "Attitudes and the Educational Process." *Journal of Educational Sociology*, 1946, 19:365–375.

Chen, W. K. C., "The Influence of Oral Propaganda Material upon Students' Attitudes." *Archives of Psychology*, 1933, 23, No. 150.

Closson, E. E., "A Study of the Factor of Information in Race Prejudice." Unpublished Master's Thesis, State University of Iowa, 1930.

Cole, N. E., "The Personal Attitudes of High School Pupils in Colorado toward Alien Nations and Peoples." Unpublished Master's Thesis, Colorado State Teacher's College, 1932.

Collier, R. M., "The Effect of Propaganda upon Attitude following a Critical Examination of the Propaganda Itself." *Journal of Social Psychology*, 1944, 20:3–17.

Doob, L. W., "Some Factors Determining Change in Attitude." *Journal of Abnormal and Social Psychology*, 1940, 35:549–565.

Droba, D. D., "Education and Negro Attitudes." *Sociology and Social Research*, 1932, 17:137–141.

Dunham, H. W., "Topical Summaries of Current Literature: Social Attitudes." *American Journal of Sociology*, 1940, 46:344–375.

Eschen, C. R. v., "An Evaluation of a Secondary School Course in 'Contemporary Problems' from Certain Stated Points of View." *Journal of Educational Research*, 1941, 34:265–271.

Ford, R. N., "Scaling Experience by a Multiple-Response Technique: A Study of White-Negro Contacts." *American Sociological Review*, 1941, 6:9–23.

Garrison, K. C., and Burch, V. S., "A Study of Racial Attitudes of College Students." *Journal of Social Psychology*, 1933, 4:230–235.

Gilbert, H. H., "Secondary Science and Pupil Prejudice." *Journal of Educational Research*, 1941, 35:294–299.

Green, G. H., "Have Children a National Bias?" *Discovery*, 1932, 13:44–46.

Haag, H. L., "Study of Racial Attitudes of High School and University Students." Unpublished Master's Thesis, University of Michigan, 1930.

Harlan, H. H., "Some Factors Affecting Attitude Toward Jews." *American Sociological Review*, 1942, 7:816–827.

Hartmann, G. W., "A Field Experiment on the Comparative Effectiveness of 'Emotional' and 'Rational' Political Leaflets in Determining Election Results." *Journal of Abnormal and Social Psychology*, 1936, 31:99–114.

Hay, D. G., "Measurement of Attitudes of an Audience." *School and Society*, 1935, 41:543.

Horowitz, E. L., " 'Race' Attitudes." In Klineberg, O., Editor, *Characteristics of the American Negro*. New York: Harper, 1944, pp. 139–247.

Jones, V., "Attitudes of College Students toward War, Race, and Religion, and the Changes in Such Attitudes during Four Years in College." *Psychological Bulletin*, 1936, 33:731–732.

Knower, F. H., "Experimental Studies in Changes in Attitudes: I. A Study of the Effect of Oral Argument on Changes of Attitude." *Journal of Social Psychology*, 1935, 6:315–347; II. "A Study of the Effect of Printed Argument on Changes in Attitude." *Journal of Abnormal and Social Psychology*, 1936, 30:522–532; III. "Some Incidence of Attitude Changes." *Journal of Applied Psychology*, 1936, 20:114–127.

Korczak, J., and Paznanska, A., "Plebiscyty Zyczliwosci i Niecheci [The Psychological Conduct toward the Mental Test]." *Polish Archives of Psychology*, 1933–34, 6:241–262.

Kroll, A., "The Teacher's Influence upon the Social Attitude of Boys in the Twelfth Grade." *Journal of Educational Psychology*, 1934, 25:274–280.

Kulp, D. H., "Prestige as Measured by Single Experience Changes and their Permanency." *Journal of Educational Research*, 1934, 27:663–672.

LaPiere, R. T., "Attitudes vs. Actions." *Social Forces*, 1934, 13:232.

Longstreet, R. J., "An Experiment with the Thurstone Attitude Scales." *School Review,* 1935, 43:202–208.

Lorge, I., "Prestige, Suggestion and Attitudes." *Psychological Bulletin,* 1935, 32:750 (Abstract).

Manske, A. J., "The Reflection of Teachers' Attitudes in the Attitudes of their Pupils." *Teachers College Contributions to Education,* 1936, No. 702.

Marple, C. H., "The Comparative Suggestibility of Three Age Levels to the Suggestion of Group vs. Expert Opinion." *Journal of Social Psychology,* 1933, 4:176–186.

McNemar, Q., "Opinion-Attitude Methodology." *Psychological Bulletin,* 1946, 43:289–374.

Millson, W. A. D., "Problems in Measuring Audience Reaction." *Quarterly Journal of Speech,* 1932, 18:621–637.

Millson, W. A. D., "Audience Reaction to Symposium." *Quarterly Journal of Speech,* 1935, 21:43–53.

Minard, R. D., "Race Attitudes of Iowa Children." *University of Iowa Studies in Character,* 1931, 4, No. 2.

Moore, G. W., "Social and Political Attitudes of Students at North Carolina State College." Unpublished Master's Thesis, North Carolina State College, 1931.

Murphy, G., and Likert, R., *Public Opinion and the Individual.* New York, 1938.

Murphy, G., Murphy, L. B., and Newcomb, T. M., *Experimental Social Psychology.* (rev. ed.) New York: Harper, 1937.

Myers, I. M. A., "A Study of Anti-Negro Prejudice." *Journal of Negro Education,* 1943, 12:709–714.

Nettler, G., "The Relationship between Attitude and Information concerning the Japanese in America." *American Sociological Review,* 1946, 11:177–191.

Newcomb, T. M., "The Influence of Attitude Climate upon Some Determinants of Information." *Journal of Abnormal and Social Psychology,* 1946, 41:291–302.

Peterson, R. C., and Thurstone, L. L., *The Effect of Motion Pictures on the Social Attitudes of High School Children,* New York, 1930.

Porterfield, A. L., "Education and Race Attitudes." *Sociology and Social Research,* 1937, 21:538–543.

Ramseyer, L. L., "Factors Influencing Attitudes and Attitude Changes." *Educational Research Bulletin, Ohio State University,* 1939, 18:9–14.

Reckless, W. C., and Bringen, H. L., "Racial Attitudes and Information about the Negro." *Journal of Negro Education,* 1933, 2:128–138.

Remmers, H. H., "Propaganda in the Schools—Do the Effects Last?" *Public Opinion Quarterly,* 1938, 2:197–210.

Rosander, A. C., "Age and Sex Patterns of Social Attitudes." *Journal of Educational Psychology,* 1939, 30:481–496.

Rose, A. M., "Army Policies Toward Negro Soldiers." *Annals of the American Academy of Political and Social Science,* 1946, 244:90–94.

Rose, A. M., *Studies in Reduction of Prejudice* (mimeographed). Chicago: American Council on Race Relations, 1947.

Rosenthal, S. P., "Change of Socio-Economic Attitudes under Radical Motion Picture Propaganda." *Archives of Psychology,* 1934, No. 166.

Saadi, M., and Farnsworth, P. R., "The Degrees of Acceptance of Dogmatic Statements and Preferences for their Supposed Makers." *Journal of Abnormal and Social Psychology,* 1934, 29:143–150.

Samelson, B., "Does Education Diminish Prejudice?" *Journal of Social Issues,* 1945, 1:11–13.

Schlorff, P. W., "An Experiment in the Measurement and Modification of Racial Attitudes in School Children." Unpublished Doctor's Thesis, New York University, 1930.

Sims, V. M., and Patrick, J. R., "Attitudes toward the Negro of Northern and Southern College Students." *Journal of Social Psychology,* 1936, 7:192–204.

Smith, F. T., "An Experiment in Modifying Attitudes toward the Negro." *Teachers College Contributions to Education,* 1943, No. 887.

Smith, M., "A Study of Change of Attitudes toward the Negro." *Journal of Negro Education,* 1939, 8:64–70.

Smith, M., "Attitude Homogeneity and Length of Group Association." *Journal of Abnormal and Social Psychology,* 1940, 35:573–578.

Smith, M., "A Second Report on Changes in Attitudes toward the Negro." *School and Society,* 1943, 57:388–392.

Stager, R., "A Note on Education and International Attitudes." *Journal of Social Psychology,* 1942, 16:341–345.

Thurstone, L. L., "Influence of Motion Pictures on Children's Attitudes." *Journal of Social Psychology,* 1931, 2:291–305.

Thurstone, L. L., "The Effect of a Motion Picture Film upon

Children's Attitude toward the Germans." *Journal of Educational Psychology*, 1932, 23:241–246.

Tuttle, H. S., "The Campus and Social Ideals." *Journal of Educational Research*, 1936, 30:177–182.

Watson, G. B., *Orient and Occident: An Opinion Study*. Unpublished work on file at Institute of Pacific Relations, New York City.

Whisler, L., "Changes in Attitudes towards Social Issues Accompanying a One-Year Freshman Social Science Course." *Journal of Psychology*, 1940, 10:387–396.

Wiese, M. J., and Cole, S. G., "A Study of Children's Attitudes and the Influence of a Commercial Motion Picture." *Journal of Psychology*, 1946, 21:151–171.

Williams, D. H., "The Effects of an Interracial Project upon the Attitudes of Negro and White Girls within the Young Women's Christian Association." Unpublished Master's Thesis, Columbia University, 1934.

Willis, E. E., "The Relative Effectiveness of Three Forms of Radio Presentation in Influencing Attitudes." *Speech Monographs*, 1940, 7:41–47.

Young, D., "Some Effects of a Course in American Race Problems on the Race Prejudice of 450 Undergraduates at the University of Pennsylvania." *Journal of Abnormal and Social Psychology*, 1927, 22:235–242.

Zeligs, R., "Influencing Children's Attitudes toward the Chinese." *Sociology and Social Research*, 1941, 26:126–138.

Zeligs, R., and Hendrickson, G., "Racial Attitudes of Two Hundred Sixth Grade Children." *Sociology and Social Research*, 1933, 18:26–36.

Subject Index

Index of Authors

Index